JUST THE WAY THINGS WERE DONE

A POLITICAL HISTORY OF BLUE ISLAND

VOLUME I: 1920 to 1965

REVISED EDITION

By

Joseph Thomas Gatrell

JUST THE WAY THINGS WERE DONE

A POLITICAL HISTORY OF BLUE ISLAND

VOLUME I: **1920 to 1965**

By

Joseph Thomas Gatrell

Published in the United States

ISBN-13: 978-1495223198
ISBN-10: 1495223191

ACKNOWLEDGMENTS

The author would like to thank the following people and organizations. Each of them was essential to the publication of this book.

Atop the list are Carol von Raesfeld, Marci “New York” Metz, Dorothy Hardy, and Robert "Cutout Guy" Osborn. They worked on the most essential tasks of this project.

The Blue Island Public Library provided archives of information and photos. Those most helpful staff members include Deb Beasley, Sarah Cottonaro, David Boras, Mary Kay Tueth, Sophia Sierra-Aguillera, Lisa Johnson, Dan Carroll, Viviana Salgado-Hernandez, Mike Byrne, and Darren Thompson.

The City of Blue Island provided access to city council minutes and records. Those who assisted include former City Clerk Pam Frasor, Linda Podgorak, Betty Harmeyer, Linda Ortiz, Barb Nagel, Abby Leiva, and current City Clerk Randy Heuser. Also from the City of Blue Island: James Reihel, Jason Berry, and Mary Poulsen provided historical insights and information.

Very important biographical data was generated by Philip Hernandez and the staff of the Hallinan Funeral Home and Clay Krueger and Marsha O’Brien Rauch of the Krueger Funeral Home.

Finally, the underrated and often overlooked Blue Island Historical Society provided access to photos and documents, and it generated publicity for this author and his work. The president of the organization, Mike Kaliski, was helpful in these endeavors.

THE COVERS

The concept came from the creative mind of Robert "Cutout Guy" Osborn. Dorothy Hardy used her great skills to refine it and get it into print. The back cover photo of City Hall is courtesy of the Blue Island Historical Society. The back cover photo was taken by George Partin III. The Blue Island Public Library provided the photos of the mayors. The photo of Babe Tuffanelli courtesy of Shirley and Dawn Marie Tuffanelli. Mike Moller snapped the photo of Lefty and Joe on a beautiful June morning on Western Avenue in Blue Island.

TABLE OF CONTENTS

TABLE OF CONTENTS [cont.]

TABLE OF CONTENTS [cont.]

Part IV

FOREWORD

The Bumpy Ride into Blue Island History

This project began for me in Blue Island during the late 1960s. It was during an early autumn weekend when I spent the night at the home of my best friend, Leo Rangel. It was exotic enough for a 13-year-old to discover how others lived (They eat toast in the morning just like we do!), but on that weekend there was a special event. On that Saturday morning, Leo and I accompanied his older brother, Chuck, who we called "Chotter," as he delivered bundles of newspapers for the Blue Island News Agency.

Chotter drove the News Agency's beater of a pickup truck from vendor to vendor and Leo and I bounced around in the back with the bundles. I remember Chotter laughing at us because we didn't know any better than to be in hog heaven: two grinning teenagers riding around Blue Island in the back of the dilapidated pickup as if we'd made the big time. That bumpy ride was the next leg of a different journey for me. At age four, I had begun reading the newspaper over my father's shoulder. Since then newspapers have been special for me. They always hold a treasure: information.

During that trip with Leo and Chotter, one of the newspapers—a section of the *Blue Island Sun-Standard*, somehow escaped from a wire-bound bundle. I picked it up and read as we were jostled around town. The part that fascinated me most was a column written by *Sun-Standard* sports editor Don Rizzs. The column was about a baseball game between the Cubs and Pittsburgh Pirates that had a controversial ending. "The Homer in the Gloamin'" the headline read. The umpire ruled that the home run hit by Cubs catcher Gabby Hartnett landed in fair territory, but later it was revealed that actually it was foul because the woman struck by the ball was sitting in foul territory.

That column by Mr. Rizzs motivated me to become a sportswriter. Leo and I never did bounce out of that truck. We survived and Don and Julie Rizzs's youngest son, Ricky, became one of our best friends. Because the writing bug never left me, several years later, I asked Ricky to ask his father if he could get me a writing job with the *Sun-Standard.* He did and I began writing high school sports, which led to local sports, local government, crime news, and politics.

A funny thing happened on my way to a career in journalism. I went away to college and forgot completely about skills, ambition, romance, and money, and I became a teacher. I did not completely forget about writing. I was conned by the recruiter for Augustana College who assured me that the school had a journalism major. It did not; I majored in English, but it wasn't the same. For years, my desire to write bubbled beneath the surface like a volcano. Every once in awhile, Leo or Ricky or another friend would bring it up and I might write something, but there was no quick return to writing on a serious or regular basis.

During the 1990s, my volcano finally erupted and blew the top off of the mountain. Because the *Sun-Standard* had been absorbed by a larger area publication before completely disappearing in the mid-1980s, I began by writing for another local publication before starting my own newspaper, *The Blue Island Sun*, in 1997. It was then I received an education about the real Blue Island. I was aided in this endeavor by none other than Don Rizzs, who had retired and was writing and lecturing on local history. Between Mr. Rizzs' history lessons and what I learned covering the Blue Island city council and writing obituaries (that fascinating subset of history known as biography), I became hooked on local lore and I began investigating. My inquiries invariably led me to something else, which led me to something else, which has led me to the project that started in the back of that pickup truck driven by Charles B. "Chotter" Rangel back in the 1960s.

I would like to thank everyone who contributed to this project—from those who contributed to the history to those who shared recollections to the readers who encouraged me. Also, this book would not have been possible without the archives at the Blue Island Public Library and at the City of Blue Island, the former for its collection of newspaper files and the latter for its City Council minutes and records dating back to the organization of Blue Island as a village.

This book is dedicated to the Rangel Family, the Lopez Family (Cecilia Rangel was a Lopez. Her brother Mel was one of my basketball coaches at St. Benedict Grammar School), the Rizzs Family, and the Galatti Family (Julie Rizzs was a Galati. For many years, she helped make that great pizza at the annual St. Donatus Feast).

These great contributors to Blue Island helped make our community the kind of place where a kid could grow up to be a Major League Baseball broadcaster (Ricky), a doctor (Leo), or a sports writer turned teacher turned historian.

Joseph Thomas Gatrell
August 22, 2010

Part I
When the Fix Went In

There have been fixes for as long as there has been larceny in people's hearts and opportunities. There are books and movies about great crimes, and where do you think those plots and subplots came from? Art imitates life and there was no place better for this version of flattery than Blue Island after the turn of the 20th Century. Little did anyone know that the community of that era would attract an outsider named John M. Hart, who would become mayor and leave his indelible imprint on Blue Island. Mr. Hart was so forceful a personality and his decisions were so long-lasting that Blue Island has not been able to change what he created, to undo what he willed upon it.

Blue Island was on its way to becoming a metropolis during the 1920s and 1930s. Even the Great Depression could not stop it. Blue Island was a farm community being transformed into a large city with a business district and major industry. During this transition, however, there was a leadership vacuum and you know what nature does to a vacuum. It fills it. Just as dirt roads were created, then filled with cinders and gravel and eventually with concrete and finally asphalt, so was the Blue Island leadership vacuum filled. Early in its history, Blue Island had a series of strong leaders who seemed to care only about the community. When weaker men followed, a leadership vacuum was created. At first it was filled by men who were not up to the task of leadership. Eventually it was filled by a man with a very strong personality and a barely hidden agenda who posed as a savior, John M. Hart.

Had life imitated art, John M. Hart would have been the gambler and con artist bent on fleecing his prey of everything they owned. From the time he stepped off the train in Blue Island, the checkered-suit clad Mr. Hart would have used his poker skills and scams to relieve the rubes who lived in Blue Island of their money. Along the way he would have met a good woman, (think Clark Gable and Lana Turner in "Honky Tonk") fallen in love with her, and experienced a life-changing transformation that convinced him it was better to go straight and be a poor-but-honest hero instead of a wealthy and unloved crook. He would have become the heroic mayor who cleaned up the community and turned corrupt Rubeville into a modern, model metropolis. Because life did not imitate art in this case, Mr. Hart's destiny was to be a wealthy hedon who died virtually alone.

The political history of Blue Island is not limited to sadness and tragedy, of course. There is so much more to the story. The fix went in for Blue Island prior to 1920, at least seventeen years before John M. Hart assumed power, and it never went off. Mayor Hart understood the fix and embraced it. The conniving corner druggist turned politician knew how to use the fix to his advantage and did so better than anyone else. This is one reason why Mr. Hart's era is as interesting as the legendary mayor was crooked. To fathom the story of John M. Hart, one also must understand the community and the surrounding area physically, morally, culturally, and politically. There also is a legacy. Mayor Hart left office in 1965. He died in 1974. Why has Blue Island never been able to escape him or its past? The fix went in a very long time ago in Blue Island. How did John M. Hart imbed it so securely that it never has been off?

To answer this and other important question, it may be best to revisit the scene. Perhaps if we know what Blue Island and its people and the surrounding area were like before John M. Hart came to power, we may better understand why.

"A Synonym for the Lowest in Vice and Crime and Human Rottenness"

The Notorious Wigwam

Blue Island once flourished, among other things, as *the* mecca of hedonism south of Chicago. Long before there was Las Vegas, there was Blue Island. Yet despite a proclivity for vice and pleasures of the flesh, Blue Island was not Sodom or Gomorrah. Those cities were destroyed by fire. Blue Island was not so lucky. Its eternal punishment was for it never to change.

Old Blue Island had a proper and conservative veneer. After the turn of the 20th century, its business district was the biggest thing between Chicago and Joliet, and everyone in the area shopped here. Blue Island had an elevator and it was not a mechanic apparatus that provided vertical transportation. Blue Island was in transition from farm community. The Klein Elevator provided goods for the many farms in and around it.

As early as 1918 and depending upon whose figures you chose to believe, Blue Island had more than 10,000 residents, a sizable population for that era, and the community-in-transition was a dichotomy. Blue Island was starched white collar, well-to-do, God fearing, and church going. It also was blue collar, living paycheck to paycheck and sinning with impunity. Blue Island had many churches, even more saloons, and plenty of reasons to attend each. The temptations included gambling, booze, and prostitution. The city motto could have been *Let's have another round! What's your name, honey? Hey, hurry up and deal them cards 'cause I'm feelin' lucky! What? It's Sunday mornin' already? Damn it! I mean, amen.*

No one worked harder, played harder, or got dirtier than the men who toiled in the six brickyards in and around Blue Island around the turn of the century. The most historically important of them to Blue Islanders was the Purington Brick Company, which manufactured the paving bricks that compose the streets of the older sections of the city. Those Purington bricks have withstood the tests of time physically and symbolically. Like Blue Islanders themselves, the bricks are stubborn and tough. They lie not far beneath the surface of the city, covered by asphalt and waiting for someone to expose them and the truth about Blue Island past.

Purington had two brickyards at 119th Street just northeast of Blue Island. When brickmaking was at its peak, many area men worked at local yards, an estimated 600 according to the *Sun-Standard.* The days in the brickyards were long. Very early in the morning the men went into a hole in the ground and they literally did not come out of that hole until the end of the workday, which may have been 12 hours later.

My great-grandfather came to Blue Island [in the] early 1890s and both great-grandfathers worked at Purington brickyards that used to be around 119th Street. "My grandfather did too," said former Blue Island resident John Juby in a "Blue Island Back in the Day" post on Facebook. "The family home was at 127th and Hoyne. My great-grandmother used to start making dinner when she saw her husband climb out of the hole at the brickyards.

There was nothing to obscure her view from 127th to 119th!"

Eventually the Illinois Brick Company acquired the Purington yards and those immense holes in the ground. Illinois Brick endured as the only survivor of the six producers until it was determined to be a major polluter and was closed by a decree from Illinois attorney general in 1975.

As for its early business history, Illinois Brick had two yards on the borders of Blue Island. Yard 22 actually was two clayholes at 123rd Street and Ogden Avenue (now California). One big clayhole with enough water to lure swimmers, boaters, and fishermen was on the south side of 123rd Street. Another bigger clayhole that also doubled as a garbage dump was on the north side of 123rd. Illinois Brick Yard 17 was on 119th Street. The other parameters of Yard 17 were Wood Street, 123rd Street, and Ashland Avenue. By 1918, the main brickmaking operation was winding down at Yard 17. So much clay had been extracted that the hole in the earth was enormous, but it no longer was profitable for brickmaking purposes. Eventually the brickmaking plant and a blockmaking plant were installed at Yard 22.

If you were a Blue Islander who grew up between 1890 and 1975, you knew your clayholes well. They were huge, colorful excavations that appeared to go on forever in every direction, and this was part of the allure that attracted people, especially boys, to them. Kids and adults swam and boated in the clayholes that were filled with water. People fished there. This leads to a question: how did fish get into an industrial excavation? Lifelong resident

Harry Robertson, age 93, who visited the clayholes as a boy, has a theory.

"No one stocked the 119th Street clayhole with fish. The fish got into the clayhole naturally," said Mr. Robertson during a June 2013 interview. "Birds ate fish and fish eggs elsewhere. When they flew over the clayhole, they expelled the eggs. The eggs hatched and that was it.

"The fish that were in the clayhole were carp. I never ate fish from the clayhole, but we'd go down there and catch them. Once I sold a string of fish I'd caught to a local fish monger," Mr. Robertson said. "We'd also go over to the clayhole at California Avenue. There was a garbage dump there and we would shoot rats with a .22."

For almost as long as there was water in the clayholes, there also were drownings. Most of the victims were children or young adults. On July 9, 1915, William Rosco Waugh and his brother Clarence Henry Waugh left their home on Burr Oak just east of Western and went to play at a 119th Street clayhole. The Waugh brothers drowned there. They were ages eight and six, respectively. Unfortunately, there were many more drownings at the 119th Street and at the 123rd clayholes after the Waugh brothers.

Those clayholes held such great allure that people who didn't engage in local water sports or rodent hunting sometimes came by just to stare at the great excavations. If those gawkers never saw the Grand Canyon, it may not have mattered. The clayholes were Blue Island's version and for generations they remained wonders of the urban world as long as those who lived in that world did not go beyond the city limits and until the clayholes finally were completely converted to garbage dumps—at which point they became a different type of wonder.

Truth be told—and please note that Blue Islanders never have allowed the truth to ruin a good story (Thank you, Earl Ebers Jr.)—the east tract of Yard 17 was in the Village of Burr Oak and the west tract was just outside of the Blue Island city limits. The unofficial dividing line between Burr Oak and unincorporated land was Wood Street. By 1919, that enormous excavation loomed and there was another reason to visit that location. According to the *Sun-Standard*, Mike "de Pike" Heitler operated a business, generously referred to as "a cabaret" called the 'Wigwam" at 119th and Wood streets. When the *Blue Island Sun-Standard* newspaper referred to it using an adjective, the word "notorious" almost always preceded the name of the cabaret. Heitler's joint was "the notorious Wigwam" and it was appropriately and conveniently situated on the precipice of the clayhole that was in the Village of Burr Oak. Now if the Wigwam was notorious, what was Mr. Heitler, who reportedly was a "White slaver" who forced women into prostitution? According to the *Sun-Standard*, from the day he acquired the Wigwam, Mike Heitler always had six to ten female sex slaves there whose job was to entice patrons into one of the private rooms at the back of the joint.

Prostitution was installed at the notorious Wigwam during the summer of 1918 before the entrepreneurial Mike Heitler came along. The Wigwam, a ramshackle two-story frame structure that had "suites" in the back, was slightly less notorious during 1917 when it was purchased by two Chicago underworld figures referred to only by their last names, Harris and Barnes. According to the *Sun-*

Standard, almost immediately Harris and Barnes transformed their cabaret into a combination gin mill-gambling joint-brothel. That's when the trouble began, but not because of law enforcement or public indignation. It was the result of a personnel decision.

Harris and Barnes imported a well-known prostitute from the Levee District of Chicago. The woman was the girlfriend of another Chicago hood. One evening, the hood and his associates arrived for her and for retribution. The waiters at the Wigwam also were hoods and they carried guns. When the mobsters from Chicago burst in with their guns drawn, the Wigwam went from cabaret to shooting gallery. "The interior of the cabaret looked like a European battlefield" is how the *Sun-Standard* described it. There was no report of casualties or what happened to Barnes, but Harris was arrested. What he did while in custody or awaiting trial may have inspired a famous scene from the movie "The Untouchables." Harris reportedly committed suicide by leaping from an upper window of the Criminal Courts Building in Chicago.

Thereafter, Mike the Pike assumed ownership—terms of acquisition never were divulged—and he brought in his brother, Coleman "Dutch" Heitler, to help him run things. That was when the Wigwam became "notorious." The legal euphemism for the establishment during that era was "disorderly house." Before either of the Heitlers ever showed up and until 1937, Blue Island and the surrounding area had quite a few disorderly houses. Before or since, there never has been any house as disorderly as the notorious Wigwam, though not for lack of trying. The notorious Wigwam was the Poinciana on steroids.

Just imagine the colorful, albeit unsavory scene at the man cave that was the notorious Wigwam. The dirty, sweaty men who toiled in Yard 17, baked bricks, or who worked in nearby brickyards, factories, fields, or railyards wanted a place to unwind. They worked long hours and in shifts. They came in at all times of day and night. Underneath the dirt and grime, they were White, of European descent, and uneducated. Some of them may not have spoken English well or at all. There was, of course, the universal language based upon money, consumption, and desire. The men wanted alcohol! The favorite concoction may have been the old country combination shot and a beer. Sometimes they wanted women or to gamble. Gambling was illegal, but it was accepted. Respectable women did not enter saloons. That was why women who had lost their souls were imported from locales such as the Levee District and why back room suites were invented.

Blue Island was different from the rest of the world, and it was the same. Legitimate industries such as brickmaking and railroads begat others that were less legitimate and nowhere near as savory. The term "on the border" is appropriate because some of them were, literally and figuratively, on the edge of Blue Island and legitimacy.

James Hackett was the gambling czar of Blue Island at that time. Mr. Hackett had a lot of clout in Blue Island and he was allowed to operate with impunity in town. For those who liked to gamble and drink, his roadhouse was conveniently located on the far edge of town, nowhere near main street, and just within the city limits at 119th and Vincennes. Mr. Hackett was a respected entrepreneur. He and his family were members of St. Benedict Parish. His place of business was not a disorderly house. Mike Heitler's joint was across the border in every way. The notorious Wigwam was located on the edge of a chasm—physically, culturally, and morally—outside but well within reach of Blue Island proper.

The intersection of Vincennes and 119th was where hypocrisy met arrogance. The question can be asked: was it also the birthplace of its philosophy and personality? Was it Blue Island's Fertile Crescent of accepted vice? For as long as anyone can remember, Blue Island has been a victim of the falsehoods of its own perception. It never has seen itself as a community defined by booze, gambling, proximity to disorderly houses, misogyny, or segregation. Blue Island always has thumped its chest as a community based upon hard work, integrity, friendliness, and Christian beliefs. Newspapers outside of Blue Island did not view Blue Island this way. They reported the good and the bad. When they did, Blue Islanders patted themselves on the backs for the good and denied there was any bad.

Perhaps Blue Island's own newspaper, the *Sun-Standard,* should share some of the fault for allowing Blue Island's head to get too big, for allowing it to live in denial. Too often the newspaper printed news that it was fed by local politicians and businessmen, that Blue Island was the biggest, the best, and its light shined the brightest.

Take, for example, the reports of construction of factories. It is a legend that the political and business leaders who controlled Blue Island did not want industry within the city limits. To do so would have caused Blue Island to grow out of the farm community so easily under their control. Yet new industry did come and most of it was beyond Blue Island borders. When they did, the *Sun-*

Standard always reported them as "in Blue Island." When a factory that was to be built at 125th and Ashland during 1920, the *Sun-Standard* reported this as "new Blue Island industry" even though it was not within the city limits.

These were not merely the doings of John Volp and his newspaper, although he did publish those falsehoods. The information was provided by elected officials, bankers, and members of the community who practiced one of the favorite Blue Island pastimes that contributed to the demise of the community: gossip. The bragging and the falsehoods were absorbed by those in the community and beyond. That Blue Island preferred to gossip and thump its chest about "new Blue Island industry" instead of ensuring that it was within city limits would lead to its decline.

Here is a difference between perception and reality: located at 119th and Wood streets, "the notorious Wigwam" actually was closer to Blue Island than that new factory at 125th Street and Ashland Avenue. The factory was in Burr Oak, but in those days there was not much of a Village of Burr Oak for anything to be "close to" it. The village that would become Calumet Park after 1930 was a small farm community and the location and lack of identity of Burr Oak was convenient for Blue Island. Almost every time there was a negative story, the *Sun-Standard* was very specific that the offender or offense was elsewhere. Thus the factory was "new Blue Island industry" and "the notorious Wigwam" always was located in Burr Oak.

Publisher Volp and his editors are deserving of some credit. When they were made privy to it and if it did not involve a friend or local big shot, they published crime news and named names. They kept Blue Island and the surrounding area informed. As for friends and local big shots, James Hackett was both and he always received a free pass from the *Sun-Standard.* Mr. Hackett controlled all of the gambling, primarily slot machines and bookmaking, in Blue Island until the day he died. Yet his name was never mentioned in stories about gambling raids.

When the Transfer Inn, his roadhouse at 119th and Vincennes, was raided—rarely and on those rare occasions by outside law enforcement agents, but never by Blue Island police—James Hackett was not credited as its owner. Oh, there might have been a few lines in the *Sun-Standard* about "a raid at Mr. Hackett's Transfer Inn" as there was in the December 25, 1925 edition of the *Sun-Standard.* According to the story, "the gambling house at 119th and Vincennes" and the Blue Goose Inn were raided just before Christmas by the state's attorney. The doors and windows [of the Transfer Inn] are tightly nailed and a watch is kept." Apparently that watch was either quite lax or the fix superseded it. Unlike the Blue Goose Inn (another notorious brothel located in Burr Oak!), the Transfer Inn quickly re-opened for business. With the exception of one very loud hiccup, the establishment thrived until 1937.

The hiccup was dynamite bombing that occurred in the wee hours of November 9, 1927. It did not stop Mr. Hackett or his operation. The opposite occurred. The Transfer Inn was closed only long enough for repairs and the heroic actions of James Hackett added to his legend. According to that legend, after the bombing he completely took over the police station and directed rescue and investigative efforts. At least one part of the story, as it pertains to the bombing, is not accurate. The Transfer Inn was not dynamite bombed by bootleggers who wanted to force Mr. Hackett to purchase their product. The bombing most likely was perpetrated by operators of Chicago gambling houses whose casinos had been shut down during raids by Chicago police. In its reporting of the bombing, the *Chicago Tribune* called this a "dog in the manger" tactic. The Transfer Inn was a Blue Island establishment, which made it untouchable by Chicago cops. It was not out of the reach of Chicago gambling bosses whose message reportedly was *If we can't operate, neither can you. Ka-boom!* Yet operate everyone did. The raids were for publicity. The fix went back in for Chicago gambling the day after the raids. The gambling houses re-opened, as did the Transfer Inn after repairs to its frontage.

Like his Transfer Inn, James Hackett was a larger-than-life figure who seemed indestructible. That he and his establishment not only survived the bombing, but flourished contributed to his legend in progress. James Hackett was an entrepreneur, philanthropist, sports enthusiast, and money lender. According to the *Sun-Standard*, Hackett provided "valuable assistance" in the acquisition of the 6.75 acres known as Becker's Woods which would become Centennial Park. He also promoted local semi-professional baseball when he helped organize and fund the group known as the Blue Island "Fans." Jimmy Withers, the uncle of a future mayor, was the Fan's president. James Hackett golfed and took fishing trips to Canada with other prominent Blue Islanders such as George Roll, Christian Krueger, Andrew L. McCord, and publisher Volp. He acquired money and property from some of them too, either through loans or gambling. James

Hackett owned prime real estate on Western Avenue, and his slot machines graced the local saloons, but not only saloons. The Hackett Family was a member and big contributor to St. Benedict Parish. For decades when there was a St. Benedict fundraiser, the Hacketts allowed the church the use of their slot machines.

Everyone knew James Hackett. Everyone knew who owned the roadhouse. He was a friend and supporter of mayors Klenk, Kasten, and Hart. In Blue Island, James Hackett helped put the Fix in and keep it there. The Fix was good for business and that was good for Blue Island. There was no need to mention James Hackett in a story about anything unsavory. The dynamite bombing of a place of business could happen to anyone. So it should be no surprise that in the passage devoted to the Hackett kidnappings in his FIRST HUNDRED YEARS, Mr. Volp respectfully refers to James Hackett as a "reputed gambler and well-known man about town."

So Blue Island was corrupt and clannish and arrogant and it took care of its own. As any Blue Islander would tell you, "So what?" About James Hackett, they would say, "He's a good guy." If someone on a far-lower rung of the ladder such as Mike "de Pike" (also known as "Mike the Pike") did business just across the border in the Village of Burr Oak, Blue Island didn't care. It was Burr Oak. If you have your head tilted upward and your nose high in the air, you pretend not to see the garbage or smell the stench no matter how close it is.

Taking a step back in time, even those who assumed this odd posture must have noticed the interesting twists that began during the first week of November 1919. They provided entertainment and amusement.

As reported by the *Sun-Standard*, that was when three officers from the office of the Cook County Sheriff raided the notorious Wigwam and arrested everyone on the premises—"the Pike, fifteen johns, and four prostitutes." Among the johns were two murderers and four car thieves. Everyone was charged, some with more serious crimes than others. Heitler was cited for "operating a disorderly house," although his operation actually was quite orderly. Male customers and crooks on the lam knew exactly why they went to "the notorious Wigwam," how much it would cost them, and prior to the unexpected raid, that there was a good chance they were not going to be arrested.

Hence an interesting question: why were Heitler and the others at the Wigwam arrested in Cook County where, like Blue Island, the Fix always was in as long as you either paid or knew someone?

Well, the reason may have been that Mike Heitler was more despised and mistrusted by those who operated outside of the law than by those who upheld it. The Pike sometimes undercut and double-crossed his fellow mobsters. Over the years, among those Heitler eventually ratted on for profit or to save his own hide was rival mob-pimp-turned-Outfit-accountant Jake "Greasy Thumb" Guzik. The Outfit did not yet exist. There was a disjointed collection of rival mobsters at that time, not the structured organization created by Capone a few years later. In 1919, instead of having him killed, any mobster or rival who had a beef with Mike Heitler may have ratted on him or paid a little more to put him out of business. In this case, perhaps an elected official or members of law enforcement did not receive their payoff. Still another possibility was the three

Cook County Sheriff's police may not have known who they were arresting. Finally, as farfetched as it would have been for the time and place, someone actually may have decided to enforce the law rather than ignore it.

Stranger things did happen, although not very often, and occasionally there was public indignation to consider. Some residents of Burr Oak were outraged that the notorious Wigwam operated in their community and they complained to local elected officials and police. As for those who received the complaints, they probably were paid off by the Pike, but once in awhile they had to feign indignation and pretend to provide law and order. This could have led to Mike Heitler being arrested, which would have caused him to become indignant. *How dare anyone arrest someone who paid off not to be arrested!*

At that point, Mike Heitler fought corruption with more corruption. After his arraignment in Oak Park, he reportedly summoned the Burr Oak Justice of the Peace, Henry A. Wolske, who the *Sun-Standard* alleged was on the Heitler payroll as a bartender, and had him issue warrants for the three arresting officers. The Pike must truly have been upset because he put Mr. Wolske in his car and drove him downtown to the County Building to serve the warrants. For reasons never specified, the Justice of the Peace chickened out and didn't approach the officers. Afterward, Henry Wolske denied to the *Sun-Standard* that he was a bartender at the Wigwam, although he did not deny that he issued the bogus warrants for false arrest or that he was on the payroll of a pimp.

Because he was arrogant and perhaps because he already had paid off at least once, Mike Heitler refused to pay the $200 fine issued by another Justice of the Peace,

Frank A. McKee of Oak Park. He opted for a trial. That hearing was delayed, however, because the witnesses for the prosecution could not be located. Eventually, Mike the Pike was convicted and paid a fine, but he received no jail time. Yet he continued to operate the notorious Wigwam during and after that court case until he was arrested and put on trial again, this time in Chicago Circuit Court. According to the *Sun-Standard,* Mike Heitler lost this bigger case and was given the option of jail or leaving Cook County. He chose the latter and he announced that he was leaving the United States for Cuba and that he had sold the Wigwam to Abraham Weinstein. Dutch Heitler stayed behind to look after his brother's interests.

Abe Weinstein was a front, of course, and nothing changed at the notorious Wigwam except the presence of The Pike, if that since there is no record of Mike Heitler ever departing for Cuba. There is a record of the notorious Wigwam being raided by federal agents on February 26, 1920, exactly 57 days after Prohibition became the law. During the raid, it was revealed that in addition to booze, prostitution continued to be available in the back rooms under the direction of an African American madam. Abe Weinstein, Dutch Heitler, the madam, the working women, and the johns were brought before Blue Island police magistrate Peter Heintz. Charges were filed, bond was set, and the case was assigned to federal court in Chicago.

That's where the fix temporarily ended for Abe Weinstein and Dutch Heitler, although not for lack of effort on their parts. Despite some of the evidence—eight bottles of whiskey—disappearing on the way from the notorious Wigwam to Chicago, the defendants were in the wrong venue against the right judge. In federal court against the legendary Judge Kennesaw Mountain Landis, they didn't stand a chance. According to the *Sun-Standard*, Judge Landis found both men guilty and sentenced each to six months in the House of Corrections. And Judge Landis was not finished. He inquired as to whom had been in charge of the evidence that disappeared. Told that the police officer abruptly had resigned and moved to Richmond, Virginia, the judge ordered that he be brought to his courtroom to explain.

This still was not the end of the notorious Wigwam, perhaps because of the gap between determining the law and enforcing it. The operators of the brothel announced that it was a soft drink emporium. This designation was not unusual. Virtually every saloon in and around Blue Island converted to a "soft drink emporium" after Prohibition took effect. In Blue Island, the soft drink emporiums, all licensed by the city, actually were sanctioned gin mills and bookie joints. Gambling and booze were part of the fabric of Blue Island and were universally accepted. Many stills operated in Blue Island and there was no shortage of supply. As for the "resort" as Burr Oak Mayor John Synakiewicz referred to the notorious Wigwam, it continued to operate with impunity and to make news. During the week of July 4, 1920, five couples caught in the act of being, ahem, disorderly were arrested on the premises. That caused Burr Oak officials to announce they'd had enough. Subsequently, on July 13, 1920 there was a special village board meeting presided over by Mayor Synakiewicz and covered by the *Sun-Standard.* The notorious Wigwam "had brought shame on the village," said some in attendance. It had "caused property values to fall," said others there. It also must be noted that during the same meeting, someone from Burr Oak stated that "when Mike 'the Pike' ran the Wigwam, at least it had been operated with some semblance of decency." Now what's a little shame and diminished property value amongst neighbors?

Oh, yes, in post-World War I America, some things still were in short supply. Burr Oak was not different than Blue Island in this and decency was one such limited commodity. Or was decency simply in the eyes of the beholder? And what if the beholder was intoxicated or on the take? Nevertheless, there was a raid on the notorious Wigwam the next night, July 14. Among those who barged in and made the arrests were village officials, Cook County Sheriff's police, and two members of the *Sun-Standard* staff who managed to get themselves deputized in order to get a firsthand view of the action. The following is a portion of the account filed by the journalists.

> "A score of men and girls were found seated at tables at the café. There was no shooting. Several individuals protested and offered bribes to be let go and to no avail. A search of the back of the hotel yielded one couple."

As a symbolic gesture, arresting officers confiscated the business license. Also symbolic—and because local law enforcement agencies of that era had virtually no budgets and thus few vehicles and virtually no equipment—was that everyone arrested was taken to jail in taxis. They were bailed out by Dutch Heitler, who either had received an early release or who had not yet begun to pay his six-month debt to society. There was no mention of who paid the cab fares.

What ensued was a series of continuances for various reasons in Burr Oak Court before bartender and Justice of the Peace Wolske. The first two court calls, Weinstein claimed to be ill. The next two calls, police magistrate Henry Buhring, who for years was the Blue Island city attorney, was on vacation. Finally, on August 17, all were in attendance, the case was presented, and there was great theater. According to the *Sun-Standard*, Abe Weinstein claimed he was being railroaded and screamed. When he did, Henry Wolske, who either found religion or was a showman, told him to shut up and pronounced him guilty. The latter may have been the answer because Magistrate Wolske had the best lines in the production. When Mr. Weinstein shouted, "Not guilty! You're framing..." Mr. Wolske cut him off before he could finish.

"Shut up!" he told Abe Weinstein.

When Weinstein later began to defend himself with "I run a high class, respectable..." Wolske again cut him off. "Fifty dollars you're fined! You're guilty!" He added, "You should have known that none of that stuff gets pulled off in a village such as Burr Oak."

Of the four men charged, one was a bartender and another was a waiter. The two customers arrested were railroad employees. One was a watchman, the other was a switchman. The defense listed the dissolute women by another occupation. Wolske took note and said, "*Hmmm.* I notice how you ladies are dance instructors. You should make quite a little money teaching young

America to shake its hoof, hey? You are hereby fined $10 apiece along with the four men." Weinstein wailed. The defendants that the *Sun-Standard* called the "Wigwam Ten" joined him in protest.

Wolske said, "Maybe ten [dollars] more for contempt of court." The complaining ceased.

While the fines may not seem like much, they were substantial in 1920. That was two dance lessons apiece for the women, who paid their fines and departed. The Justice of the Peace concluded the proceeding with a less believable pronouncement when he said, "We got 'em. Now Weinstein's got to get out. He's operating now under a temporary permit because he's turned the Wigwam over to a new management who will run the place in a respectable, high-class fashion."

Yes, for reasons never explained, the notorious Wigwam was allowed to operate. It did so the only way it knew how, with impunity, though for only a short time longer. The end had nothing to do with the legal system or that the Heitlers and Weinstein were in exile. Something more potent than the legal system finally put the Wigwam out of business.

Appropriately, on the morning of Tuesday, October 14, 1920, the notorious Wigwam went up in flames. Arson was not the cause. Reportedly it was a cook who threw a still-lit cigarette butt into a corner that caused the wooden structure to ignite. The *Sun-Standard* was merciless in its report of the demise of the notorious Wigwam, which included a recap of its sordid history.

"Some denizens of Chicago's underworld came to Burr Oak when Chicago refused any longer to hold them and erected a two story frame building—a "crime castle"—at 119th and Wood Sts. That was several years ago. From that time on the two-story frame building has been a synonym for the lowest in vice and crime and human rottenness. With it have been connected men whose names caused honest citizens to shudder."

The newspaper also ripped proprietors Weinstein and Heitler in its reporting of the fire. The *Sun-Standard* said:

"Today the Wigwam is only a mass of charred timbers. The 'hotel' at the rear, for years used for immoral purposes, also is practically destroyed. Abe Weinstein, vice baron who inherited the Wigwam estate from the notorious Mike 'de Pike' Heitler, is furious. Peaceable citizens of Burr Oak and Blue Island and county, state, and federal officials are overjoyed.

"Weinstein discussed the fire as he was wandering disconsolately about the ruins Monday afternoon. He refused to state whether he would attempt to rebuild the resort. 'All the clothes I've got in the world except what are on my back were burned,' Weinstein said. 'They were in my room in the second story. There was about 200 bucks in cash there too and that was burned.'"

Fire finally put an end to the notorious Wigwam, but it did not stop Mike "the Pike" Heitler and his cohorts. The White slaver rode the flames into Blue Island and continued his business on a larger scale.

"In Five Years, I Had a Snug Fortune"

The Burr Oak Hotel and Bootleg Booze

Things got hot at City Hall in Blue Island, too. Late in 1920, Mayor Edward N. Stein pontificated against gambling in the city and announced that something had to be done about it. In its December 20 edition, the *Sun-Standard* praised Mayor Stein for this stance. Thereafter, the newspaper and everyone else in town who opposed gambling waited and wondered. What would Mayor Stein do? The wait was approximately three months because Mayor Stein departed for California immediately after his announcement, reportedly for health reasons, and he did not return until March.

Decades before Paddy Bauler and like Chicago, Blue Island was not ready for reform.

Alderman E.B. Bronson served as mayor pro tem during the absence of Mayor Stein and he was besieged by Western Avenue business owners who wanted protection not against gambling, but against crime. Robberies were regular occurrences in the business district and were bad for business. Gambling was not. Mayor Pro Tem Bronson and aldermen received a petition signed by 32 business owners who wanted the city to approve "special police" (security guards) to protect them. Business owners were so serious about their proposal that they submitted names of the men they wanted to hire and offered to pay for them. The city council voted unanimously to reject the proposal.

At about the same time, residents of the north side of town registered similar complaints. While the notorious Wigwam had been outside of Blue Island, its proximity had caused problems for nearby residents. A few of the details appeared in a January 1921 *Sun-Standard* story about the north side of the city. It was bad enough that city officials virtually had ignored that part of Blue Island to the extent that some neighborhoods still had dirt roads, paths instead of sidewalks, and no sewer or water connections. Local law enforcement failed to ensure safety.

"People here have no protection whatsoever. Our neighborhood is like a desert isle," a female resident told reporter Alfred O'Connell. "When the Wigwam café was running, people were rushing up and down 119th Street at all hours of the night firing revolvers. Many residents have been held up and other crimes have been committed."

Perhaps to further protect his health, Mayor Stein did not seek re-election in April 1921. On the other hand, gambling enjoyed quite a long and healthy existence in Blue Island. So did bootlegging and the availability of alcohol-making ingredients. Anonymous providers shipped large quantities of alcohol-making ingredients to the Blue Island rail yard for pick up by fictitious businesses. Occasionally those shipments were intercepted by federal agents. More often bootleggers managed to get them through. Stills of all sizes seemed to be everywhere and the *Sun-Standard* occasionally ran stories of raids on the basements and garages that were supposed to conceal them. When the operations busted were large in scale, the name linked to them usually was Lorenzo Juliano, the feared local mobster who was rumored to control all of the bootlegging in the area. Occasionally, Mr. Juliano was taken into custody, but he never was convicted of bootlegging or any other major crimes.

Yes, there were many booze and gambling raids in Blue Island during Prohibition. None were staged by Blue Island police. One raid took place during mid-1921 when Ben Brodsky's saloon was raided and federal agents posing as customers observed a gambling game and that alcohol was being served. According to the *Sun-Standard*, Brodsky and seven patrons were arrested. They pleaded guilty and paid fines. Brodsky did not lose his business license. Instead, after a very short time, he resumed business.

In its February 9, 1922 edition, the *Sun-Standard* detailed another raid on local "soft drink emporiums" by federal agents. "The wettest place on the Prohibition map, otherwise known as Blue Island, ain't quite so wet this week, and the cause is two score of dry agents who motored to this city for exercise and visited the watering places from start to finish. About one barkeeper or saloon proprietor for every two dry agents was arrested and taken to Chicago for quizzing."

The federal agents posed as real estate salesmen and carried maps and blueprints. When they entered an establishment, they said they were cold and wanted something to help them warm up. When they were served alcohol, the arrests began. Among the proprietors and bartenders taken into custody and charged were John Kruse, Daniel Chamberlain, James H. Dertz, Herman Groskopf, Edward Groskopf, Pa, and Fred J. Wigenton. All reportedly pleaded guilty, paid fines, and were released. Then they went back into business.

Again, city officials looked the other way when it came to booze. To allow the proprietors to sell beverages, albeit illegal beverages, without licensing them would have been politically and financially foolish. So the city sold them business licenses and then looked the other way. All of the soft drink emporiums were licensed. When, not if, one or more of the proprietors was indiscreet enough to be busted by federal agents, he may have been forced to close his doors briefly and pay a fine. When the federal heat was off, the proprietor resumed business as usual. City officials never did figure out a way to license bootlegging and gambling, but the possibilities actually were discussed publicly and usually by accident when an alderman would forget that the rest of America did not do business in the same manner as Blue Island. After the indiscreet alderman was reminded by the city attorney that illegal activities could not be licensed and assured by the police chief that no such things existed in Blue Island, the subject was dropped. As the old timers said, "It was just the way things were done."

As for prostitution, the one vice Blue Island apparently wanted to get rid of, not the demise of the notorious Wigwam, complaints, arrests, nor any other legal action changed the situation. Mike "the Pike"

Heitler continued his profitable business at a better location. Blue Island was a boom town, a metropolis in the making. It had a large population for that era, a shopping district, and a railroad terminal. Mr. Heitler was a savvy businessman and he relocated his operation approximately one mile south in Blue Island when he took over the Burr Oak Hotel, which was at the northwest corner of Burr Oak Avenue and Fairmount Street. The location was on the fringe of the Blue Island rail yard, on a busy thoroughfare and just a few steps off of the main street.

After they knew it was being operated as a brothel—and they did because it is on the record—city officials did not close the Burr Oak Hotel. This may seem like a mystery today, but it is not. Then it was just the way things were done. Prostitution was considered to be an embarrassing crime, not a serious one. There was no moral outrage that women were being exploited since women had few rights during that era of male domination. Crimes against women were easier to commit and more difficult to prosecute or even to generate sympathy for them. There were no women in law enforcement or in prosecutorial roles. There were no women judges. There were virtually no women in the media to write about the abuses and injustices against other women.

Furthermore, in that era, law enforcement always operated underfunded, understaffed, and unprofessionally. Regarding the latter, to get anyone in law enforcement interested in a brothel beyond accepting a bribe or using its services must have been a chore. Thus no one should be surprised that instead of closing places such as the Burr Oak Hotel, local officials danced around this flagrant disregard of the law for years. When there was so much as a nod in that direction, it was precipitated by a request from a local organization such as the Episcopal Methodist Church, which was located at Burr Oak and Western Avenue, less than two blocks from the Burr Oak Hotel.

Can you imagine how church members of the Episcopal Methodist Church felt, not merely being so close to those who sinned against the flesh, but the proximity of their place of worship to where the flesh was peddled? After the congregation issued a complaint to Mayor Klenk during the summer of 1923, he denied a license for the Burr Oak Hotel, which was being operated by Phil Kimmel. Mayor Klenk also ordered an inspection of the premises. Thereafter Fire Marshall John Link announced that the hotel was not safe because of fire hazards such as debris in the basement and due to the lack of proper fire escapes.

During that inspection, Mike Heitler was on hand and he admitted to Chief Link that he actually was the owner. After Phil Kimmel's request for a license was denied, he claimed to have sold the hotel. Ben Harris of Chicago next attempted to acquire a business license. Harris tried to fool city officials by announcing that he was a married father of four and living at the hotel with his family. Mayor Klenk saw through this and Harris's license was also denied. The hotel was to remain closed for legal and safety reasons. Yet it continued to operate as a brothel just as it had during the faux transition from Heitler to Kimmel to Harris. A fourth front, a man named Ira Caesar, subsequently was arrested and charged with operating the establishment without a license.

The two guys who publicly claimed to no longer own the joint, Mike Heitler and Phil Kimmel, just happened to be arrested there at 8 p.m. on Saturday, October 13, 1923. They were charged with keeping a disorderly house. Three men and five women also were arrested and they were charged with being "inmates." The Cook County state's attorney, not Blue Island police, performed that raid and all of those arrested were hauled off to court at Forest Park. Mr. Heitler had been living at the Burr Oak Hotel while he appealed a conviction for a violation of the Volstad Act. During 1920, he had been caught smuggling 1,000 cases of whiskey and he spent the next three years appealing the conviction.

During October 1923 his last appeal was denied, as was his request for a new trial, and off to Leavenworth Federal Penitentiary went Mike "the Pike" Heitler. He didn't depart before holding a farewell press conference at the Chicago train depot. During this event, Mr. Heitler gave reporters his version of his life story. He said he came to America from Austria at age ten and lived on the Lower East side of New York City. He claimed that was where he earned the nickname "de Pike," although he did not say how. Mike Heitler explained that as a young man he ventured to the Klondike during the Gold Rush. There he struck gold, which he called "paydirt" and he also was very lucky gambling in Nome and Dawson. He came back to the States with $16,000 and opened a cigar store at 24 N. Halstead Street. There was gambling in the back of the cigar store, he bragged, and the games got big. "In five years, I had a snug fortune," he told reporters.

Thereafter, according to Heitler, they called him "Mike, the killer," "the fence," and "the White slaver." He referred to himself in the third person when he added, "Mike hasn't the heart to kill a mouse. Mike never ran a crooked game. Mike never was a pickpocket. Why call me a gunman?" He did not explain who "they" were, why "they" referred to him in those terms, or why he ran operations such as the notorious Wigwam and the Burr Oak Hotel. Those details would not evoke sympathy. When operating in Blue Island, do what Blue Islanders do. Why ruin a good story with the truth?

Heitler wore an expensive suit and he waved triumphantly as he posed for photos while boarding the train to Leavenworth. His sentence was 18 months, but he served less than half of it. Why he was paroled early was not explained. He did not get time off for good behavior or have legitimate employment waiting for him because upon his release Heitler returned to operate the Burr Oak Hotel and other such establishments in and around Cook County.

Things at the Burr Oak Hotel were no less exciting during Heitler's taxpayer-funded vacation. It was raided January 19, 1924. The proprietor of the hotel, again it was family man Harris, was taken into custody and charged with operating a disorderly house. He was fined $1,000. Also taken into custody and fined $50 apiece were eleven "inmates." The raid was conducted by officers of the Cook County Sheriff's Department. One of the arresting officers was Ferd Tuffanelli, a Blue Island resident who would become prominent for his connections outside of law enforcement. The Blue Island Police Department assisted, but most likely this was just a courtesy notification by the Cook County Sheriff.

Exactly one week later, there was another raid at the hotel that was supposed to be closed. This raid was conducted by Secret Service agents. Counterfeiters Frank Giorano and Frank Roberto were arrested. The federal agents found printing plates, paper, and counterfeit $20 notes. Giorano and Roberto reportedly ran their counterfeiting operation and prostitution out of the hotel. The Blue Island Police Department had been notified of the federal investigation and, according to Chief of Police George J. Fiedler, was asked not to stage any vice raids so that federal agents could infiltrate the counterfeiting operation at the Burr Oak Hotel. Fiedler, who had a reputation for being soft on crime, took some heat in the Chicago press for this. As for the raid itself, according to the *Sun-Standard*, prostitutes reportedly escaped via hidden doorways and secret passages.

The Burr Oak Hotel was not the only brothel operating in and around Blue Island, it merely was the most infamous. Its demise seemed to coincide with the death of Mike "the Pike" Heitler in 1930. By 1935, the property at the northwest corner had fallen into such disrepair that eventually it had to be demolished. Why the notorious Wigwam, the Burr Oak Hotel and other brothels were allowed to continue for so long never has been explained officially. In Cook County and especially in Blue Island until 1937, it was just the way things were done.

By no coincidence, during that year the business of organized prostitution ended in Blue Island. Crimes such as armed robbery and murder occurred randomly and only when someone from the outside was the perpetrator. On those occasions, the offenders often were taken into custody or they vanished. As for other illegal activities, the ones considered part of the native fabric, (i.e. profitable and pleasurable and therefore acceptable), well, it was still Blue Island. They continued to flourish.

"A Shame to Expect the Post Office Department to Make City Deliveries Under Such Conditions"

The Gospel According to Postmaster F.T.E. Kallum

The following is a letter from Blue Island Postmaster F.T.E. Kallum to City Attorney Roy Massena in response to a request by the city for home mail delivery for the north side of Blue Island as opposed to the rural mail delivery it was receiving. The letter is dated December 30, 1927. The information is interesting because it gives insight as to the physical condition of Blue Island at that time. The report has been reprinted verbatim.

My Dear Mr. Massena:

With reference to your letter of the 23rd instant [sic], referring to City delivery in the City of Blue Island lying west of the railroad tracks at Burr Oak Avenue, I beg to call attention to paragraph 137, page 23 of the U.S. Official Postal Code Guide, which reads as follows:

"City delivery limits must not be extended by postmasters without specific authority from the department. Such authority will be given only when the territory to which

it is proposed to extend service is provided with good continuous sidewalks, crosswalks, street lights, and street signs and when the houses are numbered and provided with mail receptacles or slots in the doors for the receipt of mail. Service will not be extended to any block in which less than 50 per cent of the building lots are improved and houses occupied. When two or more building lots constitute the ground of one residence, the plot may be regarded as improved. It is preferable that the new territory be contiguous, but this is not an absolute requirement."

Paragraph 138, page 23:

"When recommending an extension of service, the postmaster must certify that each of the foregoing requirements is met, and must show clearly the relation of the extension to the adjacent territory being served, the number of deliveries to be made daily, the population within the proposed exten-sion, the number of steps, the distance the carrier will travel, the time required to serve the new territory, and whether the extension can be made with present carrier force without additional expense. A sketch or map should be submitted showing each street.

"In connection with all requests for the extension of city delivery the postmaster shall, either in person or through competent supervisors, make

careful survey of the territory in question, and, in the event it meets the requirements, recommend the extension. If in doubt, the postmaster should submit to the department a detailed statement of conditions and request advice."

Now taking into consideration the conditions, as they exist in this territory, I am sure you will agree with me that there is no sidewalk at present and no crosswalks, except an attempt has been made to have a cinder walk laid, which is very unsatisfactory and has been misconstrued in many ways. Some Post Office inspectors will not accept such a sidewalk, for the reason that after delivery has been established, the owners of the property do not keep in it proper condition.

The district just south of the territory is an example of such a condition. The mud is about ankle deep, and the carrier is now compelled to walk in mud, on account of the sewers being laid the condition is abominable [sic]. I am thinking of reporting the same to the department and get a ruling thereon and ask to have the city delivery withdrawn. It is a shame to expect the post office department to make city deliveries under such conditions.

On the other hand, I will most gladly recommend extension of city deliveries as soon as the required deliveries are made. The territory you refer to is now being served by rural route number 1, out of this office, and I have received no request so far for city delivery.

I would like your cooperation to have this territory put in the proper condition and will do all I can to extend the city delivery as soon as I am warranted in doing so.

Thank you for calling my attention to the matter, and assuring you that I appreciate the interest taken on your part, I am

Sincerely yours,
F.T.E. Kallum
Postmaster

"I Also Would Recommend One Hour Parking On Western Avenue Between Burr Oak Avenue and 135th Street"

Blue Island Was Soft on Crime and Softer on Parking

Throughout the history of Blue Island, many detailed and informative reports have been issued during city council meetings. One department, however, rarely has issued comprehensive reports and it is the Police Department. This has been by design. To this day, as members of city government will admit privately that Blue Island officials do not want the citizenry to be informed when it comes to crime, primarily because they do not want the negative publicity that goes with crime.

Apparently members of the police force are in complete agreement since they are defensive about crime reports. They suspect that if accurate crime reports and statistics are issued, the public will assume either they're not doing their jobs or that they are doing their jobs too well. Each provides a no-win scenario. In the case of *not well enough*, cops would be forced to work a little harder. In the case of *too well*, they would be relegated to boring tasks that don't qualify as crime fighting. The latter is the most interesting and gives insight into the history of BIPD. Blue Island cops will chase a bank robber or a thief to the ends of the earth, but forget about getting any cop to write parking tickets in the business district. This is a matter of preference, not professionalism, and please note that the Blue Island police force today is professional and efficient.

It was not so during the 1920s and 1930s. Blue Island police were not up to the task of effective crime prevention. Not that police officers ever would have been sleeping, hanging out in saloons, having sex in squad cars, or—and this is really farfetched—perpetrating crimes themselves. Who would ever believe any of that? Anyway, when it comes to issuing monthly reports about police activity, the unwritten rule for Blue Island always has been, *What Blue Islanders don't know may hurt them, but it won't hurt the police and politicians.*

Thus citizens of that era were hit over the head and left unconscious on Western Avenue after a purse snatching. Armed men burst into the saloon where cards were being played and took the contents of the cash register and the pot. Delivery drivers were held up at gun point and relieved of their payrolls, cargo, and vehicles. Victims were beheaded and their corpses were dumped into the Cal Sag Channel. All of these types of crimes and many more occurred during the more colorful and lawless era of Blue Island and, God bless the *Sun-Standard* for reporting some of them.

For the purpose of presenting Blue Island as a safe, virtually crime-free community and perhaps to have something on paper in the event someone should ask for statistics, reports by the chief of police were issued. They were issued infrequently, however, and only when it was convenient. On those rare occasions reports were given, the details always were brief and designed to make as many as possible believe that not much in the way of crime occurred in Blue Island. Here is a report that was read during the July 6, 1931 city council meeting. The report was issued by the ever-beleaguered and soon-to-be replaced Chief of Police, George J. Fiedler. Again, before and during the Great Depression, Blue Island was rampant with crime, although you'd never know it by Chief Fiedler's very brief report. It has been reprinted below.

> *Total amount of fines collected: $729.00. Transported to Oak Forest infirmary: 2. Number of lodgers accommodated: 160. Number of burglaries reported: 2. Number of safekeepers: 60. Number of juveniles arrested: 11. Total number of arrests: 242. Transported to St. Francis Hospital: 8. Number of accidents: 30. Number of dogs destroyed: 20. Boys turned over to juvenile authorities for stealing auto: 2. Prisoners turned over to the Will County authorities for stealing auto: 2. Number of men found dead in home: 1.*
>
> *George J. Fiedler*
> *Chief of Police*

Chief Fiedler was not inept. He may have been disorganized and too nice a guy, as he was described by some, but he was not obtuse or lacking in skills. Chief Fiedler actually was quite observant and forward thinking, as the following report, a prequel to the above crime report, indicates. The report from Chief Fiedler was to Mayor Paul T. Klenk and the city council. It was submitted during the Monday, August 24, 1925 meeting. It has been reprinted verbatim.

> *Gentlemen:*
>
> *The growth of traffic in and through Blue Island makes it imperative that radical change be made in the existing system of usage of streets and highways. After careful consideration of the conditions, I respectfully urge that you cause to be drafted and passed as soon as possible, ordinances regulating the following subjects.*
>
> *1. No left-hand turns on Western Avenue between Burr Oak Avenue and Broadway Streets [sic].*
>
> *2. That Burr Oak Avenue and Vincennes Avenue be created as Thru [sic] streets.*
>
> *3. Also the turning in the middle of the block.*
>
> *4. I also would recommend the [sic] one hour parking on Western Avenue between Burr Oak Avenue and 135th Street. Especially on Saturdays and Sundays. I have noticed Automobiles [sic] standing from 3 to 8 hours in the same place; Western Avenue being a narrow street and the traffic being heavy on these days, hampers our traffic situation to a great extent.*

Your prompt consideration and action on these subjects will greatly assist the functioning of this Department.

Respectfully,
George J. Fiedler
Chief of Police

The recommendation was approved by Mayor Klenk. Upon a motion by Alderman Joseph Lentz and a second by Alderman Harold Volp, it was unanimously referred to the police committee and the city attorney. That is another noteworthy detail. Reports submitted to the city council rarely have been acted upon. In this case, only one of the recommendations came to fruition and that was #2. In Blue Island history, aldermen rarely created legislation, and they almost never passed legislation suggested by anyone other than the mayor. As for suggestion #4, the problem has haunted Blue Island for as long as motorized vehicles have operated here. From the day they did, the parking situation on Western Avenue was a never-ending problem. Aldermen simply have neglected to approve any of the many simple, but viable solutions offered to correct it as far back as 1925.

Again, even if they wanted to, neither Chief Fiedler nor his successors were allowed to issue comprehensive public reports of crime. As a result, Blue Island officially had few, if any, robberies, assaults, and purse snatchings. No stills were busted or moonshiners arrested. There were no gambling raids, nor were there raids on houses of ill repute. The bodies dumped into the canal, as reported by the *Sun-Standard*, were either figments of a writer's imagination or floated here from somewhere else. They must have been. If they existed—if any of the above occurred and in Blue Island—police reports would have been issued. In Blue Island, it's just the way things were done and not done.

There were two notable and calculated exceptions to the suppression of crime reports. One of the incidents that precipitated them was more tragic than the other. Each was symbolic. There also was an incident that may indicate precisely how out of control Blue Island crime was and that no one was immune to it. The details are reproduced in the following passages.

The Unspeakable Crime of 1929

And What It Said About the Police Department

The Blue Island city council held a special meeting on Thursday, January 24, 1929 at precisely 8:15 p.m. Mayor Paul T. Klenk opened what would be a tense meeting with the following announcement, reprinted below as it appeared in the official city council minutes.

> *Last night an unspeakable crime was committed in our City which calls for action from this body. From investigation I feel certain and positive that our police department did everything that could be done. We received splendid support from the County, State, and Federal authorities; also the Chicago and Blue Island press have done very good work.*
>
> *This is the first major crime in Blue Island in fifteen years and should not go unchallenged by the people of this community. While we can do but little we should do that little in our own way. In discussing the matter with the City Attorney we are of the opinion that the offering of a reward by the City is illegal, but that a sum should be raised by individual contributions. I am willing to underwrite a reward of at least $3000.00 but feel that this*

> *amount should be increased to $5000.00. I am certain that there are people willing to subscribe support necessary to make up the balance of $2000.00. The granting of a reward may mean little or nothing, but many times a man who knows something unless he will be personally benefitted thereby. We should not leave anything undone to apprehend the party responsible for this crime.*

At the conclusion of the speech by Mayor Klenk, some of the aldermen gave input. Rocco Guglielmucci moved that the mayor appoint a committee of five aldermen to contact all of the civic organizations in the community for the purpose of raising the balance of the $2,000. Joseph Lentz seconded the motion and it passed 11-0. The mayor appointed Guglielmucci, Lentz, Alfred Koenecke, George F. Fiedler, and William Gerdes to the committee.

Mayor Klenk added that Chief of Police Fiedler and Lieutenant Hankey were entitled to receive a $100 reward from the Illinois Bell Telephone Company and that they were willing to donate their reward money to the fund the city was creating.

More suggestions as to how to use the police department followed. Alderman Guglielmucci moved that the chief of police be instructed to station officers at the depots from five o'clock in the evening until the last train arrives or leaves the City of Blue Island. Alderman Lentz suggested that the taxi cab companies be requested to report to the Police Department at once any suspicious characters which they may be requested to haul. There were no objections and the Mayor issued the orders.

Aldermen Lentz and Rudolph Swanson suggested that another officer be placed at the police station at night and an additional police car be used in answering calls in addition to the patrol car.

It was at that point that Mayor Klenk became hesitant. These suggestions, the mayor said, would be referred to committee. This was a code. When a mayor said that an issue would be referred "to committee" that meant that it was going to disappear forever.

The mayor knew that he could authorize another car and hire another officer. He could create a fleet of police cars and a regiment of officers, and it would not be enough. He would not do so, however. Why? Well, it was obvious that, unlike his aldermen, Mayor Klenk had no faith in the police force. The mayor had many issues with BIPD during his eight years in office, chief among them that it was an unprofessional force that was unable to enforce the laws or deter crime. During April of 1928, Mayor Klenk had appointed five "town guards, all expert riflemen," to protect local banks. The town guard, not the police, would be the first called in the event of a bank robbery.

Because he believed the police department was not up to the urgent task the city suddenly faced, Mayor Klenk had asked representatives of the American Legion to be present. He said he did this because "they are familiar with the use of firearms and to try to work out some sort of plan for an auxiliary police force guarding against further crime." The statement itself was an indictment of Blue Island Police officers, some of whom carried firearms, none of whom had training, and one officer who had recently accidentally shot himself.

Veterans, on the other hand, were revered. Those who had returned from the Great War were the heroes who had defeated the Kaiser, a German archvillain. They were supermen who could accomplish anything! Now they were being asked to step down from their pedestals, take up the arms they'd been trained to use, and accomplish another herculean task.

Walter Gaboriault, Commander of the American Legion Post #50, stated that the organization would be glad to cooperate with the city council in anything it might undertake. The mayor added that as long as there were no objections, the Police Committee would meet with officers of the American Legion to see that this special force be deployed. Alderman Lentz stated that the committee of five appointed by the mayor would do so immediately and the city council meeting concluded.

Just what was this awful crime that was beyond the capabilities of the Blue Island Police Department and who were the suspected perpetrators? The crime must have been horrific if the mayor, aldermen, and chief of police refrained from giving any specifics. The foe must have been great for the mayor to appoint an armed militia separate from the police department.

Perhaps the answer lies in what happened afterward: virtually nothing.

In the history of the city council, there never was a reference to whatever happened regarding the crime and to the measures the mayor and city council announced during their special meeting. There is a record of the crime, but it does not appear in the files of the Blue Island Police Department because that file and many others which should have been preserved either have disappeared or have been destroyed. Only John Volp went into detail about the crime in the *Sun-Standard* and in his *THE FIRST HUNDRED YEARS*. A condensed account appears in the "Crimes" section, on page 279, after the sub-heading "The Murder of Laura Buchholz."

Miss Buchholz, age 27, lived with her family on Hansen Avenue, now Artesian, just north of 123rd Street. According to Mr. Volp, she rode the train from her job in Chicago to Blue Island on the night of January 23, 1929. She exited the train at 8:03 p.m. with four other passengers at 123rd Street just east of Vincennes Road and began the four-block walk to her home. The other four passengers walked faster than Miss Buchholz and quickly disappeared. Two of them, Mr. M.K. Muller and Grace McMillan, later would tell a coroner's jury that they neither saw nor heard anything suspicious or unusual. When Miss Buchholz was sufficiently alone on that dark and deserted street, someone came up from behind her, bludgeoned her into unconsciousness, and dragged her into the tall grass of the prairie behind the Paul Revere School.

There was a witness, not to the attack but to a man carrying away the bloody, limp body of Laura Buchholz. The crime occurred in front of the home of Mrs. Edna Stewart at 2262 W. 123rd Street. A teacher named Rose Hanley was a boarder in the home. She later told police that she looked out the window to check the weather because she wanted to go skating. Miss Hanley had turned away from the window, but she turned back when she heard something outside. When she did, she saw a man at first carry and then drag Laura Buchholz into the vacant lot behind Paul Revere School. There he briefly bent over the body before walking toward the school building and examining something in or on his hands. Miss Hanley summoned others in the home and they too watched. One of the people in the home telephoned Blue Island police.

Perhaps scared away by police sirens, the offender fled. Officer Frank Aubin and police wagon driver Earl Clow located Miss Buchholz, who was bloody, barely alive, and unconscious in the tall grass of the field. She was transported to St. Francis Hospital, where she died shortly after her arrival. Police scoured the area, but there was no sign of the perpetrator or clues as to who he was or where he went. It was this terrifying unknown that propelled city officials into a panic. The mayor and aldermen were concerned that a violent sex offender was on the loose in Blue Island.

Based on testimony and speculation, police quickly generated a few leads, but none of them were precise. According to Mrs. Hanley, the perpetrator wore a long overcoat. This tied into an account from George Morton, the manager of the coal chute at the 123rd Street rail yard. At approximately the time the crime was committed, a man wearing a long overcoat entered his shed and asked if there was water to wash with. Told that there was not, the man took out a handkerchief, soaked it in coffee, and wiped his bloody hands and one of his sleeves. The man then inquired of Mr. Morton if there was any danger of him being picked up by railroad police. After the coal chute manager replied that there was, the man exited the shed and disappeared into the darkness.

Perhaps the most convenient lead was provided by some passengers and railroad employees. They told investigators that a Rock Island flagman, Leonard Mitchell, was on the same train as Miss Buchholz. This testimony, that he was available, Mr. Mitchell's race, and authorities' desire to wrap up the case quickly were enough to make him a suspect. Leonard Mitchell was described as "a colored flagman" who was supposed to be on duty at 120th Street, but for reasons never explained he left his post and rode that train.

Chicago detectives had joined Blue Island police for the investigation of the murder. They had Leonard Mitchell put on an overcoat, took him out at midnight, and had him drag a body "to test the man's reactions." The body Mr. Mitchell dragged was that of Blue Island officer Wilbur LaMore. The ridiculous photo of this suspect Mitchell looking perplexed as he holds the officer by the collar and "victim" LaMore, a motorcycle cop clad in full uniform, including knee-high boots, pretending to be unconscious, appears in the February 7, 1929 *Sun-Standard.* How Officer LaMore drew that assignment was not disclosed, but he must have taken a tremendous ribbing at the police station for a long time afterward.

Fortunately for Leonard Mitchell, he must not have been convincing during his forced re-enactment of the crime. Also important, he was courageous enough to stand up for himself. He hired a good attorney and he admitted nothing, including that he was on the same train as the victim. This appears to be a lie—two Blue Island residents, Louis Postweiler and Grace Hanify testified that they saw him—but his denial is understandable under the circumstances. Suspect Mitchell also complained to the jury at the coroner's inquest that the Chicago Police detective who interviewed him "gave him the third degree."

Because authorities had nothing on Leonard Mitchell besides his race and his misfortune to be on the same train as the victim, they did not charge him. Emma Buchholz testified before the coroner's jury that her sister was not involved in anything suspicious. That ruled out a boyfriend, a jilted lover, or that she had a disagreement with anyone. Who could it have been?

Police investigators continued to pursue other leads and looked for suspects, real and imagined. One farfetched angle led them to a farmer from Orland Park, 60-year-old Ted Cramer, who recently passed bad checks in Blue Island. Fraud was not enough to make Mr. Cramer a suspect, but it was said that he had exhibited strange behaviors before he abruptly left Blue Island at approximately the same time as the murder. There also was a rumor that on the day before the murder that suspect Cramer had purchased a baseball bat. Why this would have been significant was not disclosed since the blood-soaked instrument used to bludgeon Miss Buchholz, described as a short 2x4, was recovered near the crime scene. Still, the report of the usual purchase cast suspicion in the farmer's direction.

In the meantime, the coroner's jury assigned to the case had to be disbanded. The jury, made up entirely of Blue Islanders, listened to testimony in a court first convened at the Hallinan Funeral Home. One of the jurors, Frank Pucik, was a Blue Island Police officer. The attorney representing Leonard Mitchell pointed out that someone whose job was to investigate the crime could not sit in judgment and be impartial. Officer Pucik was excused. A new jury was convened. The evidence was resubmitted.

While there never was a big break in the case, the closest to it appeared when Blue Island Chief of Police George J. Fiedler received a call from his counterpart in LaPorte, Indiana. Sheriff McDonald informed Chief Fiedler that a man there confessed to murdering a woman. The sheriff said that the suspect recently had fled Blue Island and that the victim he babbled about could be Laura Buchholz.

According to the *Sun-Standard*, Howard Coleman resided with John W. Arnolds at 2200 Des Plaines Street for four years. Mr. Coleman was an employee at the mill of the American Wire Fabrics Corporation. After the murder of Laura Buchholz, some of his fellow employees said that Mr. Coleman acted quite oddly. He appeared to be under great stress, talked to himself, and screamed aloud. Howard Coleman reportedly left Blue Island and returned to his mother's farm eighteen miles outside of LaPorte a few days after the murder. His mother became alarmed when he mentioned that he had killed a woman and referenced the Buchholz case. Her fears caused her to summon Sheriff McDonald. Thereafter, she had her son committed to the asylum at Logansport.

Chief Fiedler and witness George Morton traveled to Logansport so that suspect Coleman could be questioned and identified. The trip did not yield what the police chief needed, however. Howard Coleman could not be questioned because his mental state had deteriorated to the point that he was a babbling wreck. Here also is where history itself is contradictory. In the February 14, 1929 edition of the *Sun-Standard*, George Morton was quoted that Howard Coleman "was not that much sought after the man who washed his hands with coffee." In the account that appears on page 280 of THE FIRST HUNRED YEARS, Mr. Volp wrote that Mr. Morton "unhesitatingly identified Coleman as that man."

The coroner's jury reconvened for the last time on Valentine's Day of 1929 at City Hall. At approximately the same time, another great crime that would remain unsolved was being perpetrated at a garage on the north side of Chicago. In Blue Island, jurors Raymond Jenner, Kendall Spearing, and Edwin W. Hallinan were holdovers from the first inquest. After Officer Pucik was excused from the jury, so were Officer Earl Clow and Firefighter John Sauerbier. John McEvoy, August W. Werner, and Christian Bohne took their places. After one last round of testimony, the court was cleared and the jury sequestered.

"After a short deliberation, the jury brought in their verdict," according to the story in the February 21 *Sun-Standard.*

That final determination was announced by Cook County Deputy Coroner Frank Munday. "Laura Buchholz died as a result of shock, skull fracture, and hemorrhage when struck by a blunt instrument by persons unknown with the recommendation that the person be apprehended by police."

The term "persons unknown" indicates that when the coroner's jury interviewed George Morton, he told them that he did not recognize Howard Coleman as the man who appeared at the shed. Had he stated that Mr. Coleman was that man, the jury may have recommended that an arrest warrant be issued for Mr. Coleman. While he may have been admitted to asylum, it is doubtful that suspect Coleman could have been declared legally insane in just three weeks. Based upon positive testimony by George Morton, he could have been returned from Indiana and the determination of his sanity and his guilt could have been left to the Cook County Court.

Deputy Coroner Munday praised Blue Island police and all of the investigators who worked on the case. "The Blue Island police have worked hard. They have not neglected a single clue," Mr. Munday said. "The trouble is everyone is handicapped because there absolutely was not a scrap of evidence to work on."

In conclusion, he added, "The fact that the coroner's jury turns in a verdict of murder by persons unknown is not the end of the case. The police will continue their efforts."

Like that more sensational crime in Chicago, the murder of Laura Buchholz officially was "unsolved," but most people believed they knew the identity of the perpetrator. Unlike the St. Valentine's Day Massacre, which was talked about with glee, Blue Island officials were so embarrassed by the random act of violence committed in their city—they were very worried that it might be a reflection of their community—that they never again spoke of it in specific terms. There is no record of any follow up by the mayor or the city council. There was no announcement to the community that its members were safe. This was just as well since the community was not safe.

During the Roaring 20s and through most of the Great Depression, people much more dangerous than Howard Coleman lived, did business, and perpetrated crimes in Blue Island. Controlling the negative information about them always was more important than incarcerating them, curtailing their activities, and inter-vening against them. Why was perception by those outside of Blue Island borders trumped by the safety and security of those within in them?

As for those lawless individuals themselves, was it only because attempts to curtail or end their activities would have brought negative publicity upon Blue Island? Or was it because these men were so feared that they were allowed to come and go as they pleased and act with impunity? Was it the fix? Or was it because it was just the way things were done?

Blue Island never has been a community of easy or simple answers. Perhaps the start of finding answers lies with a look back at one of the individuals.

"A New Era That Should Help Solve Many Crimes"

The Lorenzo Juliano Murder

From the end of WWI until 1937, Blue Island was known for many things. It was a blue collar, hardworking, churchgoing, predominantly German community. There also was the proliferation of booze, all forms of gambling, prostitution, and a smorgasbord of crime that included, but was not limited to armed robbery, burglary, and murder. City officials did not know how to reconcile the two Blue Islands in the era before effective law enforcement was created.

While the Blue Island Police Department could catch a horse thief, it could not or would not ensure safety. As you have read, the police department was untrained, unprofessional, and sometimes unwilling. For these reasons and others, Blue Island was an open city which seemed to have no rules. The name of the city could have been *Anything Goes* because anything did, sometimes with a flourish and for enjoyment, and other times violently, painfully, and to its detriment.

Regarding the latter, one of the most feared local characters was Lorenzo Juliano. According to a reputation enhanced by the *Sun-Standard*, citizen Juliano was a bootlegger, bomb thrower, and murderer. It also was said that he had a lengthy arrest record and that he worked for

Al Capone in various capacities, some more dangerous than others.

How much of this was accurate? Well, the odds are that Mr. Juliano may have dabbled in some of these occupations, that he had some scrapes with the law, and that he may have formed associations with people of questionable character such as Scarface himself. Why else would most people, including police officers, be nervous around Lorenzo Juliano while others wanted him dead?

Perhaps his nationality and stereotypical guilt by association also were to blame. Lorenzo Juliano was Italian. He had to be a mobster. He must have known Al Capone, right?

Or was he a law-abiding citizen who came to Blue Island, USA to pursue the American dream?

According to newspaper reports, city records, and some of his descendants, Lorenzo Juliano was born in Montella, Italy on January 4, 1882. Immigrant Juliano came to America in 1910 and he arrived in Blue Island during 1924. Afterward, when inclined to do so, he listed his occupations as restaurateur, grocer, and salesman. There is little doubt that he was a bootlegger. Who wasn't? A Blue Island resident in 1929 almost couldn't walk down the street without tripping over a bootlegger. Of what magnitude were Mr. Juliano's skills and at what level of management was he? Who did he work for and to whom did he sell his product? These are among the questions never answered.

The legend of Lorenzo Juliano first may have been chronicled by the *Sun-Standard* on April 5, 1928. At that time, he reportedly was detained and questioned by authorities after the attempted murders of U.S. Senator

Charles Deneen and Judge John A. Swanson. Senator Deneen was the political rival of Chicago mayor William Hale Thompson, who was head of the state Republican Party. Senator Deneen also was a powerful Republican. For years he had been trying to seize the top spot of the state party from Mr. Thompson, but the subplot was more sensational and more important. Mayor Thompson was backed by Al Capone and the crime boss reportedly did not want Charles Deneen to take control of the Illinois Republican Party. It wasn't that Mr. Deneen was on the up and up. He reportedly was just as dirty as Mr. Thompson. Al Capone apparently believed that any type of change at the top was bad for him and for his organization. As for Judge Swanson, who was a candidate for Cook County state's attorney, he was an ally of Senator Deneen. Judge Swanson's political opponent, incumbent State's Attorney Bob Crowe, reportedly was on the Outfit payroll.

The homes of Deneen and Swanson were bombed within hours of each other during March 26. Al Capone reportedly ordered the bombings and Lorenzo Juliano was one of the men who authorities suspected may have carried them out. According to the April 12 edition of the *Sun-Standard*, the two-paragraph story said suspect Juliano "is now directly implicated in the recent Deneen and Swanson bombings and previous bootleg wars in southern Cook County."

The story concluded, "His local record is quite pretentious, a recent federal indictment under the prohibition law was another step while this final circumstance, if authorities succeed in making one-tenth of the present charges stick will spell finis to the rather remarkable career."

The charges did not stick. Mr. Juliano reportedly was held in custody for approximately one week. Because authorities had no evidence linking him to the bombings, he was released. According to the *Sun-Standard*, he was indicted on charges of bootlegging and freed on $5,000 bond. Upon his release, he returned to his home at 876 Wiley Avenue (now 12202 Ann) in Blue Island, which brings up another question? Why was he here?

Lorenzo Juliano may have come to Blue Island because other family members were here. Blue Island had a growing Italian population and there also may have been friends and acquaintances from the village of his birth in Italy. Perhaps it was because Blue Island was a virtually lawless, wide open town, and he could operate without fear of serious legal consequences. In summary, Blue Island may have offered all kinds of comfort and security for him.

The *Sun-Standard* never substantiated its incriminating comments about mobster Juliano and hindsight questions the accuracy of them. According to the newspaper, after arriving here with his wife and two children, resident Juliano was so feared in the community that police reportedly were reluctant to detain him when he was suspected of a crime. Yet, also chronicled is the occasion when a rookie Blue Island officer stopped the car Lorenzo Juliano was driving and did just that.

According to the front page story in the July 7, 1929 *Sun-Standard*, "Arthur Fritz, a brand new Blue Island policeman, showed his mettle Friday evening when he arrested the 'great' Lorenzo Juliano and a partner.

"Juliano was driving south on Western Avenue in a big car and Fritz, in uniform, was directing the traffic at the York Street intersection. Fritz signaled for them to stop, but Juliano drove right through and the policeman jumped on another car and crowded Juliano's machine to the curb. After prolonged argument, he got his men to the station, where Juliano gave his occupation as grocer."

Lorenzo Juliano was initially charged with driving while intoxicated. Because the doctor who examined him was not the "regular police medical expert," the charge was reduced to a misdemeanor moving violation. His partner, Sam Morelli of Chicago Heights, was charged with disorderly conduct. Police Magistrate Carl J. Carlson fined each man five dollars and released them on $25 bond. Both men apologized to Officer Fritz.

That was the newspaper version that came out immediately after the incident. According to a later report, rookie Officer Fritz didn't know Juliano from Garibaldi. So he did not know that he had arrested the most feared mobster in the community. The veteran Blue Island officers there laughed nervously when Officer Fritz brought Lorenzo Juliano and Sam Morelli into the station. *They* recognized the "great" Juliano. Uneasy pleasantries were exchanged. Mr. Juliano was polite. He and his companion were processed and released. The rookie officer subsequently was informed of Lorenzo Juliano's reputation and told never to pick him up again. There was no follow-up story in the *Sun-Standard* of the follow-up hearing or if there ever was one.

If he truly was involved in various crimes and unsavory activities, it did not cause Lorenzo Juliano to be more cautious. Thus, he remained in the news. During the late 1920s, when a still or bootlegging operation was busted in Blue Island—always by the feds or the state and not by Blue Island police—Lorenzo Juliano was rumored to be the operator. One such event was detailed by the *Sun-Standard* in its October 28, 1928 edition after the feds busted "an enormous brewery" in a brick building at what is now 2558 Broadway. Upon entry, federal agents discovered five 500-gallon vats and six 100-gallon vats, many of which contained beer and four 400-gallon ice coolers. Two men with Italian surnames were arrested at the site and charged, but alleged bootlegger Juliano was nowhere to be found. That is, because they were Italian, they must have worked for Juliano, right? And Lorenzo Juliano had to be the operator of the bootlegging operation, despite the fact that there was no evidence.

The sensational stories were entertaining, but how accurate were they? Was Lorenzo Juliano so feared that Blue Island officers did not want to pick him up, even for questioning? If that was the case, how did he acquire a local arrest record that was "quite sensational?" If he operated so brazenly, how is it that no law enforcement agency could catch him in the act of making moonshine? Why couldn't the Feds make just one of their charges stick?

The most logical conclusion may be that most of the rumors about Lorenzo Juliano were false. There were other, more prominent, well-connected, and organized bootleggers. They must have been happy that Mr. Juliano received most of the publicity. While the spotlight was shining on Lorenzo Juliano, they could continue to operate in the shadows. One of these men operated so stealthily and was so crafty that he would rise to the top and control Blue Island for decades. As for Lorenzo Juliano, indications are that he was not a big time operator. He did not own property. He did not own a car. When he had to go somewhere, he borrowed one. There are conflicting reports as to whether or not he carried a gun, although this portion of his legend may be misleading. In that lawless era, even law-abiding citizens carried guns for protection. All things considered, Mr. Juliano simply may have been a tough hustler trying to make a buck in a very competitive, albeit illegal industry.

At least that may have been his situation when he encountered the wrong people on June 19, 1930.

Late on that afternoon, Lorenzo Juliano borrowed a car from a friend. He informed the friend he needed transportation to go to a meeting and that he would return the vehicle afterward. The friend loaned the car to Lorenzo Juliano, who drove away. That was the last time anyone except those at his never-disclosed destination ever saw him alive.

Perhaps the retelling of what followed is best related by the official report issued by Chief of Police George J. Fiedler, who gave the summary to the Blue Island City Council during its meeting on Monday, June 23, 1930. It appears verbatim.

> *Honorable Mayor and City Council of the City of Blue Island, Illinois*
>
> *Gentlemen:*
>
> *I herewith wish to make a report of the activities of the Police Department and myself following the murder of Lawrenz Juliano.*
>
> *On June 20th at 10:15 a.m. a phone call was received. Mr. Hanify who was working at the City garbage*

dump reporting that at the clayhole at 123rd Street and California Avenue there was a car in the hole with a man lying in it covered up with canvas. He did not know whether the man was dead or drunk. I sent officers Jones and Lamore with Dr. Roemisch to the scene with patrol driver Besgen, instructing them that if it looked like murder to them they should not touch anything or let anybody disturb anything, to get the license number and report to me at once. About ten minutes later officer Jones called from box 55 stating that the car was an Oakland Sedan with license number 477-523 and the City of Blue Island vehicle license number 2420. I told Jones to go back there and stay with Lamore until he heard from me. Upon investigating the license, I found that it belonged to Dan Lamorte of 12824 Winchester Street, Blue Island. I instructed Sergeant Schultz to notify the coroner's office, which he did, and was informed they would be here in about forty minutes and left word for me to wait for them. In the meanwhile, I went to Lamorte's home. As I was nearing his home I met him on Union Street and brought him to the station. Then I went to the clayhole and looked the scene over and came back to the station. While I was in the station Louis Tiberi of 121st Street, a son-in-law of Juliano, came in and stated that

Juliano had been missing since yesterday afternoon.

About 11:15 Coroner Bundeson came out in person and he and I went to the scene. Upon arriving there he got in the car, removed the canvas from the man's face and asked me to look at him, and I identified him as Juliano. We had the car pulled up on 123rd Street, and the body removed to the County Morgue by Officer Jones. While we were taking the body out we found that the back of his neck had been beaten by some blunt instrument. After the body was taken away we moved the car to the Fiedler Mohr garage with instructions that no one should handle or touch the car. The coroner and myself came back to the station and questioned Mr. Lamorte about his car.

We then went to one of the soft drink parlors which was frequented by Juliano and Coroner Bundesen and myself went through the basement and upper floor and questioned the proprietor and a number of others regarding Juliano's activities of the previous day. They were all released by the coroner and some were requested to be at the inquest at 2 o'clock the following afternoon at the County Morgue. Officer Lamore and I attended the inquest.

Officer Lamore and I had a report about the same cars being at the brickyard about 10 o'clock that evening (the evening of June 19) we went to the Wall Brothers' clayhole and upon making an investigation found that these cars had been there but belonged to the contractor who was working on Kedzie Avenue.

We have been investigating basements and garages of acquaintances of Juliano in an effort to find a trace of the instrument which was used in murdering him.

We also made inquiries at a number of hospitals regarding the blanket that was found. We finally went to Oak Forest and were informed the blanket had been at the Infirmary about six or seven years ago. This information was turned over to the State's Attorney's office. Following inquiries made concerning the canvas, we found that it had been taken from the Rock Island. The Rock Island promised they would report to us if they could trace the canvas.

We are still checking up in this vicinity and any further developments will be reported to the Council.

Respectfully submitted,
George J. Fiedler
Chief of Police

The following letter was read during the Monday, June 30, 1930 city council meeting. It has been reprinted verbatim.

June 27, 1930

Hon. George J. Fiedler
Chief of Police
Blue Island, Illinois

My dear Chief:

I have been quite busy during the past few days or I would have written to you sooner, which I intended to do immediately after the Juliano murder. I want you to know that I deeply appreciate the fine cooperation that you gave this office, the promptness with which you notified this office, and the safeguards that you threw around the available evidence to see that none of it was destroyed.

It is indeed gratifying to have police departments in Cook County show such intelligent handling of cases as you did and I want to repeat that I am grateful for it. This is a new era that should help us solve many crimes.

Please feel free to command us at any time we can be of service.

Yours very truly,
Herman N. Bundesen
Coroner

The popular local legend, still retold in Blue Island, has it that the bullet-riddled body of Lorenzo Juliano was found in the 123rd Street clayhole. *Rat-a-tat-tat!* Blue Islanders love to pretend they are firing a tommy gun as they relive it. As you have read, however, victim Juliano did not die in a hail of bullets. He was beaten to death. He was struck with a heavy instrument and kicked and stomped. Because mobsters sometimes liked to send messages, there also was the irony of, well...you could call it his final resting place.

The story and photos of what happened to Lorenzo Juliano appeared in the June 26, 1930 edition of the *Sun-Standard.* William Kent, a local scavenger, told watchman William Hanify that there was a car sitting atop a pile of junk in the clayhole. The police were called. Upon investigation, the bloody corpse of Mr. Juliano, wrapped in a blanket and canvas, was found wedged between the seat and the dashboard. Coroner Bundsen arrived rather quickly and by the time he did, news of the sensational murder had spread throughout the community. The curiosity seekers who literally descended upon the crime scene included elected officials and residents. Coroner Bundsen literally had to push some of them away from the car.

As for those photos, a very good likeness of Mr. Juliano appeared on page one. If you did not know of his reputation and you saw it, you may have thought he was a restaurateur, a salesman, or a grocer. He was well-dressed and appeared to be a peaceful law-abiding citizen, and with the exception of the traffic stop, he may have been.

The inside photo of the crime scene was worth much more than a thousand words. It showed the Oakland Coach, a very large four-door auto, atop the debris that had been strewn along the bottom slope of the hill. The doors of the vehicle were open and investigators were looking inside the car and at the victim. A few spectators stood closely behind them. Exclusive of its new designation as a crime scene, the clayhole was spectacular. It was a very large excavation with foliage around its slopes and its base is filled with water. If you did not know specifically what you were looking for or at—a dump site turned into a crime scene—you might have been fooled into believing it was a scenic lake or pond.

The last day Lorenzo Juliano was above ground was just as sensational, according to the *Sun-Standard.* The funeral began at the family home at 12202 Ann Street. The number of mourners outside and inside the Juliano home was estimated to be in the hundreds. It was believed there were 75 vehicles in the procession to St. Donatus Church. At the church, there also were numerous floral arrangements from loved ones, friends, and associates. After the mass, mourners gathered around his gleaming casket at Holy Sepulchre Cemetery, that there was frantic weeping by his wife, Filomena, and children, Salvatore and Carmelia, and that the family asked to see the face of Lorenzo Juliano one last time before it was covered forever.

Things did not get better for the Juliano family afterward. The Julianos were forced to move from their beautiful home. No money had been left to them. There was no insurance policy. Lorenzo Juliano died as did some of his era and his alleged profession—sensationally, but broke.

Crime, both random and organized, had been a major issue long before the murder of Lorenzo Juliano. It would continue to be so afterward. Precisely how out of control, occasionally ridiculous, and even indiscriminate Blue Island crime was may best be illustrated by one incident. It did not involve anyone or any place notorious, but the first family of Blue Island, Paul, Caryl, and Teddy Klenk and their beautiful home at 12914 Elm Street. The Klenk home reflected the family's status as Blue Island aristocrats.

"They had a beautiful garden in the backyard tended by a professional gardener. They had a maid that they would summon with a bell. "I still have that bell," said Teddy's widow, Joan Klenk. They liked to travel and visited Cuba with some other couples."

After a trip taken during the 1920s, the Klenks returned to a surprise. Furniture and other possessions had been stolen from their home. The items had been hauled out in broad daylight and whisked away in a large truck. The neighbors told them that a moving van pulled up to the house. Men went inside, removed items, carried them out to the truck, and drove away.

"The neighbors didn't think it was a burglary. No one thought anything beyond asking each other, 'Is the mayor moving?'" said granddaughter Paula Klenk Everett. "Whoever did it was never caught."

While that crime is ironic because Paul T. Klenk was the mayor, it is just as symbolic as the Lorenzo Juliano murder because the 1920s was a lawless decade which featured less-than-adequate law enforcement and brazen criminals. It was a reminder that law enforcement was ineffective, not only in Blue Island but everywhere and that no one was immune to crime. No one was safe.

It also must be noted that Mayor Klenk never attempted to improve the Blue Island Police Department beyond getting its members into uniform. Police services were not a priority. Because it was just the way things were done, BIPD was insufficiently funded and managed, and continued to operate inefficiently.

Mayor Klenk's priorities were elsewhere. His focus always was on the growth and physical improvement of Blue Island. He paid great attention to finance and infrastructure, gave some attention to annexation, but he gave very little consideration to law enforcement. Mayor Klenk always seemed cautious, yet judicious when commenting on police services. Let's go back three years before the Lorenzo Juliano murder. Note Mayor Klenk's choice of words and the condition of the Blue Island Police Department in the portion of his annual message of February 21, 1927 that has been reprinted below.

> "Because of the lack of funds above mentioned, the Police Department is not now and has not in the past been properly manned. The administration recognizes that additional police protection should be given to the community, but during the past year vacancies in the department could not be filled due to lack of funds; yet the department

has functioned as well as could be expected. Complaints have been very few and the absence of crime has been very marked when consideration is given to surrounding communities.

In order that the Council may appreciate the low per capita cost for police protection, the following comparison with the City of Chicago is submitted: 1926 police protection cost per capital, Chicago $4.89 and Blue Island $1.95.

"Police fines have not materially increased and the administration believing that it is not within the province of any police department to trap motorists, but that the motorcycle police should be utilized for patrolling the streets and alleys of the entire community.

"At the present time the squad car which is now used is in very bad condition and it is recommended that in the very near future a high speed squad car be purchased. The use of such a car during the past several years has demonstrated not only its usefulness, but also its present necessity. No doubt through cooperation of local financial institutions, the purchase of such a car can be made possible without thc expenditure of a great deal of City money.

"Also the recent order of the Council that the entire department be properly uniformed and that regular inspections be held, will raise the morale of the department and increase the effectiveness of its work."

Flash forward again from Mayor Klenk's address to the investigation of the murder of Lorenzo Juliano. Bloody fingerprints were taken from the Oakland Coach. Yet there never was another mention of them. Nor was there mention of a link between the murder and an event that occurred just one half mile away at approximately the same time. A vacant house at 12835 Sacramento Avenue, one used by bootleggers, was completely destroyed by fire. All that was found among the charred remains were the parts of a still. This was quite odd. No, not the remains of the still. It was well known that bootleggers used vacant houses as distilleries. They would set up a still inside, leave so that they would not be apprehended while the apparatus worked its magic, and return to collect the product. Occasionally those unattended stills in the vacant houses blew up. Later you will read that this type of incident occurred in Blue Island during 1935, that house did not burn to the ground, however. Was the incineration of the home on Sacramento Avenue a message and should it have been tied to the murder of Lorenzo Juliano?

As for who carried out the execution of Lorenzo Juliano—ordered it may be better terminology—authorities did not have to look beyond Al Capone himself. Previously, the boss of the Chicago Outfit had issued an ultimatum to bootleggers. Come to work for me, go out of business, or suffer the consequences. According to published reports, by 1930 Al Capone had all of the bootlegging in Cook County under his control. Lorenzo Juliano may have attempted to operate independently and suffered the consequences. Thus, if morale in Blue Island did improve at all during 1930, some credit may be given to Al Capone and his local representatives.

The year 1930 produced a variety of challenges for Blue Island. The Great Depression was one of them. There also was an inevitability that for the first time began to sink in for some members of the community. It was a concern that while solved short term, the community would struggle with for decades.

"Mr. Ruel is of the Idea You Are Prejudiced Against Him."

The Negro Invasion, Dagos North of 127th Street, and Mexicans On Top of the Hill

During its history, someone in Blue Island has been against everything. Opposing arguments ranged from legitimate to absurd. The issues have been real and imagined. Can you imagine anyone opposing a slight increase in revenue that would keep the high school from closing? How about artwork that represents ethnic pride? Would you have opposed a new aperture system that would greatly increase water pressure for everyone in a community whose low water pressure was an inconvenience and a life safety issue? Have you ever been stuck waiting for a passing train at Vermont Street? A free overpass there would have alleviated the delays at the city's busiest rail crossing. All of these and more were opposed by some Blue Islanders. Yes, hindsight is no worse than 20-20. Yet the issue that may have raised the greatest fear was manufactured in 1930 and it was as controversial as it was ridiculous. It involved the threat of what was referred to as a "Negro invasion."

The seeds of the embarrassing episode were planted during 1928 when there was a rumor that a lumber mill and yard were to be built in the far northwest corner of Blue Island. That area was sparsely populated, but the few residents who lived there did not want this type of business in their neighborhood. They complained to their elected officials. Thereafter, Mayor Paul T. Klenk and his aldermen acted quickly. They actually convened on a Sunday morning at the rumored site and inspected it. Then they *haarrummphed*, drafted an ordinance, and approved it. The section in question, the 19000 block of Maple Avenue immediately west of the B&O Railway tracks, was rezoned First Residential. There would be no lumber yard and mill.

This would have been the end of it if the parcels in question were not owned by a pesky and unscrupulous realtor named John Robertson. When it came to making a buck, Mr. Robertson stopped at nothing. He was not afraid to manufacture rumors, make threats, and create controversy if they got him what he wanted. There are no existing photos of John Robertson, but feel free to imagine him as a fast talker wearing a checkered coat.

During 1929, after Paul T. Klenk left office and Mayor Frank Kasten was in the executive chair, realtor Robertson contacted the city. It has been said that there are three versions of a contentious story: your version, my version, and the truth. In John Robertson's case there were versions of his versions. They began in an August 15, 1929 letter to Mayor Kasten.

Hon. Frank Kasten
Mayor of Blue Island, Illinois

Dear Sir,

I am the owner of the 4-½ acres at the S. W. corner of 119th and Maple Avenue. During the last week I have had three offers for this property. A Mr. Bliss, who claimed to represent the Shell Oil Co., offered to buy the north half of it; the Ruel Lumber Co. offered to buy all of it for a lumber yard; a Mr. Francis who said he represented a syndicate backed by the Binga Bank, 35th and State Street, said they would pay me my price for it.

The taxes and specials run me close to $1000.00 a year on this property and I cannot afford to hold it, so I am writing you to ask that you see if the property can be zoned back to First Industrial as it was until changed last year so that I can sell it to Mr. Ruel of the Ruel Lumber Company.

I understand the Supreme Court of the United States has ruled that property once zoned cannot be changed without the owner's consent. This being so I can go into court and get it zoned back to First Industrial, but why should I be asked to go to this expense. [sic]

I surely do not wish to sell the property to undesirable people, but I cannot afford to hold it and pay $1000.00 a year in specials and taxes.

> *I have done a great deal of business in Blue Island and while I have benefitted by it, so has your town, for I have sent over a hundred families to live there.*
>
> *Yours very truly,*
> *John R. Robertson &Company*
> *John R. Robertson*

Mr. Robertson's letter was read during the September 3 city council meeting. The matter was referred to the plats committee, the Fifth Ward aldermen, and the zoning board of appeals for the purpose of meeting with the relentless realtor. There is much on the public record as to John Robertson's intentions, his reputation, and his threats. He successfully sued the City of Chicago Heights for allowing the pollution of the Calumet River. The claim was the damage to the river prevented him from making sales there. He later was cited in Midlothian after he was caught inflating water bills. He had inserted clauses in properties he sold there. The unsuspecting homeowners suddenly learned that they were forced to pay far more for water than their fellow residents because Robertson retained the water rights.

As for his dealings in Blue Island, had John Robertson actually brought 100 families to town, he would have been welcomed as a great partner and city officials would have bent over backward for him. Instead, Blue Island twice had to intervene on his blighted properties. Most egregiously, he abandoned his real estate office at Prairie and Fairmount (now Irving) and neglected the building to the extent that it was missing doors and windows and was occupied by vagrants. The city had to force John Robertson to tear down the building.

The city council and its committees deliberated for the next few months without any indication they would convert the zoning to First Industrial. A rumor that Mr. Robertson would sell to African Americans had spread through the city, however. During the November 4 city council meeting, "a large portion" of residents showed up and a petition with 293 signatures was submitted. The petition called for the property to be rezoned to its previous status, First Industrial. Mayor Kasten informed those in attendance that "a committee of eight" was working on the problem and would report back shortly. Frank Kasten was The Great Appeaser. He put everything in place to bring about resolution, including a committee of citizens to work with a committee of aldermen.

According to city council minutes, it was before another large crowd during the November 12 city council meeting that "the problem of the threatened Negro invasion and of rezoning the 4½ acres south of 119th Street and west of Maple Avenue then arose." George J. Landgraf was a very capable city clerk who often exceeded his duties and intervened in decision making. Sometimes this was good. This time, it was not. Mr. Landgraf suggested that "a blanket agreement be sent to all property owners in Blue Island with an affidavit attached declaring that they will not sell, lease, barter, or exchange or in any way dispose of their property to anyone not of the Caucasian race for a period of 21 years." The city clerk's proposal included all agreements to be attached to the owners' deeds and filed with the Cook County Clerk. According to the city council minutes, Mr. Landgraf further stated he "thought this would be a very necessary and important move and that he would be willing to begin action."

While George J. Landgraf's vigor and bigotry are alarming, even in retrospect, neither his views nor his suggestion of an affidavit were new. The "Caucasians only" codicil had been part of Chicago real estate transactions for many years. Until then, no one ever thought it necessary in Blue Island. Actually, it was not necessary. There was a tacit understanding that anyone not German or Swedish was forbidden to live On the Top of the Hill. African Americans were not allowed to live anywhere within the city limits.

In this situation, however, Blue Islanders in general and the city council in particular were not thinking clearly. That is what fear and misunderstanding do. After Mr. Landgraf's speech, aldermen voted 14-0 to grant the city clerk "the authority and necessary help to proceed with this work." At the suggestion of Alderman Rocco Guglielmucci, it also was unanimously agreed that John Robertson would be invited to attend a special meeting November 14. The realtor showed up for that special meeting and gave his version of what had transpired and what he needed. Mr. Robertson often changed his stories to suit his needs, such as on this occasion.

> *I am very sorry this matter came up the way it did. Chicago is not so far away that people living there cannot be*

notified of what is going on in Blue Island. This rezoning was done without my knowledge and consent. I am on your tax books; I pay taxes on 25 or 30 different pieces of property in Blue Island. No one notified me of this rezoning to residential. I don't know if it would have done any good since it seems it might have been done for spite work—but let that pass.

This thing dragged along until August of this year. We had advertized this property for factory purposes. You gentlemen know this is not residential property. I never found a white man who wanted to live against a freight road. Of the 175 families I sent here to live not one of them would have bought property adjoining a railroad track. You know selling property is no snap. Your former Board put me up against the impossible without notifying me. We have a lot of salesmen in our office who get paid by commission. Sometimes it is a long time between commissions.

My son-in-law, Mr. Brown, had been trying to sell to the Ruel Lumber Company a piece of property in Midlothian. He thought he had it sold when the company decided not to take it. Then they heard about my piece in Blue Island. When they talked to me about buying my property they stated they would like to use it as a lumber yard. The deal was closed, as I did not know the property had been rezoned.

True, I did hear something some time ago to the effect that it had been rezoned, but I paid no attention and said if it were true I certainly would receive official notifi-cation from the City Council or the Board of Appeals. After the deal was closed with the Ruel Lumber Company my attorney informed me this property had been rezoned to Residential district. He said I could take this matter up in court and have the property changed, but said it would cost a couple of thousand dollars and take two or three years before I get action.

There were three parties who wanted this property. One was an oil company who wanted half the property for oil tanks. Then we had a colored man looking at the property, Mr. Terrell. He said he could get a syndicate to pay cash on residential property. The third party was the Ruel Lumber Company.

At the time the City contemplated putting improvements in this district, Mr. Rauhauf came to my office and wanted to know what I thought about it. He urged me to be in favor of improvements which, of course, meant heavy special assessments. I told him I did not think I could afford it. But the paving was started and while my objection was tried in court this property was rezoned. They told me it was done because I did not want the paving.

The city fired a shot over Robertson's bow when City Clerk Landgraf cited the petition that recommended the property be rezoned First Residential. Mayor Kasten followed by announcing that the City of Blue Island did give notice to Robertson. The Mayor pointed out that state law provided that if an Appeals Board considers re-zoning a property and the fact is announced in a local newspaper fifteen days in advance, the property can be rezoned without the owner's consent. City Attorney Messena citing state law and the section of the local zoning ordinance that pertained to this case. Landgraf read the proceedings of the September 18, 1928 meeting of the Board of Appeals during which the zoning was changed.

John Robertson didn't have a leg to stand on, but he supported himself on his wiles when he responded, "This notice came to me on September 16th, at which time I had other plans for the 18th which could not be changed. I instructed my attorney to be there. I thought he had attended; in fact, I paid him for being there." Asked whether he would sell to the "colored syndicate" if Ruel Lumber did not purchased the property, Robertson must have shocked everyone in attendance when he said, "I would carry out the verbal agreement with the colored people because I want to get rid of the property. I have no desire to sell to colored people. I sold properties to 175 families in Blue Island and all the deeds or abstracts have a 99-year clause against selling to Negroes, but I must sell to get rid of this property."

Just the mention of "Negroes" must have alarmed Blue Islanders. Mayor Kasten was the first to waver. He may have reminded some of Pontius Pilate when he said, "If you stand at 119th Street and Maple Avenue and look as far south as you can you will see that this is one of the best vacant residential sections left. Another thing I am interested in, although the actual rezoning was done before I took office, was the petition presented by the people and the fact that there are only two or three signers who live in the immediate vicinity."

Mr. Taylor, who said he represented the owners of the ten acres immediately south of Robertson's property, Mr. and Mrs. Buttles, also attempted to scare off Robertson. Mr. Taylor said re-zoning to First Industrial would "impair the value of the Buttles' property." According to attorney Taylor, the Buttles purchased their land as a residential tract and had $10,000 invested in it. When John Robertson purchased his tract, it was zoned industrial. Asked whether in his contract with Ruel it was specified the land would be used for a lumber yard, he admitted he had only verbal assurance as to use.

John E. Steinhart had been appointed chairman of the citizens committee. A realtor himself, Mr. Steinhart suggested that the meeting be adjourned until November 25, at which time his committee would issue a report. The meeting was adjourned, but Mr. Landgraf, who was the city council liaison to the citizens committee, did not wait eleven days to act. He explained during a city council meeting held four days later that he had sent a communication to John Steinhart that stated the citizens committee had been formed "for the purpose of barring Negroes from Blue Island." The city clerk announced that he asked Mr. Steinhart to convene a meeting as soon as possible and to prepare papers to be attached to land titles. Proof that George J. Langraf's ideas were gaining traction was supplied by Alderman Charles Mosel, who added that residents of the recently annexed property near Posen also would like "anti-Negro riders" attached to their abstracts. City Attorney Roy Massena said that if the residents formed a group and wanted the documents drafted at once, he would be glad to prepare them.

Mr. Steinhart also was president of the local real estate board. During the November 25 city council meeting, he submitted a resolution from his organization. According to the resolution, the real estate board held a meeting attended by people who owned property adjacent to or in the vicinity of the land known as "the Robertson 4½ acres." The resolution requested that the zoning remain First Residential and that the property not be used for any other purpose. In support of the resolution, a petition was submitted as a petition. It contained the signatures of forty-two people who said they owned property between 123rd Street and 119th Street and east of the Baltimore and Ohio tracks and west of Western Avenue. Whether the citizens committee met since November 14 was not stated, but Mr. Steinhart announced he would convene a meeting "as soon as possible."

The crafty Robertson must have been following the proceedings because he wasted no time in turning up the heat prior to the December 2 city council meeting, which he attended. City Clerk Landgraf read into the record Robertson's letter to the "citizens' committee on rezoning," which was dated November 26. The letter is in italics and has been reprinted verbatim.

Gentlemen:

I hope the Citizens' Committee appointed to study the zoning of my land at 119th Street and Maple Avenue will report so that the Council can make a decision in this matter next Monday, for a feeling is developing among Mr. Terrell, the colored agent, and his friends that they can get all the land there that they want.

He was to see me today to find out what was done last night and he told me that he now has 17 properties on Maple Avenue and streets east of Maple that he can get if he gets my 4½ acres. He also spoke of the large amount of tax title property there that he could get.

I am afraid I have started something that may be hard to stop if the Council does not decide soon.

Condemning my land for a park as the Real Estate Board is proposing according to his speech last night, is not going to help much if colored people settle east of Maple Avenue. If there is any intention of making a park there, it should be done before Mr. Terrell's syndicate gets control, or Blue Island may be in the same position that Washington Heights was in. They decided to make a park of the area along the Pennsylvania Railroad between 107th and 111th Street, but before going far they realized it would be a colored park, so they dropped the matter.

I am taking the liberty of calling your attention to several Supreme Court decisions on zoning.

These decisions give me every reason to think I would get a like decision if I took this matter to court and from my point of view it seems just as unfair for the City of Blue Island to force me to spend thousands of dollars (and Blue Island also to have to spend thousands) and lose a good profitable sale, because I am denied my legal rights, as it is for colored people to locate there.

I know of no surer way of discrediting zoning than to destroy public sentiment by unjust and arbitrary use of the authority conferred by the statute. But no matter what is to be done, it should be settled now. This matter has been hanging since August, and I am losing control.

Very truly yours,
John R. Robertson

There is no mention in the city council minutes of the identity of Mr. Olson or the idea of a park to which he referred. Blue Island big shots were lining up against John Robertson in this controversy. So he may have been Arthur G. Olson, the secretary of the Blue Island Savings & Loan Association. Other members of the citizens committee included Christian Krueger, who was president of the First National Bank and former mayor Paul T. Klenk. FNB cashier Philip Seyfarth was secretary of the organization. John Robertson knew this and was bold enough also to address the letter not to Mr. Steinhart, but to the trio that may have been three of the four most powerful men in Blue Island: "The Honorable Frank Kasten, Christian Krueger, and Paul T. Klenk." James Hackett was the fourth and to his credit, his name never came up in this matter.

John Robertson's letter so alarmed Alderman Guglielmucci, however, that as soon as the city clerk finished reading it, he moved that the matter be referred back to the Board of Appeals for the purpose of re-zoning the property First Industrial. This was as ridiculous as it was hasty. The veteran alderman should have known better and appeared to be passing the buck. The Board of Appeals made recommendations. It had no authority to re-zone. Only the aldermen had the power to establish zoning. Mayor Kasten seemed not to mind giving into John Robertson, but wanted the city to get something in return. The Mayor tempted Mr. Robertson with infrastructure when he asked if Ruel Lumber would be satisfied if 120th Street, which did not exist west of Maple Avenue, was extended. This was crafty on the mayor's part since Ruel would have to give up some of the land for his proposed lumber yard for that portion of the street to be dedicated. John Robertson took the bait and said he would have to consult with Ruel. This led to a dialogue which revealed the realtor could not live up to his end of the bargain. Robertson subsequently admitted that the 99-year "Caucasians only" provision was not yet part of his contract with Ruel. At that point, Alderman Guglielmucci's motion was withdrawn and all other action was tabled.

Robertson, Ruel, and Buttles were invited to attend a special city council meeting on December 6. The embarrassing episode continued.

Mr. Ruel accompanied Robertson to the December 6 special city council meeting. Mr. Buttles and his representative, Mr. Taylor, also were there. The city council chamber also was packed with citizens anxious to learn whether their new neighbors would be White, African-American, or wooden. After Mayor Kasten announced that the purpose of the meeting was to consider the re-zoning of the land at 119th and Maple, Robertson spoke. The realtor's first comment was ironic in its terminology as it was ridiculous overall. Did he expect Blue Islanders to beg the lumber company owner to come into their community?

"Mr. Ruel is of the idea that you are prejudiced against him and he does not want to come in here with a lumber yard if the people have ill feeling against him."

Prejudiced, yes. Against Mr. Ruel, no. Ruel Lumber was an unwanted necessity. It was considered the lesser of two evils.

It was the politics of fear. There would be insults, but no begging, and there would be give and take. Mr. Ruel was asked if he would consent to insert the 21-year clause "barring the negro" in his deed and if he would give land for dedication of 120th Street. Mr. Ruel was agreeable on the former, but not the latter. The businessman replied that he would consent to a 99-year clause, but that he "needed every foot of ground and did not see his way clear to give thirty-three feet for street purposes."

Mr. Ruel further alarmed city officials when he inquired if other industries could be located in an industrial district. There had been rumors that gasoline storage tanks would be installed at the site. City Attorney Messena read the sections of the ordinance that indicated what was allowed. Mayor Kasten asked if Mr. Ruel planned to install gas storage tanks. Ruel said he "did have that in mind although he may not use the ground for a lumber yard."

With the cat out of the bag—Ruel Lumber would be able to do whatever it wanted with the land no matter what city officials said—John Robertson attempted to put city officials on their heels with an accusation. They saw through this and returned the subject to the lumber yard. It was obvious that Blue Island wanted a business, almost any kind of business, instead of African Americans. City officials simply wanted to know specifically what that business would be and they wanted it on reasonable terms. Only the Buttles were opposed to the lumber yard at that point. Their representative spoke for them.

"Mr. and Mrs. Buttles feel that a great hardship would be placed upon them if this property would be rezoned. It would be particularly disadvantageous to them because the property was assessed as Residential District," said Mr. Taylor. "If they had thought this piece of land would be changed to Industrial District, they might have wanted theirs rezoned so that they could have received benefits for industrial business. They are up against a proposition that presents many hardships if the Robertson property is rezoned. They would like to know what is best in the holding of their property. If the land next to them is rezoned it will impair their property."

The possibility that 120th Street could be extended did not appease the Buttles.

"If the street remained closed it would not be available for industrial purposes of any class and they would not know how to make use of their land. The idea was that if the Robertson property should be changed there should be some plan whereby Mr. and Mrs. Buttles would be protected," Taylor said. He conceded that a solution might be for the Buttles to use some of their property for industry.

This caused John Robertson to make an accusation against the Buttles, the refuting of it by attorney Taylor, and a non-solution to be suggested by Alderman Guglielmucci, who never allowed a conversation to go very long before he stuck in his two cents. City Clerk Landgraf re-focused everyone when he said, "I think the question is, 'Do we want the Negroes or the lumber yard?' Mr. Robertson says he will keep his promise to Mr. Terrell if he cannot sell to Mr. Ruel."

The unscrupulous realtor had convinced a key player, the city clerk, that he was unwavering in his threat. The Buttles also were unwavering. They said they would not sign a "Caucasians only" agreement. They were alone on the issue, however. Everyone was ready to bow to the unscrupulous realtor and his demands. Charles Van Wie, who lived nearby on the 12100 block of Ann Street summed it up when he interjected that he "would rather have a lumber yard than Negroes in his neighborhood at any time and thought that every other person felt the same way about it."

Ultimately, every other person, (i.e., the city council), did feel the same way about it. Aldermen reversed themselves and rezoned the Robertson property C-1 so that a lumber yard could be installed there.

Except a lumber yard never was installed there, although it was not because of anything done by the city council. Most likely, the Great Depression did what city officials were not crafty enough or courageous enough to do. As for "the Negro Invasion," it was thwarted until after 1977, when Babe Tuffanelli was gone, Marvin O'Lena was ousted as chief of police, and renters no longer were subject to "gun in the mouth" scare tactics. Until that time, Blue Island lived by a slogan often repeated by old timers: *The sun will never set on the head of a Black man in Blue Island.*

While there is no evidence that a Caucasians only clause ever was inserted in Blue Island land deeds, African Americans still could not live in Blue Island proper. They could live near the landfill on the northeast side of town and they could live across the Cal Sag Channel. African Americans could go to school and work in Blue Island, although according to legend, they had to "be on the last bus out of town." It never was explained how these two slogans possibly could coexist since the last bus departed after sunset, further proof that the slogans were boast, not rule. The slogans were repeated by some Blue Islanders because to repeat them made them believe they were in total control.

While the Negro invasion would be thwarted for another 50 years, xenophobic Blue Islanders were not as successful against two other groups who were victims of prejudice: Italians (who some lifelong Blue Islanders still refer to as "EYE-talians") and Mexicans.

The reasons may be that these two ethnic groups had the will, skills, and the beliefs. Italians and Mexicans worked mainstream professions during the week. They toiled as laborers on the railroad and in the factories. On Sundays, they and their families sat in church pews next to Germans, Swedes, Irish, and Poles. Eventually, Mexicans and Italians were welcome at St. Benedict Church, which was decidedly German; at St. Isidore, the Polish Catholic Church at Burr Oak Avenue and Wood Street; at the Swedish Covenant Church at Collins and Greenwood, and at other local places of worship. By 1931, there would be a new St. Donatus Catholic Church at Union and Divisions streets. The church was named in honor of the parish of the same name of Ripicandida, Italy, from which so many Blue Islanders came.

Mexican and Italian children attended the same schools and competed on the same athletic fields as those whose families had come before them. Germans, Swedes, Poles, Mexicans, and Italians socialized, fell in love with each other, married, and had children.

The history of Italians and Mexicans is similar to that of Polish immigrants who preceded them, but with a few differences. Poles already worked at jobs in local brickyards and rail yards, which meant that there were fewer jobs for ethnicities that followed, both because of availability and design. From almost the time they arrived, however, the earning power of Italians and Mexicans, meager as it may have been, did enable them to acquire property in Blue Island as long as it was not at the Top of the Hill. At first, Italians lived below the hill on the east and south sides where there already were German and Polish enclaves. Later they were bold enough to populate the north side where some Swedes settled, but most Germans shunned. The Collins Street and Greenwood Avenue area was referred to as "Swede town" because so many Johnsons lived there. When Mexicans and especially Italians moved there, The People on the Top of the Hill were alarmed, according to Jack Heuser whose family moved to Blue Island during the late 1940s.

"Calling them 'stubborn old Germans' is being kind to them," Mr. Heuser laughed. "After my father went to work at State Bank of Blue Island, he told everyone at the bank, 'If you work here, I think you should live here.' So he went to lunch with John McNulty, who was the realtor in town. My father said, 'John, we really love Blue Island and we want to buy a home here.' John McNulty got a very serious look on his face and said, 'I wouldn't recommend that. I give the town five years.' After my father asked why, McNulty told him, 'The Dagos have moved in north of 127th Street.'

"I used to tell that story when I spoke to groups as head of the Blue Island Chamber of Commerce. It's always been 'five more years for Blue Island,' " concluded Mr. Heuser, who was Chamber president, operated the Blue Island Nursing Home, and whose son Randy was elected city clerk during 2013. "And people today think immigration started with them."

Italians and Mexicans arrived in Blue Island because of the railroad. One group rode it and the other worked on it. Old-time Italians in the community tell the story that their ancestors from the village of Ripicandida came to America and stopped in Pennsylvania. The railroad from Altoona, for example, provided transportation to Blue Island. That is how many of the first Italians arrived and settled here. The community was a railway stop. Thereafter, they sponsored relatives and friends from the Old Country and the Italian population grew.

The first Mexicans to arrive in Blue Island, attracted by promises of jobs and housing by the railroad, were no more welcome than the Italians, but they were less mobile because they did not have the means. Wages paid to Mexican workers were low, even when Mexican laborers held the same jobs or did more work. Without means and because railroad officials failed to live up to their promise of providing suitable living conditions, the first Mexican families here were forced to live in box cars and shacks—if they were lucky. If not, they lived in tents, boxes, or completely outdoors. They did not live anywhere close to the Top of the Hill. They were permitted to walk up the hill at first to shop and later to worship and attend schools.

"My brother, sister, and I came here around 1930 with our parents," recalled Antoinette Pinto. "I was about seven years old. Not long afterward, my parents died. Another family took us in. We were poor. For awhile, we lived in a box car at Chatham Street. Later we lived in Gypsy Town. If you were Mexican, you couldn't live near the Top of the Hill."

Mexican children were permitted to attend schools, however. Because they were every bit as industrious as their fellow Blue Islanders, Mexicans slowly acquired the means to give them the more mobility. As the decades passed, all they needed was for time and the People at the Top of the Hill to cooperate. Finally, during the early 1950s, a half-Mexican family, the Alvarados, was able to live at the Top of the Hill. According to Sonny Carter, in 1952 his grandfather and grandmother were permitted to move into a home on Grove Street directly behind the Post Office.

"The neighbors had a meeting to decide whether or not we could live there," Mr. Carter recalled. He marveled at the recollection. "Can you believe that?"

He added, "Fortunately, there were some very good families on that block such as the Nordstroms and the Runges. They welcomed us. That block was a good place to live."

Sig Nordstrom, who has lived on the 2400 block of Grove Street for over 60 years, said he did not attend such a meeting and does not recall if there even was one. He does know something about both immigration and relocation because he came to America from Sweden in 1928 when he was seven years old.

"My father was a shoemaker. He decided to come to America at the suggestion of his uncle, who had a shoe repair shop on Maple Avenue just north of Collins Street," recalled Nordstrom.

Even though he does not recall anything about a 1952 block meeting, he has the highest regard for the Alvarado Family, who lived next door for many years.

"Years ago, I was making some improvements to my home and I had it up on jacks. One day, early in the morning, I heard something outside and went to check. It was Manuel Alvarado, my neighbor. He was working on my house. He was digging a foundation for my basement," Nordstrom said. "Manuel told me, 'It looked like you could use some help, so I thought I'd come over and give you a few hours.'

"Manuel had to be at work at eight a.m., but he put in about three hours working on my house. What a great neighbor! How could anyone not like someone like that?" Nordstrom concluded.

Yes, how could they? Well, they could do it by not allowing "someone like that" to move in. Thus progress was slow for the Italian Americans, slower for Mexican Americans, and did not exist for African Americans almost until the early 1980s. This was because African Americans did not have the proximity or the mobility of the others and even after African Americans acquired them, there continued to be block meetings into the late 1980s because Blue Islanders still mistakenly believed they could dictate who lived where and otherwise stop progress. By then the meetings were held only when African Americans moved in.

Except that whatever was decided at that meeting, African Americans were moving in anyway. There was nothing that could be done about it. Just the way things were done no longer could be done. For years Blue Islanders had prevented change. Some still work to prevent it, though race no longer is the issue. Nevertheless, change in the form of progress continues to be painfully slow to cross the borders of Blue Island and climb to the Top of the Hill.

The View from Washington

Blue Island in 1931

The following is a report issued by the War Department issued March 5, 1931. At that time, the federal government was considering widening the Cal Sag Channel for the purpose of making Blue Island a major port that cargo ships could access via Lake Michigan. Creating additional ports for shipping was the idea of Herbert Hoover when he was U.S. Commerce Secretary. After Hoover was elected president, the federal government began to implement the idea. The report was read during a hearing in connection with the examination and survey of the Calumet River. It was titled "Facts with Reference to Blue Island, Cook County, Illinois, and Its Environs." The report actually was a combination of fact, observation, and generous estimation. If the report appears favorable, that may have been because the War Department very much wanted the installation of a port at Blue Island. There certainly were no objections to the report by Mayor Frank Kasten or the twelve aldermen who listened to the reading of it by City Clerk George J. Landgraf. They wanted Blue Island to become a port and they wanted the installation of the proposed Route 52, which would have created a highway through Blue Island using Broadway or creating another thoroughfare nearby. Unfortunately, plans for neither the port nor Route 52 came to fruition because of the Great Depression.

The report from the federal government was entered into the official minutes of the Monday, March 9, 1931 city council meeting. With the exception of the footnotes, it has been reprinted verbatim.

> 1. Location: Blue Island adjoins the City of Chicago on the South, extending from 119th Street to 139th Street and is bounded by Ashland Avenue on the East and Sacramento on the West. It covers approximately five square miles.
> 2. Population: The population of Blue Island is approximately 17,000.
> 3. Industries:
>
> a. Railroads:
>
> (1) Chicago, Rock Island & Pacific, including the freight yards and shops of that railroad.
>
> (2) Illinois Central.
>
> (3) Baltimore & Ohio Chicago Terminal.
>
> (4) Grand Trunk Western.
>
> (5) Indiana Harbor Belt, combined with New York Lines.
>
> b. Brick Yards: Three yards of Illinois Brick Company and one of Tuthill Brick are immediately adjacent to the City. When operating, the daily capacity of these yards is 1,500,000 bricks per day.

c. Libby, McNeil & Libby—food products.

d. Modern Die & Drop Forge Company—forgings.

e. American Wire Fabrics Company—wire for screens.

f. Public Service Company of Northern Illinois:

(1) Gas manufacturing plant and gas storage tank.

(2) Plant for production of electric current.

(3) Illinois Cooperage Company—production of barrels.

(4) Briggs & Turivas—reclaimed car parts and scrap iron.

(5) Hutchins Lumber Company—wholesale lumber.

(6) Hawkeye Compound Company—boiler compound.

(7) Chicago Haydite Units Company—concrete blocks.

(8) North American Car Company—manufacture and repair of cars.

(9) Western Pipe & Steel Company—steel pipe.

(10) Rogers Galvanizing Works.

(11) Commercial Acetylene Plant.

(12) G Manufacturing Company—wire products.

(13) Chicago Copper & Chemical Company—boiler compound.

(14)Borden's Dairy Company—general plant.

(15) Blue Island Specialty Company—dealer specialties.

(16) Klein Elevator

(17) Klein & Schroth—wholesale meats.

(18) W.W. Koehler Paper Company—wholesale paper.

(19) Thoeming Brothers—wholesale grocers.

(20) Werkman Concrete Works—concrete blocks.

(21) Nine coal yards handling coal and building material.

4. People employed in above industries: about 5,500.
5. Tonnage received and shipped by above industries (see separate list).
6. Highways—hard surface roads radiate in all directions through Blue Island as follows:

a. Dixie Highway—north and south—State Routes # 1 and #49.

b. Cicero Avenue—on west—State Route #50.

c. Halstead Street—on the east—new Route #1.

d. Burr Oak Avenue—east and west.

e. Proposed Route 52 along the Sanitary District Channel.

(1) Municipal Airport—lies west of Blue Island.

7. An industrial community favored by:

f. Hard surfaced roads for trucks running in every direction.

g. Railroads—truck lines in every direction.

h. Variety of industries.

Part II

Mayor Hart's Immediate Predecessors and Their City Councils

Paul T. Klenk

Born April 18, 1893
Elected Mayor April 1921
Mayor Number 7
Served Until May 1929
Number of Terms: 4
Died March 29, 1950

In its modern history, Blue Island has had two great mayors and five mayors who were forceful and who could be considered leaders. Paul T. Klenk has the distinction of being a member of each group. Mayor Klenk was great because of all he accomplished during his eight years in office.

As a champion of infrastructure, he oversaw the formation of modern Blue Island. His contributions were not confined to the physical, however. Mayor Klenk was a great drafter of legislation. Perhaps all of the mayors that followed him combined did not oversee passage of as many necessary ordinances as did Mayor Klenk during his four terms in office.

Paul T. Klenk also had leadership qualities. For a mayor to be truly effective, the egos of the aldermen must be kept in check and their focus must remain on the task of keeping the city moving in the proper direction. Because Mayor Klenk was focused, organized, and forceful, his aldermen were not allowed to stray from their tasks and there were few squabbles amongst members of the city council or in the community. Thus the Klenk era was a period of collegiality and great accomplishment.

While not all of the major construction that took place between 1921 and 1929 can be credited to Mayor Klenk, a strong case can be made that his energy and philosophy were contagious. Among the projects were the Masonic Temple Building and the creation of Memorial Park during 1921. Eagles Hall was built in 1923. State Bank of Blue Island and St. Benedict School were completed in 1925. Also during 1925, the first Whittier School was demolished and construction began on its successor. There was an addition to City Hall. The new First Evangelical Lutheran Church hall was dedicated during 1926. The Mother of Sorrows Institute was completed during 1928, two years after its orphanage came into existence. A large apartment complex was built on the 2400 block of Walnut Street and it was christened Lucerne Court. The 31-unit building was owned by Charles J. Schrage. Another complex, Birdsall Manor, was created at Birdsall Street and Burr Oak Place (now Artesian).

All of the changes were not in the form of brick and mortar. Lifelong resident Harry Robertson can tell you precisely when trolley car service disappeared from Blue Island because he was there. It was the evening of April 23, 1927. Harry was seven years old and his father took him to the corner of Grove and Western to see the last run of the Chicago Interurban Traction Line.

"I'll never forget that night. The trolley went past us. It was a giant green train, much larger than other trolley cars you've seen," he recalled.

The Chicago Interurban Traction Company went out of business, but Mayor Klenk and his city council took steps to make sure that bus service was instituted. Commuters eventually were able to ride the bus to Kline's Department store, which opened June 30, 1927. Also during the eight years Paul T. Klenk was in office, improved electric street lighting was installed. Parts of Western Avenue and others streets were resurfaced incrementally as their composition went from dirt or gravel to concrete.

Most likely is that these positive changes occurred because of Paul T. Klenk's foresight, diligence, and dedication to his hometown. It was the skills and leadership of Mayor Klenk that enabled Blue Island to begin the transformation from farming town to vibrant modern community. Mayor Klenk drafted ordinances that updated building and zoning codes and he made sure they were approved by his city council. He created and planned vital infrastructure projects that provided better water and sewer services and made sure they were approved by his city council. He did not only resurface the streets, Mayor Klenk oversaw the installation of new streets and alleys. Perhaps most amazingly of all, he kept city government running smoothly and efficiently. This was no easy task during the seemingly lawless Roaring Twenties in a town where reason always seemed to take a backseat to pleasure, profit, and ego.

That was another thing about Mayor Klenk. He appeared to have no ego. Of course, he must have had great confidence to perform at a high level of efficiency as an attorney and a chief executive of a city, yet he kept his ego in check. Evidence of arrogant public displays and pronouncements by elected officials line the pages of Blue Island history, but there are none by Mayor Klenk.

Paul Theodore Klenk was born April 18, 1893 in Blue Island. He was the seventh child born to Paul and Louisa Krueger Klenk. The birth was at the family home and according to the "birth book" at City Hall, Mrs. Klenk was attended by a midwife named Mrs. Hoffman. Paul Sr., age 48 and a native of Germany, owned and operated a store at the southwest corner of New Street and Western Avenue, where the El Molino Bakery is today. The Klenk Family has a scrapbook with photos, press clippings, and other memorabilia. Among the items is the business card used by Paul Sr. It announced that he was a "dealer in dry goods, notions, clothing, hats, caps, millinery, and ladies and gents furnishing goods" and "all goods sold at lowest Chicago prices." Louisa Klenk, age 39, was born in Blue Island and was a member of a local pioneer family. Her grandfather was Christian Krueger Sr., the patriarch of the Krueger Family. Louisa's father, Ludwig, was the oldest surviving son of Christian Krueger Sr. Ludwig, his wife, three of their daughters, and his younger sister and brother were the first of the Krueger Family to arrive in Blue Island. That was during August 1851. Paul T. Klenk's uncle, Christian Krueger Jr. may have inspired him to public service. Christian Krueger Jr. held many elective and bureaucratic offices in Blue Island. Most prominently, he was president of the village board from 1880 until 1883.

Paul T. Klenk displayed his leadership and competitive skills early. At Blue Island High School, he was class president all four years, played on the football team, and a graduate of the Class of 1910. During an era when only the wealthy or the most serious students went off to college, he attended the University of Michigan as an undergraduate. For reasons not explained, he transferred to Northwestern University and completed his undergraduate and graduate work there. He was admitted to the bar in the same year he graduated from NU, 1915. Thereafter, young Paul quickly earned a reputation as a very good attorney. Before long he was considered an expert, perhaps *the* expert of his era, in one of his specialties—municipal law.

He married Caryl Nickerson on October 11, 1916, and he became city attorney in April, 1917. City Attorney Klenk took leave from that position to enter the U.S. Navy and serve during World War I. He earned the rank of ensign and after discharge in 1918, he returned home to resume his city attorney duties. Then he stepped away from local politics and government for two years before being anointed the mayoral candidate of Blue Island's ruling political party and only enduring faction—the Greater Blue Island Party. Bright, young Paul T. Klenk was the perfect Blue Island candidate. He was German, a conservative Republican, and the member of a prominent local family. He was well-respected, popular, and active in local organizations. On the day after his birthday in 1921, he was elected mayor when he defeated Aldermen E. B. Bronson and Charles J. Olson. The totals were 1,869 for Klenk, 1,442 for Bronson, and 1,371 for Olson. At age 28, Paul T. Klenk reportedly was the youngest mayor ever elected here. Newspapers outside of Blue Island dubbed him "the boy mayor," even though he was almost 30 and appeared to be serious, not boyish, in photos.

Mayor Klenk was sworn in by legendary bartender and City Clerk George J. Landgraf at the start of the city council meeting on Monday, May 2. Change was in the air and the rookie mayor immediately began to make things happen. He and his capable city attorney, the bespectacled, Vandyke-wearing Roy Massena, instituted new rules of order for city council meetings. They also quickly introduced new ordinances and rewrote existing ordinances that they deemed inadequate. In doing so, Mayor Klenk went beyond setting professional standards for the city councils over which he would preside for eight consecutive years. The changes in rules and methods he introduced have withstood the test of time and still are practiced in Blue Island and other communities today.

Procedural rules and city ordinances do not guarantee respect, of course. Leadership does. Mayor Klenk was not merely a leader, but *the leader* from the moment he took the oath of office. His aldermen respected him, he respected them without kowtowing to them, and there was order and decorum during the Paul T. Klenk era of Blue Island government. This did not mean there was always agreement amongst aldermen, however. In one early episode, during September of 1921, the three aldermen who comprised the plats committee disagreed with six of their counterparts over a building code violation. Alderman Henry J. Schnurstein announced that work had been stopped on the home of A. H. Rohe at 245 Burr Oak Avenue (now the 2400 block) because the construction was not fire proof. Alderman Schnurstein was chairman of the buildings, plats, and grounds committee and his fellow committee members backed him on the decision. So did City Attorney Massena, who said so publicly during a city council meeting. Apparently Mr. Rohe was not happy. Perhaps because he was a big shot who owned a lumber company, he had friends and sympathizers, some of whom were aldermen. According to the *Sun-Standard*, by a vote of 6-3, the Rohe backers on the city council "rebuked" Alderman Schnurstein, who then "bitterly complained" to the newspaper. The end result was that during the October 3 city council meeting, Aldermen Schnurstein, George F. Fiedler, and J. P. Wiessner resigned in protest from the plats committee.

Mayor Klenk seemed to understand completely that this was petty local politics and that a solution had to be negotiated. This took approximately one month. In the interim, the mayor accepted the resignations and appointed new committee members. After the aldermen made peace, the new plats committee—E. H. Hopf, Charles J. Anderson, and Arnold Myers—respectfully resigned and urged the mayor to re-appoint the previous members and he did so immediately. As for the project by A. H. Rohe, apparently it was not completed. There is no listing in the Blue Island Directory of a home at 245 Burr Oak.

What happened is significant for two reasons. One significance of the squabble is that it marked the beginning of a change in Blue Island building codes. During the four terms of Mayor Klenk, the rapid growth in Blue Island could have veered out of control. Keeping it under control required new ordinances for building, zoning, and all else that would physically determine a modern community. Another significance is that during the time he allowed the spat between aldermanic factions to exhaust itself, at least in public, Mayor Klenk was criticized by the *Sun-Standard*. The newspaper called for greater "transparency" and said Blue Island had "one-man rule" under Mayor Klenk. Whether these shots came from publisher John Volp or editor Myron Jones is not known. Volp and his publication were great assets to the community, but you did not want to get on his bad side. Harry Rohrbach, a very successful and well-respected local businessman, learned this the hard way when Volp opposed him and his organization, the newly formed Blue Island Chamber of Commerce. The Chamber actually was very beneficial to the community, but Volp, who also had a printing company, reportedly was angered because the organization had printing done by an out-of-town company. There also was a rumor, never substantiated, that Mr. Rohrbach had refused to co-sign a loan for Mr. Volp's business. As for Mayor Klenk, he did not engage the *Sun-Standard.* Instead, he ignored it and went about his business. This worked well. Just as Mr. Volp and Mr. Rohrback eventually made peace, before long the newspaper returned to supporting Mayor Klenk.

There was a second public dispute, the last during Mayor Klenk's eight years in office and the only one involving the mayor himself. The disagreement could be blamed on Prohibition, which Blue Island was more opposed to than Communism. The city council went so far as to pass a resolution requesting that the federal government repeal the ban on alcohol. Not that anything as insignificant as an amendment to the United States Constitution would stop anyone in Blue Island. After Prohibition went into effect January 17, 1920, local saloons became "soda pop emporiums" and the city council winked and approved licenses for them.

People here needed to drink and the city needed revenue. This is the way Blue Island interpreted the 18th Amendment. What was good for Blue Island was good for the nation.

Blue Island police never checked to make sure saloons-turned-emporiums served anything stronger than near beer, but the federal government did. Agents actually raided quite a few local establishments during Prohibition. When they did, arrests were made and fines were issued. Early in his tenure, Mayor Klenk moved to suspend the business license of the offending business owner. Usually he was able to do this. Once, during 1921, his aldermen voted not to allow him to suspend a license. The matter quickly was resolved, as were all things under Mayor Klenk. The aldermen were able to flex their muscles on behalf of a connected local businessman, but it was the only time over the next eight years they would do so. Thereafter, disputes pertaining to alcohol disappeared because everyone adhered to the First Commandment of Blue Island: *Thou Shalt Not Be Found Out.* So on the public record, there were few mentions of soda pop emporiums being raided and none of proprietors being stripped of their licenses.

Yes, Mayor Klenk knew how to solve problems and he always was judicious and unflappable in doing so. He did not criticize, complain, or panic. He rarely commented beyond official pronouncements. He imposed his will where he could and these impositions always based upon laws that had to be—okay, in the case of Blue Island, that could be—enforced. His decisions were not personal. Where did he learn to be so cool under pressure? Why was he so fair? Most probably it was his upbringing. His legal training also must have helped since he quite obviously was reasonable yet persuasive, had good negotiating skills, and knew how to broker a deal. All must have been quite useful during a notable and insightful episode that was a great test and a learning experience for Paul T. Klenk. It occurred at a city hall outside of Blue Island.

His tenure as attorney for the Village of Robbins overlapped with his election in 1921 and the incident offers insight into the character of Paul T. Klenk, of race relations during that era, and of politics during any era. Attorney Klenk had no qualms about working for a community that was African American, which during the 1920s most Whites of any profession would not do. Nor did the elected officials of Robbins have any issues with hiring an outsider who was White. The law may appear in black and white, but it should have no color.

While Paul T. Klenk may have been colorblind and capable, he was not immune to politics. Thus Village Attorney Klenk's tenure in Robbins came to an abrupt end after the election of a new village board president and board members. According to the October 13, 1921 *Sun-Standard*, because there was bad blood between the incoming and the outgoing, Village Attorney Klenk was ordered by the new mayor to audit the books and find improprieties perpetrated by his predecessor, John Kellar, and former board members. According to the *Sun-Standard*, "Throw them all in jail" is what Mayor Robert Bryant ordered his village attorney to do. Paul T. Klenk carried out part of this order by reviewing all of the business transacted by the village during the tenure of former president Kellar. Upon completion, Mr. Klenk announced that the previous village president and the board were clean. This was not what Board President Bryant wanted to hear and he ordered Village Attorney Klenk to bring the old mayor up on charges anyway. He refused. According to the *Sun-Standard*, he announced, "I decline to prosecute innocent men." Subsequently, Paul T. Klenk was fired and an African American attorney, J. Harold Mosely of Chicago, was hired. As for Klenk, he may not have laughed all the way to the bank since it was not his style, but he did go there. Per his contract with the Village of Robbins, he received one year of salary in severance.

That is not where the episode ended. Attorney Klenk's work was thorough and accurate. His successor as village attorney, Mr. Mosely, was unable to find anything. Charges never were filed. Also, there was no public protest or indignation from outside of Robbins that African American elected officials dare fire a White village attorney. To the victors went the spoils.

Of note about that era: Robbins and Blue Island had a good relationship and news from Robbins, the all-Black community, regularly appeared in the *Sun-Standard*, the publication of the all-White predominantly German community. Residents of the village shopped in Blue Island and Blue Islanders did business in Robbins. Some Robbins residents worked in Blue Island and there was a Robbins-based cab company that served Blue Island. It was not until after World War II—when there was a baby boom, African Americans began their quest for equality and Whites who did not understand their plight began to view them differently—that the bond between White and Mexican Blue Islanders and African Americans became strained. The increase in African American enrollment at the Blue Island High School and the inability of school officials to ensure coexistence between Black students and other ethnicities finally broke that bond.

There was no controversy in Blue Island under Mayor Klenk, whose slogan was "A Greater and Better Blue Island." To this end, even conflicts of interest could not stand in the way. One that actually helped was a doozy. During his era and for many decades afterward, the city had a Board of Local Improvements whose job was to recommend local government projects to the mayor and the city council. The members of the Board of Local Improvements were appointed by the mayor. Perhaps because he believed no one loved Blue Island more, but probably because there was no one more trustworthy, Mayor Klenk appointed himself chairman of the Board of Local Improvements. Thus he and the other two very capable members, R. B. Hammond and Vertus B. Roberts, decided exactly what was to be done, where, by whom, and for how much. They decided on projects, solicited bids, and made recommendations to the mayor and city council when all aspects of the project were ready.

Mr. Hammond and Mr. Roberts had knowledge of infrastructure. Infrastructure was their area of expertise. Board chairman Klenk most likely put the specifics of the job into writing and drafted the legislation. These recommendations he submitted in a letter to Mayor Klenk and the aldermen, who always approved them. Yes, *Chairman* Klenk wrote official letters to *Mayor* Klenk. They appear in city council minutes and Blue Island grew in many ways thanks to this conflict of interest.

Miles of streets were paved; water and sewer lines were installed. Fire hydrants and sidewalks were added. Dead-end streets such as Union just west of Highland Avenue and California Avenue were opened to the west and south, respectively. Additional streets and alleys were created. Many of the streets were illuminated. The improvements may have been most important for the north side of Blue Island (the unofficial dividing line was Burr Oak Avenue), which was neglected before Mayor Klenk and would be considered a haven of the working (i.e., lower) class for years after him and despite his efforts. Mayor Klenk gave the same attention to the east side and the far south side that he gave the north side. He made sure that streets were paved and that sidewalks, connections to the water main, and sewers were installed. The city council minutes for that eight-year period may be the most boring in the city's history. They contain page after page of ordinances and specifications for projects. If the introductory words, "We herewith submit an ordinance" isn't enough to put you to sleep, the seemingly endless lists of project measurements and price quotes may be.

All numbers were not preceded by dollar signs, of course. Some numbers pertained to street addresses. At the urging of Postmaster F.T.E. Kallum, it was the Klenk administration that passed legislation bringing the local numeric system into alignment with Chicago. In a letter to Mayor Klenk and the city council, the perceptive yet tactful Mr. Kallum started the ball rolling when he gave as reasons for change the “rapid growth” of Blue Island and the “out-of-date system in use.” Mayor Klenk’s city council did not make Postmaster Kallum’s job any easier, however, when it changed the names of some streets. Prospect Street became Longwood Drive. Because Blue Island had two Division streets, one on the east side and another on the west side, the thoroughfare on the far west side became Hoyne. Apparently that western version of Division was a long and winding one, so portions of that street were changed from Division to Mozart. Ogden Avenue between Broadway and 123rd Street was renamed California Avenue. The street that was called California was renamed Francisco.

Neither rain, nor sleet, nor snow, nor multiple street names could keep them from their appointed rounds.

As for geopolitical designations, during the February 1, 1926 city council meeting, the ordinance by which Blue Island went from five to seven wards was passed and four aldermen were elected to represent the two new wards during April. Aldermen debated as to whether the bumpkins who lived in the wilderness of the north side of Blue Island should have mail delivered to their doors instead of having it delivered to a box on a post sometimes hundreds of feet away. As you read in an earlier chapter, this caused Postmaster Kallum to go to his rule book. How appropriate that Mayor Klenk met one of his few defeats by another crafty professional with a rule book.

There were far more victories for the mayor. A new accounting system also was installed very early in the tenure of Mayor Klenk. As a result and because he was frugal, the budget was balanced and the city began operating at a profit. Blue Island remained in the black for as long as Paul T. Klenk was mayor. It had been in the red during at least the five years before he became mayor. It would not be in black again for years after he left office.

Mayor Klenk presided over three annexations that enabled the city to grow on the west, east, and southeast, and he was an advocate of expansion who warned aldermen that it was essential. In his address to the city council during the May 5, 1924 meeting, he outlined improvements which had been completed and other goals that he determined necessary for the future success of Blue Island. The mayor said, “We must not lose sight of the fact that in order to properly function as a rapidly growing city which has suburban, urban, and especially industrial tendencies that we must expand territorially to properly provide for our three-fold development as above noted. We should even be willing and anxious to take in such adjoining territory which properly should be under jurisdiction so that such territory can receive Municipal [sic] benefits and at the same time bear its small portion of Municipal [sic] taxes.” Mayor Klenk continued to advocate annexation in his annual message each year.

The mayor was far ahead of his time as a champion of the environment. He repeatedly campaigned against polluters such as Illinois Brick Company, Chicago Copper and Chemical Company (which for years emitted a rotten egg smell from its location at the northeast corner of the Burr Oak viaduct), the railroads, and other local businesses such as refineries. Sometimes he cited them for illegal dumping, air pollution, or water pollution. He advocated legislation that would curb all of these problems.

There is no detailed explanation in city council minutes or the *Sun-Standard* as to why Paul T. Klenk did not seek a fifth term as mayor, which would have been a record at that time. He cited only the demands of his other responsibilities as reasons for not running in 1929, yet there was an unrelated oddity. Despite all he accomplished, there was no fanfare for Mayor Klenk upon his departure. During the last city council meeting of the mayor who may have been the greatest in Blue Island history, not one of the thirteen aldermen in attendance commented on his service. No members of the public said anything either. This was unusual because during that era, popular public officials upon election and upon departure always received lavish praise and gifts. The only reference was made by Mayor Klenk himself. According to the city council minutes he "stated he enjoyed working with the City Council during the past eight years, that because he was leaving office was no reason for his losing interest in city affairs, but that he would continue to have the interests of the city at heart at all times."

Apparently they did not understand that Mayor Klenk's greatest achievement may have been incorporating others to work for the benefit of Blue Island. The aforementioned Board of Local Improvements was invaluable and its accomplishments still are enjoyed by Blue Islanders today. In 1924, Mayor Klenk also installed the city's first zoning board. Its first appointments were Robert Krueger, Henry J. Schnurstein, and Thomas R. Foster. These men approved the private projects that still endure in Blue Island.

Mayor Klenk had good ears. He listened to his constituents, who clamored for more recreation land and activities for Blue Island youth in 1924. During May of that year, the Mayor created a playground and a recreation commission. Its first members were Dr. Frank W. Tracy, Arthur C. Seyfarth, Mrs. Jacob P. Postweiler, Henry M. Schlemmer, and future mayor Frank Kasten. Dr. Tracy, who served as president, provided a great service to Blue Island when he secured $13,500 for the purchase of the east side property known as Becker's Woods, which later became Centennial Park. The area that included Becker's Woods property was annexed.

Prior to leaving office, Paul T. Klenk was able to witness another politician assume power. During March of 1929, Mayor Klenk attended the inauguration of the new President of the United States. In the Klenk family album is the invitation. "My father-in-law went to Washington and he met President Hoover," said Joan Klenk. "He came back and told us that he got to shake the president's hand."

Unbeknownst to Mayor Klenk, with the Great Depression lurking and crime about to spike, he could not have chosen a better time to leave office. He also was serving as Assistant Attorney General of the State of Illinois, an appointment he held for eight years and at various times he represented various municipalities and taxing districts. Among them were the Blue Island Park

District, Worth, the Village of Robbins, Midlothian, and Alsip, yet he found time for recreation and to get away. In his spare time, and it is difficult to believe he had any, he built a log cabin in a wilderness area of Orland Park.

"He didn't hire someone to build it. He built it himself. I think it was during 1937 when we [Teddy and Joan] were in college," said his daughter-in-law, Joan Klenk. "There was nothing in that part of Orland Park in those days and my in-laws used it as their getaway place. He even enjoyed driving out there. He found it relaxing."

"I have a photo of him cutting the logs," she added. "He gave his cabin a name—'Serendipity.'"

The little boy who watched the trolley car pass through Blue Island for the last time grew up to be Paul T. Klenk's next door neighbor. Said Harry Robertson, "He also called the cabin 'As You Like It,' which I believe was a reference to Shakespeare."

"They had a summer cabin 'out in the country,' which is now a forest preserve in Orland Park and we used to go there as kids," said one of Franklin Klein's daughters, Linda Klein. "They had a swimming pool there, which was quite unusual for those days."

Yes, Paul T. Klenk was Lincolnesque. He was hardworking, trustworthy and creative. He was an attorney, a well-respected politician, and a railsplitter. He was an inspiration and role model. The great-grandson of a pioneer helped Blue Island become the birthplace, literally and figuratively, of many great attorneys, some of whom also became experts in municipal law. They included great attorneys now all but forgotten: W. Otto Wielgorecki, Henry Buehring, Carl H. Carlson, and Roy Massena. Mr. Carlson eventually became a Cook County Court judge.

Among those who followed Paul T. Klenk by approximately two decades were Paul Schreiber and Franklin Klein. Mr. Schreiber was the city attorney for almost the entire 28 years John M. Hart was in office. For a few years, Attorneys Klenk and Klein were associates of former Illinois Attorney General Carlstrom. In 1936, Klenk & Klein became a law firm. Their offices were at 111 W. Washington in Chicago and in the First National Bank Building in Blue Island. Franklin Klein would succeed Paul T. Klenk as *the* attorney to see on issues pertaining to school district law.

"They were tireless workers," said one of Franklin Klein's daughters, Linda Klein. "They eventually became experts on school bond law and issues of those bonds. They were legal counsel for many school districts."

Among the attorneys closer in age to Paul T. Klenk, but whose expertise was in other aspects of the law was Henry Seyfarth, whose specialty was labor law on the side of management. What would you expect from a conservative Blue Islander, who founded a very successful international law firm that still flourishes and who for many years controlled First National Bank? There also was Henry Gentile, "the dealmaker" who was at various times a crafty criminal defense lawyer, a litigator, a prosecutor, and also the city attorney for several municipalities. Attorney Gentile came along in the 1940s. By the early 1960s, he became one of Paul T.

Klenk's successors as Alsip Village Attorney. Henry Gentile eventually became a Cook County Circuit Court judge.

According to those who knew him, another successful local defense attorney, Larry Petta, used his clout in Cook County to get Judge Gentile his appointment. Attorney Petta also was a city prosecutor, first for Calumet Park and later for Blue Island, where he also wrote ordinances on building code enforcement. Perhaps most notably, Mr. Petta was a wily and feared (some say ruthless) strategist with strong political connections.

While Maurice Schultz may have been the most respected, Earl Ebers Jr. may have been the most crafty for the personal business and political deals he brokered. In 1961, Mr. Ebers, with his wife Loretta and brother-in-law Louis Tiberi, organized a campaign that helped him defeat incumbent city prosecutor Gentile. Said Mr. Tiberi, "We went door to door all over town campaigning for Earl. Henry Gentile must have thought he had it in the bag because he did not campaign hard. After the election, I ran into Mr. Gentile. He looked at me and said, 'I know you.' I told him, 'You had me in court.' And he did. I appeared before him when he was magistrate. He said to me, 'You helped beat me in that election.' I said, 'Yes, sir, I did.' We kind of laughed about that. Henry Gentile was a good man. He didn't hold any grudges."

In 1964, Earl Ebers Jr. succeeded another local legend, Paul Schreiber, when he was appointed by Mayor John M. Hart to be his last city attorney.

Speaking of last, but absolutely not least, after his discharge from the service, a professional musician named Romie Palmer passed the bar exam, relocated to Blue Island, and opened a practice here. Eventually Mr. Palmer was the first city attorney appointed by Mayor Richard W. Withers. Mr. Palmer left that position after he was elected to the Illinois General Assembly from here. Eventually he became a Cook County Circuit Court judge.

As skilled and successful as they were, none of the aforementioned may have been as accomplished an attorney. They certainly were not as diversified as Paul T. Klenk.

"Paul Klenk also was an expert in cemetery law," added Harry Robertson.

At some point in his career, Paul T. Klenk became president of the Mount Greenwood Cemetery Association and therein lies a peculiarity, perhaps another conflict of interest in his business and political history. Long before it became Blue Island's signature park, Memorial Park was Blue Island Cemetery. It was founded in 1850, but quickly fell out of favor. Burials reportedly were banned there by 1898. By the end of World War I, the cemetery was in great disrepair after years of neglect. In 1921, as an attorney, Paul T. Klenk represented Blue Island Cemetery and Mount Greenwood Cemetery. As mayor, he wanted to create a park to honor veterans. So Mayor Klenk, Willis N. Rudd, and others were instrumental in the public acquisition of the cemetery and surrounding property that would become Memorial Park. As for the conflict of interest, many of the remains interred at Memorial

Cemetery were transferred to Mount Greenwood Cemetery. Thus Mayor Klenk benefitted as an attorney too. Years later, businessman Klenk became a major stockholder in the cemetery and was its president. Eventually, he acquired Mount Greenwood Cemetery. His family still owns and operates it today.

Yet for all of his successes and renown, it seems that few people knew him intimately.

"I knew of him, but I didn't know him well," said Harry Robertson. "We said hello, but we didn't socialize or talk much. He was quite a bit older."

Actually, none of the neighbors of that section of the 12900 block of Elm Street spoke to each other much, but it was not because they were not interesting or interested. Everyone on the block was quite successful. In addition to Mr. Robertson, who had a career in manufacturing and investments, at the opposite end of the block was Pete Jenin, who owned Raceway Park. In between the Klenk family and the Jenin family were Adeline Hackett and Francis Hackett Walton, the widow and the daughter of gambling boss, James Hackett, who owned and operated Navajo Hills Country Club. While there is one story of animosity that led to a lawsuit, reportedly over a property dispute between Mr. Jenin and Mrs. Hackett, there are no stories of socializing or collegiality—or other problems—amongst the neighbors.

Paul T. Klenk probably was too busy with his career and his family to socialize outside of either. What else could he have had time for?

"My grandmother said that Mrs. Hackett lived there, but she never mentioned any more about her," said Paula Klenk Everett. "I don't think they associated, but not because of any particular reason. They were just neighbors."

Paul T. Klenk was personable and outgoing, however, and he did have a sense of humor, according to Linda Klein.

"In his library at the cabin, there was a book entitled EVERYTHING I KNOW ABOUT WOMEN. My dad used to love to pull that book out whenever we were there and open it up and show us the inside, which was all blank pages. He and Paul would laugh and laugh about that."

Paul T. Klenk was a founding member of American Legion Post 50 and he also was a member of the Lions Club, the Elks Club, the Masons, the Odd Fellows, and the Moose Lodge. He served as vice president of Navajo Hills Country Club after it opened in 1930, before James Hackett acquired it. He was a member of the Chicago Bar Association and the Blue Island Bar Association. He was vice president of the Illinois Municipal League and chairman of its legislative committee. During World War II, Paul T. Klenk continued to serve his country and Blue Island by serving as head of the local draft board and by taking charge of the first bond drives in the community.

Paul Klenk suffered a heart attack during 1946, but recovered. While being treated for a throat ailment in 1948, he was diagnosed with lung cancer.

"He smoked all the time, which eventually did him in," said Linda Klein.

The former Blue Island mayor was a patient at St. Luke's Hospital in Chicago for the final two months of his life and died there March 29, 1950 at age 56.

Visitation was at Krueger Funeral Home and the service was held at Grace Methodist Church. Paul T. Klenk was laid to rest at Mount Greenwood Cemetery.

How did a strong leader such as Mayor Paul T. Klenk contribute to the election of John M. Hart? Well, without the structure and direction provided by Mayor Klenk, during the next eight years, the city council almost self-destructed and took city government down with it.

Frank Kasten

Born January 13, 1878
Elected Mayor April 1929
Mayor Number 8
Served Until May 1935
Number of Terms: 3
Died December 12, 1946

Frank Kasten was Mayor Paul T. Klenk's successor and he may have been the unluckiest mayor in the history of Blue Island. He could not have been elected at a worse time politically or economically. He inherited an unprofessional police department that was distrusted by the community and ridiculed by the press. He presided over a revolving door of fourteen aldermen who were arrogant and seemed able to function only with the strongest of direction. Quickly added to this double whammy was the denial of tax revenue.

At the conclusion of the Roaring Twenties, Frank Kasten became chief executive of a sanctimonious, yet morally wide-open community that enjoyed drinking, whoring, gambling, arguing, racial and ethnic divisions, rowdy political campaigns, and casting ballots (sometimes more than once on election day), but which seemed to have an aversion to meaningful participation in local government. As the epitome of blue collar Blue Island, Mr. Kasten seemed fully aware of his community's strengths and weaknesses. Because of this, perhaps in spite of this, he never wavered as the city's biggest supporter and defender.

As for the misfortune of Mayor Kasten, well, it has been said that luck is the residue of design. This axiom seems especially true when revisiting the six years he was in office. Mayor Kasten was not an astute businessman or a visionary. He provided few positive solutions for the law enforcement and finance dilemmas, and some of his decisions actually contributed to the problems. Lack of executive leadership, a weak city council, and a citizenry that seemed to care most about having a drink and placing a bet combined to set the good ship Blue Island adrift without a rudder at the start of the most desperate decade in its history.

Frank Kasten was born in Dolton on January 13, 1878 to Louis and Caroline Gese Kasten. Like those of Paul T. Klenk, Mr. Kasten's ancestors—both his mother and his father—came from Germany. Unlike the Klenks, the Kastens possessed neither wealth nor prestige. The family reportedly moved to Blue Island during 1880, although no reason was given as to why. The most likely explanations are better living conditions and a job opportunity for Louis Kasten in one of the local rail yards or brickyards. Young Frank Kasten was industrious. He dropped out of high school at age fourteen and went to work for the Illinois Brick Company. By 1902, he had purchased the home at 2359 Des Plaines Street. In 1907, he became president of Local 3 Brick and Claymakers of America. He held that position until 1914, the same year he married Margaret Morford.

In 1917, he was elected president of the national organization, although sometimes he listed his occupation as "business agent." By any title, Frank Kasten was a respected labor leader. According to the *Sun-Standard*, legendary American Federation of Labor president Samuel Gompers once said, "There's no cleaner and finer labor executive in the United States than Frank Kasten."

On the same day that Mayor Klenk announced he would not seek re-election - February 14, 1929 - the Greater Blue Island Party met and endorsed Frank Kasten as its candidate for mayor. How and why candidate Kasten became the valentine of the most prominent local political group never was explained. One possibility is that popularity was confused with leadership. Certainly Mr. Kasten wanted to be mayor and he appears to have set himself up for a run at the office. It probably was not a coincidence that five years prior to his candidacy, the name *Frank Kasten* began to appear in city council minutes and in the *Sun-Standard*.

The first mention was May 5, 1924 when he was appointed to the playground and recreation board by Mayor Klenk. The second was August 2, 1926. Frank Kasten attended the city council meeting as president of the BCOA. According to the minutes, he was introduced at the start of the meeting. Big fish always feed first. Little fish are forced to tread water and wait for scraps. Union president Kasten, a big fish, "spoke on behalf of the brick interests of this vicinity and urged that a committee be appointed to assist in demanding that the Sanitary District use brick for the building of the West End sewer." This was a shrewd political and public relations move on the part of the future mayor. It propelled him into the public eye, demonstrated that he had clout on a local level, and promoted the brick makers that he represented. Alderman Joseph Lentz immediately moved that Mr. Kasten's request be accepted and Alderman J. P. Wiessner seconded. The vote was unanimous in favor of Mayor Klenk appointing a committee to contact the Sanitary District. That quickly, Frank Kasten and those he represented, (i.e., workers and the companies they worked for), had a new lobby group. The arrangement made great business sense. Illinois Brick Company was a thriving business and its employees lived here and spent their hard-earned money here. The more bricks made and sold, the greater the all-around revenue for Blue Island.

During the May 2, 1927 city council meeting, Frank Kasten changed roles and made a personal appearance as a loyal subject. It is important to note that in that era, politicians sometimes were treated as royalty. Old country style, they were presented gifts. On that occasion, the swearing in of elected officials, citizen Kasten presented gold stars to aldermen George F. Fiedler and Rudolph Swanson "as a token of esteem." How the aldermen had esteemed themselves and why Frank Kasten served as presenter was not explained. All that remains is speculation. Mr. Fiedler was an influential alderman who represented the south side where the future mayor resided. Later he would be Mayor Kasten's most trustworthy ally on the city council. As for the newly-elected Mr. Swanson, it may have been because Illinois Brick Company was a prosperous local company whose property bordered on his ward. The future mayor and the rookie alderman were not political allies, however. Rudolph Swanson was on the slate that opposed Frank Kasten in 1929.

It was labor leader Kasten who appeared at a special city council meeting held Thursday, March 1, 1928, approximately fourteen months before he would be mayor. The purpose of the meeting was to discuss new building codes, a signature of the Klenk administration. As president of the national brick makers union, he was asked to attend the meeting so that Mayor Klenk could give him a copy of a proposed ordinance regarding buildings made of brick. Mr. Kasten was asked to review the ordinance and make recommendations. He also appeared at special city council meeting held Thursday, January 31, 1929, during which he presented for consideration a masonry code prepared by the Common Brick Manufacturers Association.

If Frank Kasten was otherwise active in local politics, it was behind the scenes. Prior to his candidacy he rarely was mentioned in the *Sun-Standard*. Yes, Frank Kasten was a politician - probably one of only two real politicians ever to be elected Blue Island mayor - except that he never was a candidate before or after. He was a good speaker and campaigner and an energetic liaison between labor, management, and government. Near the top of his brief resume was that he was a member of the Lincoln School PTA. That was it.

It is quite possible that some of the veteran aldermen pushed Frank Kasten to acquire recognition and to run for mayor. Blue Island aldermen squirmed under Mayor Klenk, who wisely allowed them very few important decision-making opportunities. What better way for aldermen to take back the city council than by endorsing a friend willing to share governance with them?

Frank Kasten also may have been placed atop the ballot because he crossed the social and economic strata. Again he was true blue collar—a brick maker. In Blue Island yards that meant you went to work very early in the day and returned home late at night, often not sober and always dirty, so dirty in fact that the woman who scrubbed your clothes could not get the dirt and clay out of them any more than she could extract those earthly components from your veins. Your preferred drink was a shot and a beer, which you sometimes had for breakfast and for lunch. If you were lucky enough to become a foreman or a union leader, you got to know workers, management, businessmen, and political leaders. You did business with them in the brickyard, at the construction site, at the office, and in back rooms. You stood elbow to elbow with them at the saloon and you sat next to them at the company picnic, the poker table, and in the church pew. That was Frank Kasten, the common man elected president of a labor union with a large membership.

Yes, candidate Kasten had that common man image. No one was elected in Blue Island unless they had it. Until the 1970s, no one could be elected—and stay elected—in Blue Island unless he also was perceived to be practical. Furthermore, until 1935, with perhaps one exception, no one was elected unless he had the support of conservative, mainstream leaders such as Paul T. Klenk, Cook County Republican Party chairman

William Webber, Cook County Board member Carl J. Carlson, and banker John L. Zacharias. Also influential were individuals of nebulous careers such as gambling boss James Hackett.

Frank Kasten passed muster on all of the criteria. He had worked his way up from laborer to popular and influential union boss. He worked for working stiffs and with the people who employed them. He did not rock the boat and he was a cheerleader for Blue Island. This got him backing of the working class and local big shots.

In those days, Blue Island had a primary election in which candidates for the same office ran against each other regardless of party. Frank Kasten easily defeated Milard A. Rauhauf in the March primary and it appeared that he would beat him just as easily in the general election.

More than enough support almost turned out to be not enough. Milard A. Rauhauf, a popular and respected local attorney, was Mayor Klenk's last police magistrate. Mr. Rauhauf did not have the backing of Blue Island powers that be. He and the members of his slate campaigned hard amongst the masses, however, and they touched on every issue real and imagined that resonated with Blue Islanders. These included garbage pickup, the police, the city dump, and city services.

There was one odd mention by candidate Rauhauf and it alluded to race. In a full page ad that appeared in the *Sun-Standard*, Mr. Rauhauf said that he was "not a member of any organizations which belittle or deny to anyone their right or belief or membership in other organizations or churches such as the Ku Klux Klan.

The candidates of the Clean Government Party do not and will not criticize except where such is necessary."

Despite what this oddly-worded plank in the Rauhauf platform might lead readers to believe, there never has been a chapter of the KKK in Blue Island. Yet the promise obviously pandered to those concerned about race, a subject that always has bewildered Blue Islanders, and it may have generated some votes for the Clean Government Party.

There also was an oddity in the platform of candidate Kasten. This was reform of the police department, which Mr. Kasten claimed was known for "loafing around the police station." This was unusual because public criticism of the police force was an indirect shot at Mayor Klenk, who had given the Kasten candidacy tacit, not public, endorsement. On the other hand, every negative that Frank Kasten directed at the police department was accurate. Is it possible that the well-respected and influential Mayor Klenk did not care what candidate Kasten said because Kasten had to do what he could not bring himself to do—clean up BIPD? What Paul T. Klenk thought was not expressed publicly. There was no rebuttal to candidate Kasten's promise of reform.

And did this promise of reform confuse or alarm voters? There is nothing that voters fear more than change. Did Blue Islanders believe that Frank Kasten might actually make the police department worse? Perhaps enough members of the police force feared losing their jobs and campaigned against him. For whatever the reasons, after the primary, the contest between Mr. Kasten and Mr. Rauhauf went from runaway to dog fight.

By all accounts, it was a typical Blue Island election. Candidates from both political parties campaigned all over town and in churches and halls. Their rallies featured fiery speeches, bands, parades, and Vaudeville shows. They played to ethnicities. At Hahn's Hall, located at Lincoln Street and Burr Oak Avenue, a Kasten gathering featured speeches in Polish. Italians played prominent roles too. The event also featured music and a boxing card with fighters from Frank Bella's gym. Louis Lombardo, who later would become an alderman, played the banjo and fought on the boxing card at 112 lbs. At the Eagles Hall near the Top of the Hill a well-attended Rauhauf rally was in German. The Hungry Five, "the famous German band from WGN Radio," entertained. On election eve, Frank Kasten secured the support of WCFL radio and a one-hour speaking slot.

As for Blue Island on that Election Day, perhaps the best snapshots are of the polling places. The police station, two of the firehouses, and Old Main Building were logical locations for ballots to be cast. Others, such as the showroom of Fiedler-Mohr Motors (Alderman Fiedler's place of business) and Tony David's barber shop, are curious by today's standards. Not so in April of 1929, when local elections often came down to behaviors. In these, the more gruff followers of candidate Kasten were not above crossing the line. Frank Kasten was quite popular and as you would expect of any well-known working class candidate of that era, his campaign was a rowdy one. On the day before the election, a Kasten supporter set off a stink bomb inside the Masonic Hall where, ironically, the Clean Government Party was holding a campaign event. It is believed that the Masonic Temple was sufficiently aired out because it did serve as a polling place the next day.

This may have precipitated the Election Day incident at the north side firehouse on Cochran Street fire house. After receiving a Clean Government Party complaint against Kasten supporters, the Cook County Sheriff reportedly sent deputies, not fumigators, to make sure there were no shenanigans. There were not, at least after the deputies arrived, because the officers picked up the shotguns kept on the premises and wielded them. The presence of armed deputies discouraged stink bomb throwers and greatly offended Frank Kasten. A counter complaint quickly was issued and the deputies were pulled from the detail. Never explained was why the Coroner's Office got involved or why the *Sun-Standard* called the election of 1929—in which Frank Kasten defeated Millard Rauhauf, 3,951 to 3,313—"one of the bitterest campaigns in the history of Blue Island."

The 7,301 ballots cast did reflect the growth of the city. The post-election edition of the *Sun-Standard* was symbolic and it featured other signs of things to come. On the left half of the front page was a plea from Paul T. Klenk for peace between local political factions. On the right half of the page was the story of the armed hold up of the box office at the Lyric Theater.

After the smoke, stink, and accusations cleared, Frank Kasten became the eighth mayor of Blue Island, but he would not be a full-time mayor—at least not during his first year in office. According to the *Sun-Standard*, he occasionally was out of town on union business, sometimes in Washington, D.C. meeting with officials of the federal government and national business leaders. This is understandable. Mayor of Blue Island never has been a full-time or well-paying job. The mayor always had to do something to generate a real income. Labor did more than pay the bills for the Kasten family. It gave Frank Kasten his identity and helped him get elected. Why wouldn't he continue to work on behalf of labor?

Then the Great Depression took hold of America and there was no one for the brick makers to make bricks. Local brickyards shut down. With not much else to do besides tend to his garden, Frank Kasten unofficially became the first-ever full-time mayor of Blue Island. He reportedly went to his office at City Hall almost every day. Yet with all of the time he devoted to Blue Island, Mayor Kasten could not get a handle on the community's two most urgent problems—the police department and finance.

Candidate Kasten had been correct. For years, the Blue Island Police Department was a liability. In May of 1929, Mayor Kasten decided to do something about it. His something was a surprise and something that unions consider a mortal sin. The rookie mayor announced there would be a reduction in the workforce. He fired those he determined to be the most inefficient members of the Police Department.

The *Sun-Standard* referred to Mayor Kasten's plan as a "purge." He defended the move with a return to his campaign rhetoric. The mayor cited the "loafers" at "the station" who practiced "bandying from mouth to mouth." He fired desk sergeant Max Bilb and officers George E. Heatley, Dean Goulding, William Steffenhagen, and Frank Jenner. He said the quintessential Blue Island police officer, George J. Fiedler, temporarily would remain as chief, and according to a quote in the *Sun-Standard*, "He and the rest of the force have distinctly been told that it is up to them to demonstrate in no uncertain terms that they are capable."

Chief Fiedler and the rest of the force soon demonstrated what they were capable of. On the evening of June 1, according to stories in the *Chicago Tribune* and the *Sun-Standard*, there was a raid on the Burr Oak Hotel by twenty investigators from the Office of the State's Attorney. Chief Fiedler and one of his officers were taken into custody.

The *Sun-Standard* version was more entertaining and pro-Blue Island business. The account seemed to remind bordello operators and bootleggers to be vigilant against strangers and that locally the fix remained in. The story referred to the raid by the State's Attorney as "their weekly visit to Blue Island." The story emphasized the raid was conducted by "outside" enforcement officers, not by Blue Island. The *Tribune* story pulled no punches. It said that Chief Fiedler and Officer Henry Pucik were arrested along with prostitutes, johns, and the operators of the establishment. This was vehemently disputed by Mayor Kasten, who claimed Chief Fiedler and Officer Pucik were, for lack of a better explanation, just along for the ride.

The *Sun-Standard* was able to clean up their version of the story somewhat. In part, it said, "While the raid was in progress, Officer Henry Pucik of the Blue Island force dropped in and Chief Fiedler was asked for. Pucik got in touch with him over the telephone and he came right over to aid in the raid if needed."

The *Sun-Standard* also quoted an assistant state's attorney telling Chief Fiedler, "I thought the place was closed," and the chief's incriminating response as, "So did I."

Mayor Kasten "denounced" the *Tribune* story, according to the *Sun-Standard*, which he said was composed "by someone who wished to defame and drag Blue Island's good name in the dust." The mayor added that Chief Fiedler was "not technically put under arrest" and that he made the trip to Chicago with the arresting officers "merely as a matter of courtesy." He added, "The patrolman neither was arrested, but did go into the building to see that everything was run within the law." Officer Pucik further distinguished himself three months later when he accidentally shot himself in the shoulder while sitting in his car parked outside of the police station.

As for that June 1 *Tribune* story, it also mentioned the "tinkling of a battery of slot machines" during the raid of the Burr Oak Hotel. In his attempt to refute this, Mayor Kasten was at his best as defender of Blue Island. In the process, he may have caused laughter and eye rolling from the Transfer Inn all the way to the Top of the Hill when he put forth one of the biggest whoppers in Blue Island history. “That is not a fact. I am absolutely positive that there is not a slot machine being operated within the city limits of Blue Island,” pronounced Mayor Kasten.

Within the city limits? There were slot machines at the American Legion Hall, which was located on the second floor of City Hall. Mr. Kasten may have heard the tinkling from his office. Because the mayor was just as emphatic that Chief Fiedler had a case for libel against the *Tribune*, the matter was turned over to the city attorney. Nothing ever became of it, of course. Had the matter gone to court, people everywhere might have learned just the way things were done in Blue Island.

In 1929, the Blue Island Police Department may have been the prime example of the way things were done. If you wanted to be a police officer, there was no formal application process or examination. This held true even after civil service was created and until sometime after 1965. It all came down to who you knew. Someone sponsored you and three prominent citizens recommended you. The police committee approved you and the mayor rubber stamped the appointment. In 1914, George J. Fiedler was a driver of one of the Blue Island Fire Department horse teams. After someone suggested to him that he could make more money with BIPD than he could as wagon driver, Mr. Fiedler spoke to the mayor. The mayor liked George J. Fiedler, made sure it was okay with the police committee, and appointed him to the police force. His first day on the force, Officer Fiedler justified his appointment when he caught a horse thief. For this, he earned a $50 reward, which was the equivalent of one month's salary. Three years later, George J. Fiedler had risen to the rank of Chief of Police. It is not known if he ever caught another horse thief.

Is there any wonder why the police force was a rag-tag bunch? Upon hire, there was no training. No one was taught procedures, safety practices, investigative techniques, how to shoot, or the law. Prerequisites, skills, and knowledge were insignificant because after someone received an appointment to the police force, it rarely was undone. To lose your job with BIPD, you had to cross the line. On other side of the line were not any of the aforementioned. The line was a political designation. A police officer crossed it when he embarrassed or angered his sponsors or getting on the wrong side of the police committee or enough aldermen to vote him out. This seemed to happen less frequently than an appearance of Haley's Comet or a slot machine being found in Blue Island. In the event such rarity did occur, the word went from the aldermen to the mayor (behind closed doors) that he could recommend termination. The mayor would make that recommendation to aldermen during a city council meeting and the same aldermen who told the mayor what to do privately would concur publicly.

In May of 1929, the police committee relented to Mayor Kasten and allowed him to fire four officers. Someone had a change of heart, however. One of the officers, Frank Jenner, was reinstated. Not long afterward, three replacements were hired. George J. Fiedler would remain in the top spot, but only until he crossed that line.

As for those served by BIPD, they could not say they were not warned. At the start of his term in office, the Mayor told Blue Islanders to "take precautions against robbery." This was at approximately the same time that the post office was dynamite bombed by burglars attempting to gain entry. Just five months later at the start of the Depression, the mayor added, "To be candid, I am somewhat fearful of the coming winter with so many people unemployed and the consequences thereof." According to the mayor, this was because less than one-half of the industries in and around Blue Island were in operation and "many wage earners are walking the streets."

Perhaps Mayor Kasten should have warned the citizens and business owners to be wary of the police. During the February 9, 1931 city council meeting, the police committee gave a report on members of the police who refused to shape up. Chief Fiedler, then in his fourteenth year in the top spot, was described as "experienced and knowledgeable" but also "somewhat lax in the enforcing of discipline among the members of the force; somewhat careless in his personal appearance, and sometimes indifferent to his obligations to business and professional men here in the city." The officers hired after the "purge"—John Zielinski, Ernest Lunn, and John Antoine—also were found to be deficient. Patrolman Zielinski already had been reprimanded several times by the mayor and the police committee and according to the report there were "several rumors that he was open for inducements." Of Patrolman Lunn, it was said that despite reprimands he was "indifferent to the rules and regulations handed down by the police committee" and that he had "taken advantage of the good nature of Chief Fiedler." Patrolman Antoine was described as having "all the markings of a good policeman," but he "had apparently associated with the wrong people during his first year of service." Later it would be revealed that he actually was one of the wrong people and that he had difficulty controlling his libido while on duty.

Also announced was that Chief Fiedler and officers Jenner, Pucik, and Fred Schultz were in debt to local merchants. This was more damaging to a reputation than anything concocted by the police committee. In Blue Island, if you owed, you paid back in full or you made an effort to pay back. If you didn't, local gossip made certain that everyone knew about it and your reputation was ruined, which was far worse than a reprimand issued during a city council meeting.

What followed was one of the few bucks, figuratively and literally, passed by the city council during the Great Depression. Mayor Kasten acted to dismiss only one small fish, Officer Lunn, and he was quite generous in doing so. The city was broke, but the mayor gave Officer Lunn one more week on the job, essentially a week of severance pay, before he was officially terminated. All other fish were let off the hook. The Mayor also alibied for all of the debtors except Chief Fiedler, who continued to be the whipping boy. The mayor told the city council that the debtor patrolmen were victims of extenuating circumstances who were doing their best to satisfy their obligations. This may have been true. Because they did not receive regular paychecks during the Depression, many city employees received credit from local merchants.

The mayor summed up his decision by stating, "So that the police officers know where they stand and not become demoralized or their morale disrupted, further action will be taken only upon evidence showing their failure to act the part of a policeman and work for the interests of the City."

It also was Mayor Kasten and the Greater Blue Island Party looking out for their interests on the eve of an election. Voters hate major changes, especially on the eve of an election. Voters in general usually do not interpret change as positive even if that change will benefit them. Blue Islanders in particular always have been adverse to change because...well, Blue Islanders never believed they needed a reason.

The maintaining of the status quo was a calculation that paid off for incumbent Kasten and those on his slate. On April 21, 1931 he won re-election when he defeated Frank J. Boyd. The totals were 4,048 for the incumbent and 2,784 for the challenger. City Clerk George J. Landgraf and Police Magistrate Carl J. Carlson also were re-elected. John H. Ganzer replaced Edward H. Hopf as city treasurer.

Mayor Kasten and the 1931 city council interpreted this mandate as a job well done and declined to make changes in the police department or the way they handled the city's money. Nature fills a vacuum. External forces picked up the slack. As the economic situation worsened, local crime did too. There were more murders and robberies. There were stickups and purse snatchings on Western Avenue in broad daylight.

Delivery drivers were held up. Sometimes their trucks were hijacked. There were armed robberies and burglaries. Even when bad publicity did not follow, complaints did. Chief Fiedler went from whipping boy to fall guy. During the July 20, 1931 city council meeting it was announced he would be demoted. Captain William Hankey would be acting chief. The man who meteorically went from wagon driver to police chief would drop to the number three spot and serve as sergeant and detective. Sergeant Stuart Heim would be promoted to lieutenant and number two in command. Emphasized during that city council meeting were the changes made by the mayor *and* the police committee: Aldermen Joseph Lentz, Andrew Myers, and Rocco Guglielmucci. The egomaniacal aldermen wanted the public to know they'd helped throw Chief Fiedler under the bus. Perhaps if they were as efficient and law-abiding as they wanted the public to be, Chief Fiedler never would have been demoted. This leads to a very interesting story about Alderman Myers and his understanding of the law.

During an October 1932 city council meeting, when Blue Island was desperate for revenue, Alderman Myers suggested that the city license slot machines. It is believed that after Alderman Myers' surprising suggestion, there was a silence. Perhaps there was some throat clearing. A few of the aldermen may have lowered their gazes so that their expressions could not be seen. Finally, City Attorney may habroke the tension when he reminded Alderman Myers that slot machines were not legal and as such could not be licensed. Mayor Kasten added that there were no slot machines in Blue

Island. To make sure that someone did not sneak one into town, he instructed Police Chief Hankey to inspect every local establishment and report back.

The mayor's announcement actually was true several months prior, but only for a very short time. During the summer of 1931, investigators from the Office of the Cook County State's Attorney descended upon Blue Island, raided every public house, and confiscated all of the slot machines—fifty in all. It is believed that replacement slot machines arrived shortly thereafter. For the sake of accuracy and to maintain Blue Island's reputation, Chief Hankey did follow the mayor's order and make an inspection. During late October, he reported to the city council that there were no slot machines in Blue Island.

Thus Alderman Myers' suggestion was shot down. Speaking of which, perhaps a better suggestion would have been the licensing of firearms and firearms training for elected officials...or anger management.

Andrew Myers and saloon owner, Anton "Tony" Sadunas, apparently hated each other. If Alderman Myers hated Tony Sadunas and he knew the animosity was mutual, what was he doing in the Highway Café at the northeast corner of Western and Canal? Perhaps he was there to kill Tony Sadunas. During his last term in office, one evening at the Highway Café, Andrew Myers drew his gun, aimed, and fired at proprietor Sadunas, who was standing behind the bar.

Mr. Myers had a reputation as a good golfer. Fortunately for both men, he was a better golf shot than he was a pistol shot. Myers missed. The *Sun-Standard* said it was because Tony Sadunas ducked behind the bar, but it is doubtful that he was faster than a speeding bullet.

Tony Sadunas dodged a bullet and he attempted to do the same in this matter. He declined to press charges, perhaps because of already-pending charges resulting from his alleged assault of a female acquaintance. Nevertheless, Alderman Myers was arrested and charged. The case dragged on for months. Eventually Andrew Myers was convicted of a misdemeanor and fined $250.

As for Tony Sadunas, who reportedly drank heavily and became violently angry when he did, he would have a few more misadventures. He was arrested and charged by the Feds several times for serving alcohol at the Highway Café. Early one morning, highly intoxicated and with butcher knife in hand, he chased his young daughters and naked wife out of the back of the restaurant where they lived and into the street. The police were called, a blanket was thrown around Mrs. Sadunas, and Mr. Sadunas was taken into custody. Eventually his drunken behaviors got the best of him. Not long after his drunken knife wielding incident, Tony Sadunas was killed when he drove his vehicle at a very high rate of speed into a utility pole on Western Avenue south of Blue Island.

As for the Sadunas girls, one followed her father in temperament and career. Razor-tongued Helen Sadunas operated the popular restaurant Helen's Olde Lantern across the street from where her father's establishment had been. On a nightly basis, she served and entertained customers with her colorful gowns and plumes, and she excoriated the help with colorful and cutting profanity.

With a citizenry that included Andrew Myers and Tony Sadunas, how could Blue Island be dull? Yet it was according to George J. Fiedler's last report as chief under Mayor Kasten, issued in July of 1931. The fines collected totaled $582. There were 97 lodgers and 68 safekeepers. There were 209 arrests, 42 accidents, four burglaries, six juvenile incidents, 17 people transported to St. Francis Hospital, and 19 dogs were destroyed. One boy was shot accidentally and another drowned at the Tuthill Brickyard. A prisoner was held for two days and another was held for eight. If things in Blue Island actually were this uneventful, Chief Fiedler would not have been demoted. He would have been Andy Griffith. Because he was so good at spin, perhaps George J. Fiedler would have been a better fit if he had been transferred from the Police Department to the Public Relations Department.

There were two things the City of Blue Island did not have: a Public Relations Department and money. Both were needed, the latter desperately. Reaction to the lack of tax revenue proved that city officials had no more a clue as to how to manage their new financial situation than they did their police problems.

During his first year in office, Mayor Kasten assessed the financial predicament and described Blue Island government as, "In the position of a blind man seeking to discover the right way out." This was partially accurate. A blind man throwing darts and hoping one of them hits the bull's eye may have been a better analogy. For years, Blue Island bragged that it had the lowest assessed valuation in Cook County. It should not have. Because its assessed valuation was too low, Blue Island received less than it needed in taxes. They also bragged about another deficit creator: that city licenses and fees were cheap too. Adding insult to insolvency, deadbeats and scofflaws had little to fear from the city because there was no real method of collecting past due accounts. It was estimated that local businesses owed the city $20,000 in fees. Not much money by today's standards but big money in 1932. How big? Midway through that year, the city announced that it had paid employees $22,000 in back wages and that it was only a few months behind. So $20,000 was a great deal to those who were owed.

Ironically, many city employees received credit from local business owners who were delinquent on licenses and fees owed the city, which could not pay its employees in full or on time. Round and round it went without solution.

Or was this a form of solution?

Would the mayor have made things worse by authorizing a reduction in the municipal workforce? During a September 1932 address to aldermen, Mayor Kasten, the union leader, was adamant that the number of city employees *not* be reduced. He added that the salaries of city employees already were too low to be reduced. The mayor did implore aldermen to enact legislation to somehow raise revenues and mentioned what would be unthinkable in Blue Island for another 50 years—charging for services such as garbage pickup. This practical suggestion was ignored. To Mayor Kasten and his aldermen, some things were more important than warning signals. One of them was keeping as many citizens happy as possible.

Despite the fact that under his leadership public safety and municipal finance had worsened, Mayor Kasten was re-elected to a third term during April, 1933. Was it that voters again did not want challenger Frank Boyd or did they continue to fear change? Did they not understand that some change had to come, not because it was inevitable, but because in this case it was unavoidable? During October, city employees finally were told that they had to work for less or take time off. All agreed but one city employee—a police officer—and he was terminated. Part-time employees agreed to work two weeks on and take off two weeks. Department heads were told they must contribute one and one-half month's salary. The exception was the head of the Recreation Department who was terminated. This was long overdue. He was receiving a salary despite the fact that the city did not have a Recreation Department. Some of the departments that did exist were merged.

During November of 1933, a positive opportunity finally presented itself and Mayor Kasten leaped to embrace it. He had received a letter from Carter Jenkins, Inspector for Second District Park Conservation. Mr. Jenkins informed the mayor that he needed to send him a list of local projects. Upon receipt, the project probably would be approved by the federal government and local men would be hired. The Mayor was so anxious to respond that he didn't even wait for his secretary to return to the office. His letter to Mr. Jenkins follows. Note the apology.

Dear Sir:

I am enclosing outline of work we would like to do at Blue Island, as per your request *dated November 10th. I am also enclosing approximate cost of the several projects. The total material costs are $15,486, and labor costs $52,220, a grand total of $67,706.*

I am also enclosing the program as outlined by the President of the Blue Island School Board. I am sorry that the proposal is not typed, because our offices have been closed for Armistice Day. Hoping what I have submitted is what you are seeking. I beg to remain

Yours very truly,
Frank Kasten, Mayor

Mayor Kasten's submission detailed the relaying of brick pavement, reinforcing the banks of Stony Creek, and filling in low land that captured and held rain water. The mayor was very precise. He gave specific numbers of the thousands of men to be employed and he did not forget his aldermen, suggesting that they prepare lists of potential workmen from each of their wards. Mayor Kasten then followed with this message to the city council at the start of the November 14, 1932 meeting. It gives an accurate indication of just how bleak the City's finances were. The address also contained a suggestion which, if undertaken correctly, could have extricated the City from its financial dilemma.

Honorable City Council of the City of Blue Island, Illinois
Gentlemen:

I am submitting this brief message to you in the hope that through this message we may be able to relieve the distressing financial situation of our City.

We are well aware that the 1931 tax bills will soon be in the mails, but we also know that when the 1931 taxes are paid, the money that the City will receive will have to be used to cancel the 1931 tax warrants that were issued for 1931 current expenses.

All of the employees of the City loyally donated one month's work without pay, but this will not be helpful to the City until the 1932 taxes are collected in 1934. Our street, garbage, water, and electric light departments are on half time, but this state of affairs cannot continue for any length of time. The problem we must solve is the bridging of a gap of one year that all the taxpayers of Cook County are in arrears, and unless arrangements can be made for the City to be financed in some way, a most drastic cut in all of the departments of the City will have to be put into effect. In my opinion, it would be dangerous to the welfare of the City to in any way curtail any of the departments; but there is no prospect of any of the employees receiving their pay until provision is made for the one year of tax arrearages, or some financial institution will agree to advance the City money for that one year.

It may be that a number of well-to-do, influential citizens of our community may come to our rescue. I therefore request that I be given permission to

> *invite to a meeting of this Council, the City Clerk, the City Treasurer, the City Attorney, and myself, some thirty or thirty-five prominent citizens, business and professional men, and the representatives of the local banks and representatives of the local press, at the earliest possible moment. Unless a program can be adopted at a meeting of this kind, I warn you that we will be forced to discontinue giving the service we have been trying to give our citizens during the past number of years.*
>
> *Respectfully,*
> *Frank Kasten*

The aldermen agreed, the vote was unanimous to approve the mayor's request, but everyone had forgotten one important detail. Neither the mayor nor the aldermen contacted any of the city's "well-to-do, influential citizens" prior to making the announcement. Had they done so, they would have discovered that the wealthy and influential had no interest in bailing out local government. Well-to-do, influential citizens are no different than the rest of the population in that they don't like surprises, especially when it comes to their money, and they don't want anyone volunteering them for difficult assignments. So you can imagine the reaction of the bank presidents and business owners when they learned of the idea at the barber shop, the poker table, or reading John Volp's newspaper over morning coffee. *They want me to do what?* The city council was a disaster in progress. It wasted time and taxpayer money. Why would anyone who had money want to partner with it?

Nothing in city council minutes indicates a group of "thirty or thirty-five prominent citizens" ever had been formed or that a meeting was held. By the time the city council met November 28, aldermen understood that assembling as many as thirty of the city's elite was too lofty a goal. Next they authorized the mayor to form a committee of only fifteen citizens to work with them. There was no stipulation that the fifteen be well-to-do or influential. Suddenly Mayor Kasten had criteria with which he could work. During the December 27 meeting he reported that he had met with ten citizens on December 22. Unfortunately, solutions were as scarce as those influential citizens who'd taken their phones off the hooks or gone into hiding. Another meeting was scheduled for December, but if it convened, there is no record of it. The city would be denied a solution in any form until a well-to-do and influential man named Franklin D. Roosevelt was sworn in. Thereafter and thanks to aggressiveness of Mayor Kasten, the city's chief lobbyist, Blue Island was approved for government projects and some local men went to work.

Amazingly, throughout the greatest economic hardship in American history, Blue Island never lost its appetite for gambling or bootleg booze.

Louis Rauch, elected to the city council as an alderman of the First Ward in May of 1933, always was outspoken. One of the subjects often on his mind was gambling, an affinity for which seemed to be part of the DNA of many Blue Islanders. Alderman Rauch was not among them. Near the end of the October 23, 1933 city council meeting, Rauch could hold out no longer. He pointed out that his "attention had been called to several slot machines in the First Ward." He did not say by whom.

Alderman Rauch knew he did not have to name names. Anyone who went into a saloon or social club knew there were slots. Mayor Kasten reacted, not by defending illegal gambling, but by quantifying it. The mayor told Alderman Rauch that there were no slot machines anywhere in Blue Island except private clubs and that he did not want acting Police Chief Hankey to confiscate any slot machines from private clubs.

Mayor Kasten asked his rookie alderman where the slots were located. This was a signal to Mr. Rauch to back off. As if he did not hear his chief executive, Mr. Rauch responded that there were slot machines at the Eagles Hall.

Alderman Joseph Lentz entered the conversation in defense of his mayor and of the indefensible, illegal gambling. "Three or four of the finest organizations in the city have slot machines and one of them uses the proceeds for Christmas baskets for the poor," Alderman Lentz said. "As chairman of the police committee, I am opposed to raiding such places and removing the machines."

Alderman Rauch finally picked up the signal. He contradicted himself when he agreed there was no harm in slot machines in social clubs. He attempted to redefine illegal gambling when he said his objection was that the machines were prominent during public dances held at Eagles Hall.

Alderman Rauch suggested that the matter be turned over to Chief Hankey for investigation. His fellow aldermen agreed and Mayor Kasten put the police chief on the caper. The city council still awaits Chief Hankey's report.

The Great Depression raged, local government was in debt up to the top step of City Hall, and some members of the city council lacked the sense to keep their mouths shut about gambling. Mayor Kasten may have believed things could not get worse, but they did. At 2:20 a.m. on February 6, 1935 the vacant six-room frame house at 2136 W. 121st Place blew up. The explosion reportedly was so great that there was nothing left of the dwelling except the foundation and some interesting debris. A vacant lot was between the sight of the blast and the home of Mrs. Alvina Jaros at 2130 W. 121st Place. The distance between the lot and Mrs. Jaros' home might have been just enough to save her. According to the February 8 edition of the *Sun-Standard*, "A huge portion of the east wall of the house where the explosion occurred was driven right through the dining room wall of the Jaros home."

From her bed at St. Francis Hospital, Mrs. Jaros told a *Sun-Standard* reporter, "I was asleep in the middle bedroom. I heard a fizzing sound like a skyrocket makes when it goes up into the air. Then there was a flash and then an awful roar. I felt something hit my head. It streaked past in front of my eyes. I thought the bed had fallen down."

According to the newspaper, no one lived in the house where the blast occurred and as verified by utility companies, electric and gas had been shut off. Despite this fact, the announcement by Blue Island police and others was that a gas leak caused the explosion. Everyone seemed to know the truth, of course. The *Sun-Standard* said, "The place fell into the hands of alky distillers this summer and on June 16, 1934 was raided by police who found no tenants, but an expensive alky outfit and two 5,000 gallon vats of mash." Also mentioned was that the coil of a still was found in the rubble and that other homes on the block suffered minor damage, including the home of Mr. and Mrs. Babe Tuffanelli at 2153 W. 121st Place.

The finger could be pointed at some, but not at others. It pointed not several doors east, but at one of the officers responding to the scene—Arthur Fritz, who reportedly was intoxicated. Because politics was much more serious than life safety issues, especially on the eve of an election, Officer Fritz was suspended by Mayor Kasten. He was reinstated by the Civil Service Commission, however, when that three-member panel determined the five residents who testified against Fritz were less credible than the three who vouched for his character.

Was that the 1935 version of the new math or the never changing Blue Island math? Either way, things became worse yet when this letter from the "Committee of Five" was read during the February 25, 1935 city council meeting. It has been reprinted verbatim.

> *Police Committee*
> *City of Blue Island, Illinois*
> *Gentlemen:*

Pursuant to agreement reached at the council meeting of February 11, 1935, a committee of five represent-tatives from the sixth ward has been selected to act as spokesmen for the group to counsel with and make reports to the Police Committee and make regarding conditions in the City of Blue Island, Illinois.

Realizing that crime against citizenry and depredation of property have reached a point where citizens are assaulted in the course of their normal duties, and our properties no longer safe against robbery, explosion, or other modes of assault, it becomes the duty of this committee to require of the City of Blue Island, Illinois adequate and complete police protection.

If this protection be not immediately accorded, certain property owners, fearful for their safety, will sell their properties at prevailing price levels and move from this community. Such a procedure will result in additional delay in tax payments which in turn will force further curtailment of government activity.

Analysis of testimony presented to this committee indicates that the taxpayers are not receiving from the Police Department protection of value equal to the monies being spent for such purposes. Pending an analysis of Police Department activities and the submission of recommendations as to how present conditions can be cor-

rected, it is the demand of the voters and taxpayers of the sixth ward that a group of six men to serve without financial remuneration, to be selected by this committee, be given full and regular police power for a period of one year.

These men, to operate as a plain clothes investigation detail, will collect data, assist in maintaining the peace in the City of Blue Island, Illinois, and make definite recommendations to the Police Committee with a view toward rectifying certain irregular conditions now existent. Until such time as the necessity for such action no longer exists, it is the belief of this committee that these six men can best accomplish their objectives if they operate free from the uniformed force, governed by all legal limitations that apply to a duly appointed police officer, and that they report directly and solely to the Mayor of the city of Blue Island, Illinois.

Respectfully submitted,
G.S. Schnee, Chairman
E.B. Zink
Wm. C. Weiss
G.J. Cauca
John W. Kent

Commentary and discussion followed. Some of the comments were enlightening. Others were absurd. The city attorney informed the Sixth Ward residents that if special police officers were appointed they would be required to post a bond "large enough to protect the

City against any loss because of accident." Alderman Fiedler stated that "a number of years ago special policemen were appointed in each ward and because the privilege was so abused the practice of appointing special police was discontinued." He alluded to the Anton Weiland shooting when he added that "one man had been killed abusing the privilege extended to him and that was the reason for the bond protecting the City."Alderman Rauch corrected Mr. Fiedler when he said, "Three lives actually had been lost because of the privilege extended to citizens." About this, Mr. Rauch was correct. Special police officer Weiland, the man who shot him, and a child were killed in the gun battle.

Alderman George F. Fiedler was the most vocal critic of the police force. He agreed in part when he added, "If conditions in the Sixth Ward were as serious as claimed by this committee, the matter should be deeply investigated," and if the Police Department needed a "cleaning out," he was in favor of it. Alderman Fiedler also admitted there was "a laxity on the part of the night force." He apparently had temporary amnesia when he concluded that he would recommend the appropriation of any amount of money necessary to employ the Pinkerton Detective Agency or some other responsible detective agency to solve the problem. Mr. Zink, one of the signers of the letter, brought him back to reality, albeit not a good reality, when he stated that the expense would not be necessary if thc six citizens were appointed special police officers.

Near the end of the discussion, the chairman of the police committee, Alderman Lentz, attempted to defuse the situation when stated that there was a plan to divide the city into four districts with a squad car in each district. The alderman only made things more confusing, however, because he failed to explain how this would solve the problem. After some discussion, he admitted his committee was not prepared to approve the plan anyway. Mayor Kasten threw gas on the fire when he informed everyone that in addition to Officer Fritz, "two other officers had been suspended on a far more serious charge." The Mayor did not elaborate further, but did say that because BIPD was understaffed, he wanted to "appoint three young men with some police experience until the Civil Service files an eligible list with the Council, or until these three men who were suspended are either found guilty or reinstated."

The aldermen agreed with the mayor's recommendation. William McAley, Louis Panozzo, and George Farning soon afterward were sworn in "as temporary members of the Blue Island regular police force." The mayor and city council also caved into the demands of the "committee of five" and six men were sworn in as special police officers. All were from the Sixth Ward, worked without pay and in plain clothes, and reported directly to the mayor.

Crime in the Sixth Ward immediately increased. It was obvious that someone, perhaps the "alky distillers" and members of the police working together, wanted to embarrass the special police officers. Homes were burglarized and the "swag" as the *Sun-Standard* called it, was left in plain sight for all to see. Cars were stripped. Shrubbery was damaged and lawns were driven over. Despite the presence of the six special officers and increased patrols by BIPD, not one arrest was made. The only positive news from the Sixth Ward was of a staged gambling bust by police. The tavern at 12126 Vincennes was raided and a slot machine was removed. There is no record of Acting Chief Hankey amending his "no slot machines" statement to "one slot machine."

As for the "two other officers" referenced by the mayor, the city had been forced to suspend officers Fabian Mitchell and John Antoine. Mitchell's suspension on unspecified charges was for ninety days. Ultimately, the city was forced to take the almost unheard of step of firing John Antoine, who was indicted March 25 on the charge of "bastardy." According to the *Sun-Standard*, on the night of May 5, 1934 Antoine and Elsie Black had sex in a squad car while Officer Antoine was on duty. A child resulted. Ms. Black precipitated the indictment when she claimed that she was attacked, this despite testimony from other police officers that Ms. Black willingly entered a police car with Antoine on other occasions. Their attempt to save John Antoine by tarnishing Elsie Black was not enough, nor was a cover up by city and police officials. The Blue Island judiciary had refused to issue an indictment against Officer Antoine. Elsie Black had to go to Harvey, whose Justice of the Peace filed the charge that cost John Antoine his job.

Officers Fritz and Mitchell were embarrassed, but did survive. Mayor Kasten suffered before finally second-guessing himself out of office. As the 1935 mayoral election neared, each edition of the *Sun-Standard* was packed with crime news. There were shootings, abductions, and robberies all over town and even on the city's main street.

Frank Kasten decided to seek re-election. In a March 1 front page story, the mayor again promised a re-organization of the police department. This time there would be "sweeping changes from top to bottom," but only "if investigations reveal conditions warrant it." Finally conditions did. With the election just eight days away, during the April 8 city council meeting Mayor Kasten demoted acting Chief William Hankey, a popular Blue Islander, and hired John McEvoy, a man more professional, but less popular who had been chief approximately 20 years prior. The mayor praised "the personal character, integrity, and honesty of William Hankey." Explaining the need for change, however, the mayor criticized him when he said, "There is a rub somewhere in the police department. We are going to find out where. There is a lack of leadership." Mayor Kasten added that the appointment of John McEvoy was the first step in the re-organization of the police department. The change was supported by Alderman Fiedler, who stated previously that members of the police department lacked discipline and refused to cooperate with Acting Chief Hankey.

Other members of the city council disagreed, some loudly. The protest of Gus Zavadil, previously a police department critic, was "vociferous" according to the *Sun-Standard.* Zavadil said that Hankey should not be made "the goat." Rocco Guglielmucci seemed to take the change as personal instead of personnel. He said, "The mayor has supported the chief until right now and now he is putting every alderman on the spot. Aldermen

Guglielmucci and Fiedler reportedly argued and made accusations against one another. Aldermen Zavadil and Guglielmucci warned the mayor that a change should not be made so close to the election. The vote to approve the appointment was 10-2-1. Rocco Guglielmucci and Charles Ulrich were the dissenters. Gus Zavadil voted "present."

Aldermen were in total agreement that the coming election was an excuse *not* to approve something far more important—a bond issue that would have enabled the city to continue to satisfy back pay and bills, some of which were years delinquent. At the time, the city was estimated to be over $100,000 in debt—a huge sum for that era and a major embarrassment for hardworking, penurious Blue Island. As for the law enforcement problems that reached a crescendo just before the election, it is important to note that with two exceptions, police issues caused almost every elected mayor from Edward N. Stein (1921) through John D. Rita (1985) either to forego or to lose his re-election bid. The exceptions were Paul T. Klenk and John M. Hart. Mayor Klenk was so respected that he could ignore police issues and get away with it. Mayor Hart was shrewd enough to use the police force to his profit as well as his advantage.

On April 16, 1935 voters rejected Frank Kasten. Of the 7,243 votes cast for mayor, Fred A. Rice received 3,846 and Mayor Kasten had 3,397. Two wards made the difference. Rice won by 115 votes in Ward Three and by 245 in Ward Five. Ward Six, the source of so much controversy before the election, was against Mayor Kasten by only 19 votes. Less than one week after the election, the *Sun-Standard* headline proclaimed "With No Regrets, Mayor Kasten Finishes Work."

During his last city council meeting on April 22, Mayor Kasten reportedly said, "Many friendships have been made during my six years as mayor which will last a lifetime and which I regard most high. I wish to express my best wishes to the incoming administration and my thanks to the present city officers and to the council. Taking it as a whole, although at times we have had differences of opinion, we have as a whole, by and large, had a harmonious time."

After his defeat, Frank Kasten disappeared from public politics. He continued to serve as a union official and went to the office of the Brick and Claymakers Union in Chicago, at first frequently, but as time passed more sporadically due to heart problems. Frank Kasten was still a union official when he died at his home on Des Plaines Street at precisely 10:50 p.m. on December 12, 1946 at the age of 68. The cause of death was heart failure. According to his daughter Gertrude, he had gone to his bedroom to listen to the radio when she heard a thud. It was believed that by the time she rushed to her father's aid, he already was gone. Firefighters and a doctor were summoned, but they could not revive him.

In addition to his wife and daughter, Frank Kasten was survived by his son, Frank Jr. who would serve in the Army Air Corps during World War II and become a detective for the West Palm Beach Police Department. Frank Jr. would be appointed Blue Island Chief of Police in 1969 after what many consider the worst incident in the city's history. Visitation and service for the former mayor were held at Krueger Funeral Home and he is interred at Mount Greenwood Cemetery.

Fred A. Rice

Born April 7, 1865
Elected April 1935
Mayor Number 9
Served Until May 1937
Number of Terms: 1
Died July 3, 1944

When Fred A. Rice became the ninth mayor of the City of Blue Island on April 16, 1935, he may have been the most popular man in town. It seemed that everyone liked him. By the time he left office two years later, he may have been the most disliked mayor in the city's history. Fred Rice had scant public service experience and even less political experience when he took office. While there were achievements during the Rice administration, the mayor was unable to keep aldermen from bickering amongst themselves and to make them focus on the business of operating the city. That the public perceived Fred Rice to be ineffective was the final coal in the fire that stoked the election of John M. Hart.

Fred A. Rice was the oldest mayor ever elected by Blue Island voters. Born November 7, 1865—approximately seven months after the end of the Civil War, Fred Rice was 69 when he took office. Like Frank Kasten, Rice was not a native of Blue Island or wealthy. Like Paul T. Klenk, his family history was noteworthy. Fred Rice was born in Riceville, a community in northeast Pennsylvania founded by and named after his grandfather.

On September 10, 1885, he married another Riceville native, Lettice Young. Afterward Mr. and Mrs. Rice moved to Illinois and Fred Rice took a job as manager of a DuPont plant on what later became the site of Oak Forest Hospital. They moved to Blue Island where in March 1902, Fred Rice went to work for the United States Postal Service as a letter carrier. During the years he walked an estimated 81,000 miles delivering letters in Blue Island, Rice became very popular and was known as "Happy Rice" and "the Whistling Postman." Eventually he was transferred inside the post office, where he finished his career as a clerk.

Legislation forced Fred Rice to retire after 30 years and five months with the Postal Service. Somehow, before he ran for mayor, Fred Rice wound up on the slate of the Peoples Economy Party in April 1933 as a candidate for treasurer, the least vital position in city government. Others swept into office were City Clerk Louis Schwartz and Aldermen Charles F. Mosel, Charles A. Ulrich, Stewart W. Sandberg, and August G. "Gus" Zavadil. In 1935, when Fred Rice defeated three-term incumbent mayor Frank Kasten by 349 votes, the *Sun-Standard* said that the "silent voters" (i.e., disgruntled, unaffiliated, and undecided until the last minute) gave the victory to Mr. Rice.

Why did Fred Rice, a retired mail carrier, decide to run first for city treasurer and later against Frank Kasten? Well, Mr. Rice was very popular in the community. As a recent retiree, either he may have been looking for something to do or his friends may have urged him to run in 1933. When you went to the grocery store or the barber shop in Blue Island, if someone liked you and disliked the person in office, they might have suggested, "You should run for treasurer" or "You should run for mayor." In Blue Island, it was just the way things were done. Thus, Fred Rice might have mistaken popularity for qualifications and capability. As for his opposition to Mayor Kasten, the two never exchanged angry words during a city council meeting or in the newspaper. Their only public disagreement was a correction followed by a clarification, although it may have been telling.

During the January 14, 1935 city council meeting, Mayor Kasten announced that Blue Island received a tax payment from the Cook County Treasurer. At the time, Blue Island was desperate for tax money, but it had not received funds in a timely manner. For a check to have been received and the treasurer not to know about it may have appeared to be a very big deal, but it wasn't. The city treasurer had virtually nothing to do with city finance. He may have reviewed balance sheets and signed off on some inconsequential documents or reports that were handed to him. The lion's share of the work was done by the city clerk and his assistants. Anyway, during the next city council meeting on January 28, City Treasurer Rice's report to the finance committee stated, "The monthly report of the City Collector to the Council shows all moneys collected, including taxes. There has been no tax money received by him since December 28th, 1934." Mayor Kasten immediately responded that the money actually was received Saturday, January 26.

That was it. Publicly, no one pressed the matter further. Did Mayor Kasten's correction offend or motivate Treasurer Rice to run against him? While it is possible, alone it probably was not enough of a motivating factor. As the *Sun-Standard* announced months prior to the 1935 election, there was a "draft Rice" movement in Blue Island, which included influential aldermen such as Rocco Guglielmucci. Most likely, Fred Rice wanted to be mayor. As were many Blue Islanders, he may have been fed up with the way Mayor Kasten did things and decided that he wanted to do things a better way—his way.

As if Treasurer Rice hadn't been paying attention at city council meetings the past two years, rookie Mayor Rice immediately made the mistake of promoting Lieutenant George J. Fiedler, the man demoted by Mayor Kasten, to acting Chief of Police. During questioning by aldermen, the mayor defended the appointment by explaining that he had to appoint an acting member of the police department because the 1934-35 appropriation ordinance did not contain a line item for a full-time chief. On this, Mr.Rice was correct. The line item appropriated a salary of $2,240 for an "acting chief of police." Aldermen could not argue the technicality since they failed to catch the error before they unanimously approved the ordinance the previous July. As for the appointment itself, aldermen demoted George J. Fiedler once for cause. Why anyone believed that he, instead of a trained law enforcement official should be reinstalled top cop, is puzzling. Perhaps equally surprising is that there is no record of any argument or even debate about the appointment. The vote to approve was 8-5. If anyone needed additional proof that the city council was not thinking clearly, during the same meeting they sent a request to the finance committee to purchase twenty-five tickets to a charity baseball game sponsored by the Chicago Police Department. Like his predecessor, Mayor Rice deferred to aldermen and offered no opposition to the purchase, which was approved unanimously July 1, when the city was over $100,000 in debt.

The appointment of Acting Chief Fiedler was just the first political mistake made by "Happy" Fred Rice, "the whistling postman" who took office May 6, 1935. Rice lacked real foresight, as he demonstrated during his first meeting. It was announced Blue Island received correspondence that the Cook County Board had petitioned the federal government to approve $400,000 for the construction of an overpass at the Vermont Street rail yard. The majority of the aldermen were in favor of the proposal by Cook County, but Mayor Rice concurred with Alderman Guglielmucci that the project should be turned down because the widening of the Calumet Sag Channel might force a Vermont Street overpass subsequently to be removed. Why either man suggested that the federal government would be so inept in its planning that it would have to destroy an overpass that cost a fortune to build never was explained, but they had to say something.

What Alderman Guglielmucci did not say was that he had friends who owned real estate in the area and those friends opposed a Vermont Street overpass for as long as he lived. In 1935, Guglielmucci's barber shop was on the 1700 block of Vermont Street in a building owned by one such friend. Guglielmucci's friends wanted to keep their real estate holdings, so the alderman went to bat for him and others. What Mayor Rice did not say was that it was good politics to go along with Rocco Guglielmucci.

The federal government had planned the widening of the channel for years. Army Corps of Engineers set up a construction office in Blue Island during the mid-1930s and the lion's share of work on the local portion (replacement of bridges, etc.) would begin during the 1950s. After it did, no functional overpasses were eliminated. As for the 1935 offer, Mr. Rice and Mr. Guglielmucci killed it first by tabling the proposal and ultimately by sponsoring a resolution that Blue Island would accept the overpass as long as it would be able to approve the plans and that the county and state accepted all property liability. Larger bureaucracies do not like it when smaller ones attempt to dictate to them. Another offer to build an overpass at Vermont Street would not be made to Blue Island until the late 1970s.

Months later, during October, Mayor Rice and the man he appointed acting chief of police were stung by bad publicity. The Civil Service Commission recommended that George J. Fiedler be suspended for 90 days without pay after it was discovered he had someone else's license plate on his car. It never was explained how the acting chief obtained the plate registered to Frank Szinwelski of Harvey. Aldermen Stuart Sandberg, Arthur Ladwig, and Fred C. Schroeder were the most vocal against Acting Chief Fiedler and, therefore, against Mayor Rice. Aldermen Guglielmucci and Charles Ulrich supported Rice by requesting that Civil Service furnish the city council a copy of its rules.

Mayor Rice did not want his chief suspended and ordered city attorney W. Otto Wielgorecki to check into the legality of the recommendation. He also ordered that the suspension begin immediately. This was a shrewd move since there could be no request for another hearing until the suspension began and the mayor's goal was to have the ruling overturned as quickly as possible. It also was just the way things were done. Yet the machinations proved that Mayor Rice was a neophyte when it came to politics. The fix always could be put in when it came to a Civil Service Commission recommendation. Throughout Blue Island history, whenever there was a recommendation by Civil Service or the Zoning Board a mayor didn't like, he ignored it, prolonging it for the purpose of never implementing it, or generated enough votes to have the city council overturn it.

Mayor Rice informed the city council he would serve as acting Chief of Police during the suspension, but none of the aldermen questioned this dangerous and ridiculous precedent—a 69-year-old rookie police chief with no law enforcement experience—probably because they were preoccupied arguing with each other.

They had bickered for months and would continue to bicker for more months without resolution about how the city should collect delinquent water accounts. Part of the drama included Alderman Sandberg taking offense to a suggestion by Alderman Guglielmucci that Mr. Sandberg's ward be collected first. Mr. Guglielmucci retaliated with the announcement that Mr. Sandberg had a past due water bill. The rookie alderman countered by accusing Rocco Guglielmucci of the same offense. Ultimately, it was proven that Mr. Sandberg was delinquent $3.17 and Mr. Guglielmucci's account was current.

As a whole, aldermen remained oblivious to the city's financial condition and continued to approve fundraising items while approving unnecessary expenditures. Alderman Guglielmucci recommended that the city purchase raffle tickets and also to pay to enter a float in a three-day celebration for St. Francis Hospital. Aldermen unanimously approved each. Only Alderman Louis Rauch opposed an authorization of $35 for each alderman to attend the annual Municipal League Convention. Aldermen voted 7-7 (Rice broke the tie with a vote to approve) for the mayor's two "special police" appointments continue with pay. Yet the city council ignored genuine moneymaking solutions. The city council as a whole ignored a written suggestion by James Amato, a Blue Island resident in the scavenger business, that each scavenger operating in the city be charged $25 annually for a license.

Mayor Rice alienated the entire city council when he announced during the December 9, 1935 meeting that he had dumped George J. Fiedler and appointed Blue Island resident Albert Eick to the position of acting Chief of Police without informing the city council. The aldermen howled! Alderman Guglielmucci immediately called for a vote to dismiss the latest acting chief from the police department. The failure of the city council to correct the line item for police chief came back to haunt them again when city attorney Wielgorecki reminded everyone that Mayor Rice had made a temporary appointment and, as such, only the mayor could appoint or dismiss.

The only recourse was for aldermen to go to court and challenge the appointment based upon acting chief Eick's qualifications for the position. Such a challenge would have failed because he was a veteran officer of the Illinois Highway Police and served as chief of Crestwood police. Ironically, the only way the city council could declare itself on the action was to make a motion to endorse the appointment and then defeat it, which was exactly what aldermen did by unanimous vote.

Despite reports from Mayor Rice that Acting Chief Eick was doing a good job and that all was well with the police department, some of the aldermen continued to attack both men. During the December 23 city council meeting, former adversaries Fiedler and Guglielmucci united to propose that the mayor terminate Mr. Eick on January 1. Mayor Rice declared their motion out of order. During the January 13, 1936 meeting, Alderman Guglielmucci attempted to employ a tactic against Acting Chief Eick similar to the one that had been used against former chief Fiedler. Alderman Guglielmucci announced that acting Chief Eick secured a vehicle registration in the name of the City of Blue Island, but listed his home address, 2062 Market Street. Mayor Rice quickly diffused this when he informed the city council that his chief had caught the mistake and corrected it. Aldermen reverted to what they did best when they squabbled amongst themselves during the February 10 meeting. After the finance committee of Guglielmucci,

Fiedler, and Lentz recommended that payroll and expenses be approved except for acting chief Eick, aldermen voted 7-6 against the recommendation.

The light bulb did flicker once in awhile for Blue Island aldermen. At the request of Alderman Lentz, who reminded everyone that city employees had not been paid for almost eight months and that something had to be done at once "to attempt to solve the dire situation and procure finances," the city council held a special meeting February 17, 1936. During that meeting, City Clerk Schwartz gave an update regarding city finances. Thereafter, the mayor was authorized to invite approximately twenty-five prominent citizens to discuss the possibility of a bond issue. Why this failed solution was resuscitated was puzzling since the city already had been rejected by anyone considered prominent. Previously, when the mayor was a national union leader, he had been unable to persuade the wealthy and influential from loaning money to the city. How did aldermen expect a retired postman to round up bankers and other business leaders—by whistling?

During that same meeting, aldermen did tackle a problem they could handle when given a second crack at it. They voted unanimously for Blue Island to align itself with Chicago regarding its time zone. Previously, aldermen had adopted Eastern Standard Time. Thus a new ordinance was drafted by City Attorney Wielgorecki to put Blue Island on Central Standard Time. Of course, not all of the news from the city council was either dire or mundane. The February 24 meeting provided encouraging news and a lighthearted moment. City Engineer Allen L. Fox announced that Congressman

Edward A. Kelly was able to submit the city's application for a grant to build a new water storage tank and that the project was being considered by the Federal Emergency Administration of Public Works. Also, William Toosley, whose family resided on one-half acre at 12029 Maple Avenue and who owed Blue Island $3,022, requested permission to build a poultry house or chicken shed for 200 chickens. "It would enable us greatly to make this idle property pay for itself and in the near future make us independent of relief which we so much detest." Mr. Toosley concluded his letter to Building Inspector Henry Schnurstein, "Granted or not, no hard feelings. One who is trying. (signed) William Toosley."

Blue Island would get its water tank, but the Toosley family was not granted permission for its enterprise. By the way, raising poultry was not against the law in that era. There reportedly is an ordinance today, but it is not enforced. You still can walk through Blue Island—near City Hall of all locations—and hear the cock-a-doodle-doo of roosters.

During the April 27 city council meeting, tragedy struck. It was a contentious meeting during which aldermen had discussed many items of business but, as usual, reached few useful conclusions. At the close of the meeting, Alderman Guglielmucci chastised Mayor Rice, who had joked during the previous meeting that the dilapidated old east side firehouse might be used as the city dog pound. Rocco Guglielmucci indicated that Mayor Rice's comments had reached his ward, where they were taken seriously and that he "had received numerous complaints regarding such action." The mayor responded by emphasizing that he had been joking and that a location for a dog pound had been secured, "but not on the east side." The discussion was Mr. Guglielmucci's last at the city council. He suddenly became ill and was rushed home by police car. He died at St. Francis Hospital three days later of an undisclosed illness. Rocco Guglielmucci was 52. He had served as an alderman since 1919.

At the May 25 city council meeting, during which it also was announced the city owed $135,000 in back salaries and unpaid bills, a petition with the signatures of 233 residents of the Third Ward was submitted. It requested that a special aldermanic election be held. The election was held July 30 and by a vote of 712-377, Michael Guglielmucci, Rocco's son, defeated Henry E. Quade. The younger Guglielmucci took office during the September 14 city council meeting and immediately picked up where his father left off by attacking Mayor Rice.

Aldermen finally approved a bond issue during that September 14 city council meeting, but it was not to wipe out the city's bad debt. Blue Island had received news from Congressman Kelly that its grant for a water reservoir had been approved. According to the terms of the grant, the WPA would contribute approximately $37,000. The city would pay $43,000 and because there were strict guidelines as to when work had to begin and be completed, city officials had to hurry. With efficiency not seen at City Council meetings since the days of Paul T. Klenk, they quickly approved a contract with underwriter C. W. McNear & Company for $45,000 in bonds (another $18,000 was added a short time later) and solicited bids for the construction.

Was that September 14 city council meeting as telling as it was significant? There is no question that the water reservoir was one of the most important public works projects in Blue Island history. During that meeting, however, correspondence from underwriter Kerfoot & Leggett reminded the city that it could issue bonds for the purpose of liquidating miscellaneous claims (debt) without a referendum until January 1, 1937 when the state statute expired. Obviously, Kerfoot & Leggett was anxious to solicit the city's business. Still, the reminder was that the bond issue was the city's main solution, perhaps its only solution. Why did city officials fail to embrace it?

The legislation that allowed municipalities to bypass the voters seemed to be tailor-made for Blue Island, which was a proud, stubborn, very conservative, working class, Republican (it supported Wilke over Roosevelt in '36) and still predominantly German community. Did voters refuse to support a referendum approving a bond issue because it would have been a statement that the leaders of their community had not properly managed its money? Was it the unwritten rule that in Blue Island someone was against everything? Or were voters misinformed or in denial about change being necessary?

Blue Island High School was subject to the harsh reality of local indecision and misinformation. By the end of the decade, after high school officials repeatedly warned the community it needed a little more money to remain open, voters on five different occasions would defeat referendums that would have raised its tax rate slightly. School officials had already made drastic cuts to keep the school operating. When there was no more to cut and they were losing staff members, administrators warned that the school would close if it did not receive more money. They even opened the ledgers to prove it. The anti-education forces were led by disgruntled former high school board member Frank Van Overstraeten, who opposed the slight increase necessary to keep the high school open. *Make more cuts! Manage your money better!* These were the mantras of Mr. Van Overstraeten and his followers. Voters bought into the negativity and four referendums failed. The result was an indication of how much Blue Islanders valued education. Because it did not have enough money to operate, the high school would close from March 9 until April 24, 1939.

Eventually Blue Island High School received another chance. Fred Rice did not. The beginning of the end for Mayor Rice began when he granted another political favor. Desk sergeant Charles O. Smith, 65, retired February 24, 1936 due to a disability. He was kicked by a prisoner and the leg injury he sustained forced him to leave the Police Department. Some aldermen, most notably Lentz and Ladwig, emphasized that the vacancy not be filled and Mayor Rice stated that "as an economy measure," he "did not contemplate another appointment."

Because a political favor was more important than keeping his word, the mayor hired Nick Guglielmucci, the cousin of the alderman, as a replacement. Cousin Nick appeared on the city payroll during February 1937, but he lasted only three weeks until March 1st when the Mayor terminated him, reportedly after complaints from other aldermen that he added a man to the payroll when the city could not afford it, which it couldn't.

Michael Guglielmucci was every bit as mercurial and razor-tongued as his father. Young alderman Guglielmucci felt betrayed by the dismissal of desk sergeant Guglielmucci and he unleashed a torrent of criticism on Mayor Rice during the March 8 city council meeting. Among the comments by the junior Third Ward alderman were that Fred Rice was "the worst mayor the city ever had." After Alderman Guglielmucci refused to relinquish the floor, Mayor Rice responded by calling the remarks "cheap publicity campaign stuff" and threatened to have the junior Third Ward alderman removed.

Undeterred, Michael Guglielmucci said, "I want the newspapers and the other aldermen to get it straight about your dismissal of Nick Guglielmucci from the desk sergeancy. You called me about Nick when you appointed him. Then when you fired him, you said some aldermen complained about him being appointed. I would like to have the facts disclosed. Nick was a high man on the civil service examination. I didn't have to be his sponsor. You put him in. Then you let him out."

Later in the meeting, Guglielmucci attempted to retaliate against Mayor Rice by leading a revolt against accepting the financial report from the Police Benevolent Association charity boxing show. The event earned a $3,224 profit and enabled the city to purchase two squad cars. The balance, $104.24, was to go to needy families and each police officer was to receive a turkey. The report did not detail all income and expenses for the event, however, as previously promised by the mayor. On that count Alderman Guglielmucci was correct to criticize Fred Rice for not keeping his promise.

The water reservoir project was transformed into an even bigger political issue. The city agreed to purchase property on Highland Avenue between 122nd Street and 121st Place for the above-ground reservoir and accompanying apertures. (The tank below ground was installed during the Withers Administration.) The original price for the lot east of the Baltimore & Ohio Railroad tracks reportedly was $2,500. Later it was announced that the sellers, F.X. Rauwolf and A. Rauwolf wanted $4,500, which the city paid. There were rumors, however, that Fifth Ward Aldermen Stewart W. Sandberg and Fred C. Schroeder secretly owned the property and stood to profit from the deal and that local attorney Walter Briody had profited after receiving unnecessary legal work. Added to the controversy was opposition by some area residents who did not want the water reservoir at that site. The opposition was led by Otto A. Kasch of 2633 W. 122nd Street. Citizen Kasch appeared at the December 14 city council meeting and criticized aldermen about the location of the water reservoir, which he and others said should be on the west side of the railroad tracks. There is no record of anyone informing Mr. Kasch of how vital the project was to Blue Island—or that it would be more cost inefficient and foolish to install the tanks and apertures across the tracks and run water lines underneath them and back into the city—or that with the exception of a small strip, the land west of the tracks was unincorporated, not in Blue Island.

Previously, Alderman Guglielmucci voted to approve every aspect of the water reservoir project. In an effort to discredit Mayor Rice, he aided the opposition during the April 12 city council meeting when he introduced attorney Moses Kammerman, who claimed to have a petition from neighborhood residents who opposed the project. Attorney Kammerman actually had a letter which detailed accusations against Aldermen Sandberg, Schroeder, Briody, and, by implication, Mayor Rice. There were no signatures or even names of any of those supposedly against the project. Yet the damage was done because the stunt was detailed on the front page of the *Sun-Standard*.

Softball became a political football too. In 1937, the softball diamond on Western Avenue was at 121st and Western, not 123rd Street as it is today. During softball season, the privately owned facility featured games that went late into the evening. Some neighborhood residents complained about the noise and parking. April was not softball season, but that didn't prevent the matter from making it to the city council and the front page of the *Sun-Standard* the week prior to the election. "Ball Diamond Protest Goes to Council Committee" was the April 16 headline. The story below it read, "The protest of 35 residents in the vicinity of the softball diamond at 121st and Western Ave., [sic] was read at the council meeting Monday night. Charges that the diamond was being operated entirely as a commercial proposition and causing noise and inconvenience to the property owners were made."

The story itself was brief, but the newspaper made it appear bigger by listing the name and address of each resident who signed the petition of complaint, most of whom were women and some residing as far as five blocks from the softball diamond. And who cared if the diamond was run "entirely as a commercial proposition?" Well, Stewart Sandberg, the alderman who presented the petition at the city council meeting, was running with John M. Hart on the Citizens Party ticket. As to why Mayor Rice and other members of his party were getting a bashing in print, it eventually was revealed. *Sun-Standard* publisher John H. Volp was a supporter of candidate Hart. On Friday, April 16, Volp endorsed Mr. Hart in an editorial framed on the front page of his newspaper. Four days later, John M. Hart turned the retired postal worker into a one-term mayor.

Was Fred Rice any worse a mayor than his predecessor, Frank Kasten? During his two years in office, Mayor Rice pushed through the much-needed water reservoir project and he brought in a police chief who at least organized his department enough to stop the public complaints. During the second year of his administration, the city had begun to collect on some of its past due water bills and license fees.

On November 11, 1936, Mayor Rice saved a life. On that day, he went to the home of his friend Ed Rossner, with whom he was to have lunch. When he arrived outside of the residence, Fred Rice gave his trademark whistle, his friend did not answer. Mr. Rice became suspicious and investigated. In the garage, he found Mr. Rossner's car running and Rossner unconscious in the driver's seat. Mayor Rice turned off the car and in an era before CPR was common, thumped his friend on the chest to revive him. If not for Fred Rice, Ed Rossner would have died of carbon monoxide poisoning.

What became of former Mayor Fred A. Rice? "Happy" came to the saddest end of any mayor in the history of Blue Island. On Monday, July 3, 1944, former mayor Rice died of a self-inflicted gunshot wound. He took his own life because he was despondent due to ill health. One of his legs had been amputated because of complications with diabetes and he was worried that his other leg would have to be taken too. Lettice Rice preceded her husband in death and widower Rice may have been lonely without her.

Fred Rice lived with his longtime friend, Ed Rossner, the man whose life he'd saved eight years earlier and with a cat named Spotty. Their home was at 2648 New Street, just two blocks down the hill from City Hall. Apparently Mr. Rice had made up his mind about what he was going to do. He told a visitor on the Saturday before he died, "Do you know Spotty senses that I won't be here long? He won't leave me. He won't get off my lap. And Spotty is going to miss me."

He left a note of explanation for Mr. Rossner. According to the *Sun-Standard*, it said:

"Don't blame anyone for this. I just can't stand the awful pain and torture any longer. So I feel that I must end it all. Please notify police and Hallinan's Funeral Saturday, if possible. If Rev [sic] is here, let him hold the service. Be good to poor little "Spotty." I am going blind fast and am so full of rheumatism that I can hardly lift anything from stove, sink, or table."

The note was signed *Fred A. Rice.* Unfortunately, Ed Rossner was unable to return the favor his friend had performed for him. Mr. Rossner found the note on the kitchen table and was reading it when he heard the gunshot. He rushed to Mr. Rice's bedroom and found him clad in bloodstained night clothes. The former mayor had shot himself on the left side of the chest with a .38 caliber revolver, but he was not dead. Mr. Rossner called for an ambulance and Rice was rushed to St. Francis Hospital. He died shortly after arrival.

Visitation and the service for former Mayor Rice were held at Hallinan Funeral Home on Thursday, July 6, 1944. Reverend Christian Schellhase, who performed the ceremony at the golden wedding anniversary of Fred and Lettice Rice in 1935, officiated. Fred Rice is interred at Tinley Park Cemetery.

Part III

King John I

John M. Hart

Mayor Number 10
Born July 30, 1892
Elected April 1937
Served Until: May 1965
Number of Terms: 7
Died December 14, 1974

His Best Efforts in the Interests of the City of Blue Island

John M. Hart was not connected publicly to the 1937 election until February. First there were rumors in print that a committee of prominent citizens urged the corner druggist to run. Then the *Sun-Standard* in its March 5 edition said: "It was expected that a full ticket would be lined up back of John Hart, Blue Island druggist, as a candidate for mayor" and "his friends are insistent, and unless the unforeseen happens, next week will see a ticket in the field headed by the pharmacist."

Candidates for public office could file as late as six weeks prior to the election and Mr. Hart did not officially become a candidate until March 9. The Citizens Party ticket was announced March 16 and it was stocked with ten sitting aldermen and other prominent Blue Islanders such as treasurer candidate August W. Schreiber and Richard B. Seyfarth, the candidate for police magistrate. If candidate Hart's slate wasn't potent enough, its backers were. Former mayors, incumbents, the city's most respected citizens, the newspaper, and the gambling and bootlegging bosses were behind him. John Hart was getting elected. Fred Rice was getting steamrolled.

The fix was in. This may have been why candidate Hart did not run much of a public campaign. For the record, candidate Hart's only recorded statement prior to the election appeared in the March 12, 1937 *Sun-Standard.* "I will be a candidate for election for mayor of Blue Island." If he said anything publicly during the campaign, it did not appear in print. Instead, he preferred that his supporters, such as *Sun-Standard* publisher John Volp, and his campaign ads do the talking. In a front-page story under the misleading headline "Deeds Count Says Hart" the mayoral candidate did not have one quote, including the one that appeared above. Instead, after a six paragraph biography of Mr. Hart, the only words which could be attributed to him were from the Latin inscription "Facta Non Verba" which appeared on a wall in his drugstore. According to the interviewer, which may have been publisher Volp, when asked for a quote, the candidate pointed to the slogan. The translation is, "Deeds not words." If nothing else, it was an accurate description of John M. Hart's public persona. To this day, he is described by those who remember him, though not intimately, as "dour" or "abrupt" and "a man of few words." Those who knew him privately, who knew him better, say that Mr. Hart could be quite talkative, but not a good listener.

Others in the community, in addition to the influential Mr. Volp, spoke for John M. Hart, and those campaign ads for the Citizens Party hit the bull's eye with voters. Most prominent in the nine-point platform were the pledges to "establish and maintain an economical and efficient business administration" and to "effect a general rehabilitation of the police department under the guidance of a competent LOCAL police chief." The former was the only campaign promise Hart needed. As for the latter, it was deceiving. Acting Chief Eick was competent, experienced, and a Blue Island resident. As for Mayor Hart, during his 28 years in office, he did not reform the police department beyond making sure members did not siphon public gasoline for their personal use, that when he was on the town during the wee hours that someone from BIPD picked him up when he called for "a cab" and most important, that they remembered who was boss. This included stopping traffic when "His Honor" decided to cross Western Avenue oblivious to any oncoming cars. "When you see him coming, you have to stop traffic because he's going to walk right into the street. He's not going to stop," was the warning passed down from veteran officers to rookies.

Mayor Hart's police chiefs and a few lower-ranking officers were his bag men and enforcers. Rank and file cops were his chauffeurs and crossing guards. Everyone understood that the Blue Island Police Department did not work for the city. It worked for John M. Hart.

As for election 1937, some of the other seven campaign pledges also were topical inaccuracies, (i.e., cheap shots directed at Fred Rice.) "Oppose the payment in the future of special attorney's fees and all other fees unless actually earned in good faith" hammered home the false accusation that Mayor Rice allowed attorney Walter Briody to profit from the purchase of land for the water reservoir as go-between. If the rumor had any merit, why were the two aldermen who were implicated, Sandberg and Schroder, on the Citizens Party ticket?

There also were promises to "advocate the immediate reopening of the Burr Oak viaduct" and for "the ultimate erection of a permanent structure in the shortest possible time without cost to the taxpayers." Mayor Rice and a few aldermen had worked to bring about both during the last two years. Before that, city officials had tried for years to get a higher government agency or the Rock Island Railroad to repair or replace the bridge. The structure was in such disrepair that it was closed in early 1937. A major obstacle was getting an entity to admit ownership and responsibility. Finally, the Cook County Board did so and at the consistent urgings of Mayor Rice and other area officials, board chairman Clayton Smith said he "would make every attempt" to get the Burr Oak viaduct on the construction docket for 1937. Former Cook County Board member Carl J. Carlson, a Blue Island resident and police magistrate under Mayor Kasten, also was influential. Mr. Carlson's influence helped get the project on a fast track. A new structure would be completed in 1940, but not because of anything John M. Hart did before or after the election.

There was one other noteworthy Citizens Party campaign pledge. It was "eliminate the garbage dump nuisance in the interests of the health of the citizens of Blue Island." Garbage dumping in Blue Island, legal and illegal, had been going on for decades. In return for permission to pollute its air, land, and water, and to breed rats, the city received free dumping privileges from Illinois Brick and others. Mayor Hart's predecessors could have stopped it or regulated it, but they never did—at least not for the betterment of Blue Island. Mayor Hart regulated it and he did so under the table so that he could profit from it.

During Hart's first term and against the wishes of aldermen and the public, Hart brokered a deal with the Illinois Brick Company and its personal excavator and hauler that allowed garbage to be dumped with impunity at the local clayholes. Later, when John Sexton acquired the land, the deal continued. Complaints about dumping and all of the problems that went with it were brought to the city council floor often during John M. Hart's 28 years in office. When the complaints became too loud or too frequent, Hart informed aldermen that he would speak with those responsible. Whenever he did, privately, the complaints stopped for awhile. Dumping and the problems it generated never did.

An interesting note about the 1937 mayoral campaign concerns the slogan "Pay as you go," which over the years has become so identified with John M. Hart that when the name of the legendary mayor is brought up today, the speaker often follows it with the slogan. While it is true that he never allowed the city of Blue Island to enter into anything that it could not pay for, "Pay as you go" did not originate with John M. Hart. The original slogan as it appeared in a headline on the front page of the March 26, 1937 *Sun-Standard* was "Pay-As-Go," and it referred to the Worth Township Board, whose Republican incumbents bragged as the election neared that under their leadership their entity was solvent. One of those candidates was Alderman Joseph Lentz, who sought re-election as Worth Township assessor. There is no record as to how the slogan acquired a pronoun and how it became synonymous with Mr. Hart, though it came to fit him perfectly. When Blue Island paid, the money would go to John M. Hart and his cronies.

When John Hart ran for mayor in 1937, he was a local pharmacist with no previous political experience. A Chicagoan of German ancestry, he was a veteran of the U.S. Navy who served during World War I. He and his wife Verna moved to Blue Island after he purchased the Harry Dare Drug Store in 1923. He became a member of American Legion Post #50, the Elks, the Fraternal Order of Eagles, the Odd Fellows, and the Shriners. John M. Hart was such a popular character that according to newspaper reports, he had been urged to run for mayor in 1935. He also was a gambler who made no bones about his love for cards. Mr. Hart bragged that poker was how he came up with the money to purchase the drug store.

Crafty and conservative, John M. Hart did not waste time or take chances. There was a kingdom to be run and money to be made. On Thursday, April 29, 1937—nine days after he was elected, but five days before his first city council meeting—he had City Clerk Louis Schwartz administer the oath of office privately at City Hall. Whether or not he physically moved into the traditional first floor mayor's office at that time is not known. Mayor Hart did flex his muscles and keep a campaign promise. He fired Acting Chief of Police Al Eick. In a move brilliant for its restraint—the last thing a new mayor should do is upset his aldermen, Mayor Hart did not appoint a replacement at that time. Instead he waited and presented his appointment to the city council for approval. Almost 40 years to the day later, another newly-elected mayor would not practice restraint. Before his first city council meeting, he fired the police chief and city attorney and appointed replacements without city council approval and set into motion the most confusing and controversial decade in the history of Blue Island politics.

Outgoing mayor Fred Rice chose not to attend what should have been his last city council meeting Monday, May 3, 1937. For ceremonial purposes, Mr. Schwartz again administered the oath of office to John M. Hart as the first order of business during that meeting. The very first act of the new mayor was to administer the oath of office to City Clerk Schwartz, who had run unopposed. The clerk administered oaths of office to City Treasurer August W. Schreiber and Police Magistrate Richard B. Seyfarth. The city clerk also administered the oath of office to the fourteen aldermen who would comprise Mayor Hart's first city council. They were First Ward Aldermen Louis W. Rauch and Thomas Hayes, Second

Ward Aldermen George F. Fiedler and Henry J. Goesel, Third Ward Aldermen Michael Guglielmucci and Gustav Lietzau, Fourth Ward Aldermen Joseph W. Lentz and Arthur Ladwig, Fifth Ward Aldermen Harry H. Sutton and Otto A. Kasch, Sixth Ward Aldermen Thomas J. Scanlan and Charles A. Dewar, and Seventh Ward Aldermen William J. Gerdes and C. O. Williams. Only three of those aldermen—Sutton, Kasch, Gerdes—were elected from the Good Government Party of former mayor Rice. Aldermen Scanlan and Dewar ran as independents. The others ran with Hart as members of the Citizens Party. The year 1937 was the first in which officials, previously elected for two years, were elected to four-year terms with a catch: while all executive terms were four years, aldermen were to draw lots to determine whose terms would be four years and whose seat would be up in two years.

As for that historic city council meeting, after the oaths of office, it began after a call to order by the city clerk. Mayor Hart gave what would become his traditional speech to new aldermen. According to the official minutes of the city council, "Mayor Hart then extended greetings to the new Council, stating he would recognize them as a single unit with the hope that harmony would be the keynote and everyone would put forth his best efforts in the interest of the City of Blue Island." As the years passed, Hart might add a few more words, but the theme always was the same: no one alderman, not even the entire body, was more important than Blue Island. What he never mentioned was that only King John I was more important than Blue Island, but he didn't have to—it was understood.

City Clerk Schwartz presented the bond for Mayor Hart in the amount of (up to) $10,000. Pearl E. Hawk was listed as the surety. Alderman Lentz moved that the bond be approved and Alderman Guglielmucci seconded the motion. In what would become a ritual, aldermen unanimously vote their approval. Mr. Schwartz then presented his own bond for $20,000 with William Woodrich, Henry Stoeben, and Otto Ziebell as sureties. The bond for City Treasurer Schreiber was the greatest at $100,000, even though he did not handle the money—the city clerk did. Phillip Schreiber, Mamie E. Rauch, Gustav Lietzau, Arthur Rauch, Emma Rauch, Ida Schreiber, Emily Zacharias Smith were sureties for the treasurer.

Thereafter, the one and only order of business of the meeting involved proposed legislation in the Illinois General Assembly, Senate Bill 282, which would give municipalities control over their streets when dealing with public utilities such as electric and gas providers. The proposed legislation was the result of a Supreme Court decision the *City of Geneseo v Illinois Northern Utilities Company*, which municipalities did not believe favored them enough.

According to the justices, a municipality could license utilities to do business and install structures, but it could not have absolute control over them in the event a municipality wanted to oust a utility, for example. In the opinion of the justice, if municipalities wanted greater control, there would have to be new legislation. Schwartz read aloud a letter from the Illinois Municipal League, which urged this in the form of SB 282. “This action is imperative. Every inroad on home rule means that another soon will follow. It is only by a united front that we can protect ourselves. The League is depending upon you to do your share."

Blue Island aldermen agreed. They unanimously passed a resolution that "endorses and declares itself in favor of Senate Bill 282" and urged every member of the 60th Illinois General Assembly to approve it. As insignificant as this resolution was pertaining to government, it nevertheless was symbolic. Blue Island did not change. How could it? Blue Islanders did not change their philosophies after John M. Hart was elected. Blue Islanders were, and still are stubborn and conservative. No one could tell them what to do and that went double if the "no one" making the suggestion was from the outside.

Decades later, when change was suggested, lifelong Blue Islanders thumped their chests and repeated the slogan, "Don't tell me about Naperville!" They did not want to learn the way things were done in that upscale community and they absolutely did not want change in any form. Change was not progress. It was not independence. Change was a threat to their lifestyle. During the 28 years John M. Hart was mayor, this stubborn refusal would be embraced as never before. It would be demonstrated over and over against the utilities, the Army Corps of Engineers, against outsiders who wanted to tap into city water, and especially against outsiders who wanted to become part of Blue Island. Unless it could be imposed upon Blue Island or unless John M. Hart could profit from it, there was to be no change.

So you can trace back the stubbornness at least to the 1937 city council. Legislation that would give Blue Islanders what they perceived as complete control of their community (such as home rule), was exactly what Mayor Hart's first city council thought everyone wanted, yet they did not pass legislation adopting it. Why was never explained. Ironically, long after John Hart was out of office, home rule would reappear as a local ballot proposition. It would be defeated time after time when the family of a future king, bitter about re-election defeats, would successfully oppose the ballot initiative in which Blue Islanders once so strongly believed. The family did this by using the heightened form of stubbornness known as "vindictiveness." That would occur more than sixty years into the future.

On May 3, 1937 there was a resolution to be passed and a coronation to be celebrated. Aldermen unanimously adopted the "Resolution Urging the Illinois General Assembly to Pass S.B. 282" and they instructed City Clerk Schwartz to wire a copy of the resolution to the Illinois Municipal League. Mayor Hart then stated, "...there being no objections, further business would be dispensed with and the Council, escorted by the American Legion Drum and Bugle Corps, would proceed to the Eagles Hall for public inauguration ceremonies." Of course, this was unanimously approved by aldermen and the official meeting adjourned, as it had to be. America was not a monarchy. It was a republic and a democracy. If an American king was to be crowned, it had to be done in private and off the books.

Alderman Louis Rauch and Mayor Hart would butt heads over the years. They reportedly argued often during city council meetings, especially about their favorite topic—gambling, which Alderman Rauch hated and Mayor Hart loved. "Each man was a dictator who always thought he was right," recalled the daughter-in-law of the alderman, Mildred Rauch. In May of 1937, however, Mr. Rauch was a strong supporter of the new mayor and he was in charge of all of the arrangements for the May 3 post city council meeting celebration.

The historic event moved two blocks south and east, and the coronation and celebration began. King John I and his court—the other elected officials—marched in behind the drum and bugle corps. After the invocation by Reverend Garrard of St. Aiden Episcopal Church, another public inauguration took place. Tuxedo-clad Henry W. Buhring, Esq., the former police magistrate who was a long-time Hart supporter, served as master of ceremonies.

According to the account in the Blue Island *Sun-Standard*, Buhring told the enthusiastic crowd, "I wish to reverse the procedure and congratulate the citizens on their wisdom in choosing such officials." Without elaborating, Buhring added, "My only regret is that the city court, which would greatly enhance the prestige of the city, lost due to an assassin's stab in the back a day before election, but I rejoice in the fact that a majority of the people voted for the proposition, even if it did not carry by the two-thirds vote because so many people failed to vote either yes or no."

There had been a proposition to establish a city court on the April 1937 ballot. By law, the city court ballot initiative had to be approved by at least two-thirds of the voters. The final unofficial total was 3,100 in favor and 2,774 opposed. During the Tuesday, April 27 city council meeting when vote totals were approved by aldermen, city court ballots from the Sixth Ward were not available. City Clerk Schwartz was instructed to provide the ballots so final results for the proposition could be approved; however, there is no record that this ever was done. Nor are there any published accounts of the identity of the "assassin" to whom Buhring referred. What is known is that the initiative received the strong endorsement of local attorneys such as Buhring, who was elected Calumet Township justice of the peace. Perhaps city court was not approved because John M. Hart and the majority of his followers as yet did not understand how it could benefit them and, therefore, could not share their vital insight with the electorate. Later, at the urging of a real Blue Island hero, attorney Leonard Carriere, the initiative would re-appear on the ballot in 1951, but not for the altruistic reasons suggested by Mr. Carriere. King John I and his inner circle finally were fully prepared to reap the rewards.

Mr. Buhring then introduced King John I. The 44-year-old king was magnanimous. In what the *Sun-Standard* called "a short, but masterful address," he thanked the following for his election: the public, members of the Citizens ticket, Mr. Buhring, campaign manager Paul Schreiber, and former mayor and advisor Frank Kasten. He also thanked the American Legion and its drum and bugle corps for their participation. According to the *Sun-Standard*, King John I told his minions, "It was due to the fact that we had a ticket such as we did that was responsible for our victory." The king vowed to have no animosity toward those he vanquished or even those who ran as independents. After mentioning that he had fulfilled the campaign promise of removing acting Chief Eick, he stated, "I will have no idea of vengeance in my heart but the supreme idea will be to do the best for the greatest number of citizens in my appointments."

Each elected official was given an opportunity to speak and all of them did at various lengths. Some merely said thank you. Alderman Guglielmucci expressed the desire "to follow in the footsteps of his brilliant father." Alderman Ladwig gave one of the longer addresses. In it he said, "We must operate for the benefit of the taxpayers and not the politicians." William Gerdes, who would complete his term as aldermen before serving for decades as a member of Hart's public works staff, lamented the two years of Mayor Rice. "I pledge my support and my untiring efforts for making possible the council co-operation [sic] so badly needed in the last two years."

In his return to the role of loyal subject, Frank Kasten presented to Alderman Goesel a pencil and wrist watch from the alderman's Second Ward supporters. A gold star set with a diamond of .66 carat, purchased from jeweler Adam C. Kranich with money donated by friends, was given to King John I. Father Theodore Gross, pastor of St. Benedict Parish, gave the closing prayer. Upon conclusion of the formal ceremony, Nate Beasley's Orchestra began to play and the bar opened. The Great Depression, local crime, and the huge debt owed by local government were temporarily forgotten as revelers danced, drank, and celebrated their great victory.

It was a time of optimism. Blue Islanders believed they had installed a savior. The reign of John I had begun.

The Woodshed, a Snappy Conclusion, and the High Curb at the Corner of Vermont and Western

During the almost three-decade long reign of King John I, some aldermen had to be put in their place during city council meetings. That is *place*—singular. All who crossed the king went to one place. It was the same place, the woodshed, where they received a beating. The alderman first to go to the woodshed was Michael Guglielmucci, who had run with the candidate Hart on the Citizens Party ticket and who probably used the big block of east side votes he influenced to help him get elected.

You'd think he would know better because he was a Blue Islander, but Michael Guglielmucci was a young politician raised to believe in the long-honored Cook County political ways. Once politician Michael Guglielmucci did you a favor, he believed you owed him a favor forever. Ron Blouin, the former executive director of Blue Cap, knew Michael Guglielmucci in his later years and believes the old-time politician never abandoned that one-in-return-for-forever philosophy.

Said Mr. Blouin, who seemed both amused and exasperated at the recollection, "Mike was good to Blue

Cap, but he had that old-style political thinking where you owed favors. He would call me up and say, 'I'm gonna send a guy over. I want you to give him a job.' I would tell him, 'Mike, it doesn't work that way. I can't just give someone a job.' It was as if he didn't hear me. He would reply, 'Just give him the job.' "

That was during the 1970s. During May 1937, Michael Guglielmucci mistakenly believed that rookie mayor Hart owed him a favor. Except that in Blue Island from 1937 until 1965, King John I owed no one a favor and no one told King John I what to do. Cook County politics? As far as Blue Islanders were concerned, their community belonged to Cook County when it needed something, such as a new Burr Oak viaduct. When it did not wish to be bothered, as in the case of the offer of a free Vermont Street railroad overpass, Blue Island was no more a part of Cook County than America still belonged to England. Blue Island was separate from all else and King John I was even farther away on a mountain top far above it all.

Because of this miscalculation by Michael Guglielmucci, an earthly exchange did occur between him and the new king. The otherwise wise-to-the-ways Michael Guglielmucci thought he could convince the rookie mayor to issue severance pay for his cousin, Nick Guglielmucci. Mayor Rice had dismissed Cousin Nick from the police department because things were so bad financially that the mayor and the city no longer could afford the political favor and the salary. In the eyes of Alderman Guglielmucci, this was breach of contract. He had made a backroom deal with Mayor Rice. Therefore, it was an open and shut case of wrongful termination.

Cousin Nick deserved to be paid for March even though he had been terminated and had not worked during that month. If Mayor Rice would not do the right thing and honor their dirty deal, surely Mayor Hart would. Michael Guglielmucci made a deal with Fred Rice: his support of the mayor in return for a job for Nick plus favors for life. Now John M. Hart was mayor. He inherited the obligation.

Except that John M. Hart was not a mere mayor. He was King of Blue Island! As Blue Island would learn in short order, no one told King John I what to do. Thus the king and the presumptuous alderman had it out during the May 24 city council meeting and the account was reported in city council minutes and in the *Sun-Standard*. After Alderman Guglielmucci presented his case, King John I told the alderman "No." After which Michael Guglielmucci used every argument he could think of, none of them convincing. The finance committee, of which Alderman Guglielmucci was a member, backed its mayor and recommended that Nick Guglielmucci not be paid. The protesting alderman argued that because he had not attended the meeting, the decision was not valid. The iron-willed mayor said, "So what?" When the recommendation was called for a vote, Alderman Guglielmucci tried to block the motion by requesting that his cousin's situation be reviewed by the police committee and the city attorney. The king denied the requests. Finally, Alderman Guglielmucci said he wanted "a full investigation." Ah! Finally he had requested something he could have!

The full investigation took perhaps three seconds and sounded like a gavel being struck decisively against wood. *Bang!* Investigation completed. Request denied. No further appeals. It was the first public example of what happened when you opposed King John I. After that session in the woodshed, the mayor announced that Nick Guglielmucci would not be paid for time he did not work. The full city council made it official. The vote total was 12-2. Michael Guglielmucci and his fellow Third Ward alderman, Gus Lietzau, dissented. Mr. Lietzau did not say a word. The woodshed had no allure for him.

Yes, King John I immediately asserted himself as the unquestioned leader of the community and he made sure Blue Island government ran smoothly and efficiently according to his plan. He accomplished these feats, not seen in Blue Island since Paul T. Klenk, despite the fact that he had absolutely no political or governmental experience.

Prior to becoming mayor, John M. Hart never served on a board. He had not served as an alderman. There is no record that he ever attended a board meeting or a city council meeting. He operated a corner drug store with a soda fountain. He filled prescriptions and made sundaes. Away from the drug store, he played poker and belonged to social clubs. Except for receiving a business license after purchasing the drugstore in 1923, the only mentions or contact John M. Hart ever had with the city council may have been these: during July 1925, Mayor Klenk appointed John M. Hart to the health board as a replacement for Harry Dare, the man whose pharmacy Mr. Hart purchased. More than ten years later, according to the December 14, 1935 minutes, the future mayor appeared on a list of donors who had contributed to the purchase of bulletproof vests for members of the police department. Citizen Hart gave five dollars.

Prior to taking over as Blue Island chief executive, John M. Hart may have picked the brain of former Mayor Kasten, one of his most ardent supporters. He must have heard what he needed to do and what not to do from friends, customers, and other assorted Blue Islanders during his first fourteen years in town. Blue Islanders loved to complain and to oppose things. They don't mind doing it out aloud and they don't care who hears it. It's more than likely that when someone came into his drugstore to purchase a bottle of Hart's Elixer ("an all purpose remedy"), they also might have passed along some juicy gossip or a complaint.

On the other hand, John M. Hart did not take advice. Nor did he tolerate complaints or complainers. There was Hart's Elixer and there was Hart's woodshed. Lifelong resident Harry Robertson, who knew the mayor, told this story which has become part of the legend of John. M. Hart.

"One winter, early in his administration, there was a snow storm and some of the business people on Western Avenue did not like the way the city plowed the street—or maybe that it wasn't plowed. Either way, they went to see Hart at City Hall to complain," said Robertson. "Hart listened. Then he looked at them and said, 'Okay, come with me.' They followed him to the Public Works garage. When they got there, Hart said, 'Would you like to help?' They said, 'Yes, John, what can we do?' Hart pointed toward some shovels and asked, 'Do you see those shovels?' They answered eagerly, 'Yes, John!' Hart told them, 'Good! Now grab those shovels, take them up to Western Avenue and start shoveling!' None of those business people ever bothered Hart again."

They'd believed they were going to the public works garage, but they actually went to the woodshed.

From the start, Mayor John M. Hart was an aggressive leader who didn't take guff from anyone. That included the many aldermen who served him for 28 years. During that time, many an alderman was intimidated by being shouted down or publicly insulted. Behind his back, some aldermen and their wives called Mayor Hart a "tyrant" and referred to him as "a dictator" but they rarely stood up to him. Some of those who complained about him also said he was a good mayor because he kept the town clean and safe. What helped him immensely was that during his 28 years in office, Mayor Hart had a reputation as a man who was stubborn, no-nonsense, a gruff-and-tough guy. By human nature, many people shy away from confrontations with Mayor Hart's type.

Of course, many aldermen and city employees were in cahoots with the mayor. John M. Hart was a notorious grafter who shared with them just enough of the bribes and taxpayer money he siphoned off to keep them happy. He did not spend the taxpayers' money on the taxpayers if he could help it and unless it could make him look good. For the king, it was a matter of managing *his* money. He did not consider it the city's money.

Thus, during his first month on the job, the new mayor made employees somewhat happy when he recommended paychecks, not vouchers, be issued, but that the city "hold back on past due salaries pending legislation." He also announced that to save money he was "terminating" more members of the police and fire departments. He did not specify who would join Nick Guglielmucci on the unemployment line and there was a reason for this. If you were a friend of John M. Hart or took care of him, you got to stick around. If not, well, you were one of the employees terminated to save money. Except that during the 28 years John M. Hart was in office, the payroll never was reduced. The number of those who received checks grew steadily, if not spectacularly.

According to people who knew him, Mayor Hart spoke quickly and abruptly. He did not like to waste time. The May 10, 1937 session, John M. Hart's first real city council meeting, reflected these characteristics. After correspondences read by City Clerk Schwartz, in rapid order Mayor Hart appointed 26-year-old Paul R. Schreiber to the post of city attorney. Young attorney Schreiber was the son of Mayor Hart's city treasurer, August Schreiber. Because the new mayor needed a bagman he could trust, he returned John R. McEvoy to the post of acting Chief of Police.

"All of Hart's police chiefs were bagmen," a future mayor would say." The reappointment also was a nod to former mayor and Hart supporter Frank Kasten, who'd elevated Mr. McEvoy to top cop, and a slap at former Mayor Rice, who had dumped him. The attorney and acting chief appointments were unanimous. Also unanimous were Mayor Hart's reappointments of Wells Crocket (who shortly thereafter would sue the city for back wages) as commissioner of assessments and tax commissioner, R.B. Hammond as commissioner of public works, Allen L. Fox as city engineer, and Dr. A. J. Roemisch as health commissioner. The lone dissent for all appointments came from Alderman Ladwig after the new mayor reappointed Henry J. Schnurstein as building inspector. His "no" vote had nothing to do with Mayor Hart. Alderman Ladwig reportedly had a grudge against Inspector Schnurstein. The Fourth Ward alderman voted against Mr. Schnurstein when Rice presented his nomination too.

Thereafter, the aldermen had their say about issues from their wards and the meeting adjourned. Mayor Hart's first real city council meeting took approximately one hour, which was a vast improvement over the contentious sessions that dragged on during Fred Rice's two years in office. In its coverage of the meeting, the *Sun-Standard* said: "Mayor Hart in his first regular meeting of the council conducted business with a snappy conclusion lacking in the council chambers for years. The meeting was called to order at 8:20 p.m., was adjourned before 9:30 despite the large amount of business transacted."

As if there had never been a Fred Rice or petty squabbling amongst aldermen, city council meetings led by Mayor Hart became more efficient, though not necessarily more productive. During Mayor Hart's first year there were good projects. The Public Works Administration gave the city a matching grant for sidewalk replacement, which was right up the aldermen's alleys since it could help them look good in their wards. Lists were compiled of residents who wanted replacement sidewalks in front of their homes (and could afford the matching amounts). There also was unfinished business, most notably the completion of the water reservoir project, which had experienced a construction delay. It was unclear as to why the project stopped. The *Sun-Standard* reported that the men working on the reservoir went on "a secret strike the public didn't know about" and that Mayor Hart met with leaders and mediated a solution. There is no evidence to support this and there was no reason for a strike. Funds were available and all of the companies hired for the project signed contracts that work would be completed by a specified date. With the Depression far from over, workers did not go on strike for better wages or conditions. According to the city council minutes, there was a problem with one of the subcontractors because parts were not available. Whatever the real reason, the city was forced to request an extension from the WPA and 121 days was granted. The reservoir project with its new one-million gallon tank officially was completed December 13, according to city council minutes.

There were signs of things to come and requests for changes which never would come. A foreshadowing involved complaints about the swimming pool at Central Park. Built in 1917, the community's public respite from summer heat still was immensely popular, but after 20 years it also was inefficient. The problem was that because the pool did not have a filtration system, the water was difficult to keep clean. During June, Health Inspector Roemisch was dispatched to make an assessment of the situation and report back to the city council. No one closes a swimming pool during the summer. The city council fully endorsed Dr. Roemisch's recommendation that the Central Park pool was in top shape. The Central Park swimming pool would not close for another ten years and by state mandate. By that time, thanks to Congressman Edward Kelly and Park District president Edward Moroney, the Memorial Park pool was open.

The closing of the swimming pool was the beginning of the end for Central Park, however. Without a swimming pool, the park became less popular. For reasons never explained, the Park Board also began to ignore Central Park and allowed it to fall into gradual disrepair. In one of Mayor Hart's few real (though not necessarily positive) accomplishments, during 1965 he would help broker the three-way deal in which St. Francis Hospital acquired Central Park from the Blue Island Park District. It also was his last accomplishment, which was fitting since it epitomized his failure to formulate a plan for water, for sewers, for the business district, and the upgrade and expansion of physical Blue Island in general.

The mayor established his philosophy quite early. During the June 14, 1937 city council meeting, Alderman Joseph Lentz had the foresight to recommend that Blue Island annex more territory. Mayor Hart ignored the recommendation. During July, Alderman C.O. Williams sought help for the many Blue Islanders whose basements flooded when said there was a "need for an enlargement of the sewer system." City Engineer Fox agreed when he reported that the city had outgrown its storm sewer system and an upgrade was needed.

Mayor Hart ignored these recommendations too. During August, aldermen brought the complaints of their constituents to the mayor when they cited garbage dumping at the Illinois Brick clayholes. This the mayor addressed. In October, Mayor Hart told the city council, "The dump is a serious matter which must be solved, but the money is not there to solve the problem." Thereafter he ignored the problem until he was ready to profit from it.

There were some oddities that first year. One of them involved transportation. During the July 7 meeting, the South Suburban Safeway Lines made application to operate in Blue Island. It proposed a bus route that would transport riders from Tinley Park, Oak Forest, Harvey and Roseland to Blue Island for shopping and movies at the Lyric Theater and the Grand Theater. Mayor Hart was against the service, however. According to the *Sun-Standard,* he said, "I believe that the traffic problem on Vermont Street is hazardous enough as it is and it would be adding more to our problems more than we would be gaining." The Mayor and dissenting aldermen defined Blue Island logic when they suggested a one-way-into-Blue Island-only route. That is correct. The Blue Island city council actually debated as to whether the bus service was a detriment since it also could take shoppers *out* of Blue Island. Never mind that outside of Blue Island, the closest place to shop was downtown Chicago or that the consumers had to return home with the items they'd purchased here. In a perfect world, there would be a ban on return ridership.

How the bus company would feel about empty buses returning to their origins so that the drivers could make one-way runs to Blue Island was not addressed. Nor was the plight of stranded commuters. The thinking in 1937 was that it was not the city council's job to be concerned with what happened to people after they purchased goods in Blue Island or the survival of a business. The street car line had gone out of business and a bus company had come along. People and businesses always came to Blue Island and would do so forever. Blue Island was the center of the universe.

Somewhat miraculously, the majority of aldermen ultimately approved the carrier and the more down-to-earth Illinois Commerce Commission gave South Suburban Safeway Lines the green light. Buses could come *and go*. By the way, if you've ever wondered why the curb is so high on the south side of Vermont Street between Western and the alley to the west, it was installed as a partial solution to "the traffic problem," part of which was buses and trucks driving onto the curb and sidewalk. That curb, fourteen inches at its highest point, is a monument to Michael Guglielmucci. It was the Third Ward alderman who brought the issue to the attention of the city council and asked that something be done there to keep vehicles from driving onto the sidewalk.

During the January 17, 1938 city council meeting, aldermen voted 7-6 to add liquor commissioner to the mayor's powers and to limit the numbers of tavern licenses and carry-out licenses to 55 and five, respectively. Mayor Hart showed his appreciation by announcing his first veto. Although no reason was given for their opposition, Hart and the Blue Island Tavern Owners Association wanted the limits to be 50 and four. Hart and his lobby group got their way, of course, and the revised ordinance was passed March 14. While no one was suspicious of this, it became obvious that some Blue Islanders did not trust their aldermen when 80 residents petitioned the city to have public, not private, drawings for two-year and four-year terms. The request was not honored. Another request not honored during King John's first year on the throne was a petition containing names of 161 residents calling for a referendum to approve a bond issue to pay the past due bills.

There were political deals and campaign promises to uphold before important matters could be addressed. Among the first for the new city council to make good on and look good on, was the softball diamond at 121st Street and Western Avenue. Owned by Mr. A. Stacker, it was allowed to continue, but with parking restrictions and time limits as to when and how late games could be played. Among the top complaints by residents had been that women softball players were changing into their softball uniforms in their cars and this was outlawed too. Mr. Stacker was ordered to provide restrooms and changing facilities.

During June, Mayor Hart kept his promise to run the city like a business when he laid off nine city employees, reportedly saving Blue Island an estimated $11,580 per year. Among those given a pink slip was police officer George Farning. Payrolls under Hart gradually were cut during his first year in office, saving the city approximately 25 percent on salaries. As payrolls had under his predecessors, however, the number of employees on Mayor Hart's payrolls eventually increased.

Officer Farning eventually was rehired, but Nick Guglielmucci never again appeared on the City payroll. Michael Guglielmucci apparently realized he never would be able to manipulate or bully this mayor as he and his father had manipulated and bullied others. He never would have the clout he wielded during the terms of Frank Kasten and Fred Rice. Michael Guglielmucci decided that if he wanted to be a big fish, he had to find another small pond. He did so when he left Blue Island government and became an elected official in Calumet Township.

All of these things occurred during the first year the new mayor was in office and before "Mayor Hart saved Blue Island." Yes, salvation finally would come, grudgingly, because of John M. Hart during 1938.

Salvation Is in the Eyes of the Beholders

If you want to give someone credit for saving Blue Island, you may consider giving more credit to C. A. McNear & Company than to John M. Hart. The bond brokerage firm handled virtually every aspect of the transaction that enabled the City of Blue Island to finally approve the judgment funding bonds that generated the money to pay its past due bills. Yes, McNear & Company made money on the transaction, but that is what businesses do. At the very least, without the persistence and expertise of McNear & Company, there may have been an even longer delay or no bond issue at all.

A smidge of credit may be given to former mayors Kasten and Rice, to a few aldermen, and to some members of the community. The mayors at least suggested a bond issue to satisfy the city's debt to employees and vendors. The aldermen and some residents may have pushed Mayor Hart to make the deal with McNear & Company.

You absolutely must include a Blue Island resident who worked at the Office of the City Clerk. The name Helen Boeber (pronounced bay-burr) has all but faded into obscurity, but it was the legal action by Mrs. Boeber that finally forced the city council to approve the measure ensuring everyone was paid what they were owed. That distinction is very important because Mayor Hart dragged his feet on satisfying the City's obligation. Perhaps because he was such a cheapskate, he did not want to satisfy the debt in its entirety.

No, contrary to his myth—which some have mistakenly referred to as *legend*—credit for saving Blue Island from financial ruin or anything else *should not* be given to Mayor John M. Hart. With the exception of tax anticipation warrants guaranteed by taxes, Mayor Hart was completely averse to borrowing. The concept was at odds with his conservative philosophy, which he defended with the slogan, "pay-as-you-go." Borrowing any amount of substance violated his code. Ironically, among the few things Mayor Hart borrowed during his seven terms in office was that slogan.

In reality, Hart may have been worse at finance than his predecessors because he was as conservative as he was dishonest. As his predecessors did, Mayor Hart allowed the city to borrow internally, from the water fund and from other of the city's solvent funds. Unlike all but one of his predecessors and despite the fact that the city had much more money to work with than all of them, Mayor Hart failed to complete one major project in 28 years.

Mayor Hart could not save Blue Island. He seemed not to know how.

The bottom line with the bond issue to pay the past dues was that Mayor Hart was forced into it. He did everything he could to delay paying off the large debt the city had incurred. He appeared to be disinterested, if not disinclined, to pay back wages to city employees who had earned them. Later, the mayor intended to use bonds to pay everyone, but not in full. Finally, facing the Boeber litigation, Mayor Hart and the city council had to borrow via bonds because they were forced to pay in full.

Finally, after seventeen months in office, King John I announced that the city would pay. With the help of the *Sun-Standard*, on September 15, 1938 he informed his subjects that the judgment bonds were issued "to pay the claims against the city for wages and services rendered and materials used prior to the administration of Mayor Hart." The king said he supported borrowing $100,000, but he emphasized that if he did so to pay off someone else's debt. "The rock bottom fact continually bobbed up [is] that the only way to meet a debt honorably is to pay it," his highness added.

The only reason Mayor Hart went along with the 1938 initiative was because his back was against the wall. Otherwise he hated bond issues. He saw bond issues and tax increases as bad for business, bad for his image, and bad for his wallet—the three things most important to John M. Hart. Under Mayor Hart, the city spent a great deal—in fact, almost all of the city's money before he left office in 1965 and for the benefit of John M. Hart. Yet he was able to appease Blue Islanders—perhaps *fool* them is a better description because he did not allow the city to go into debt again. To Depression-era Blue Islanders, Mayor Hart's early constituency, this was enough.

As for the history of the borrowing initiative, even after it was determined bonds were the only solution, the process was not "pay as you go" but "stop-n-go."

The city council had all but finalized an agreement with McNear & Company by December 1936 when aldermen approved the plan. There were no updates or reports, however, until May 18, 1937 when McNear & Company notified the city that legislation favorable to the elimination of its debt could be coming out of Springfield. The advice was for the City to put the bond issue on hold, which it did.

The hold went off September 13, 1937 and aldermen passed an ordinance authorizing borrowing bonds. According to the minutes of that meeting, Blue Island took the action because there were "binding claims and indebtedness" incurred against the city "prior to April 1, 1937." Of the $96,645.77 reportedly owed, "wage and salary claims" were $47,727.84. One claim, a lawsuit filed by Charles Van der Wahl, a custodian employed by the city, dated back to 1931. All others dated only to 1935. There also were "miscellaneous claims for materials furnished, services rendered, or property used" in the amount of $48,917.93.

After getting the okay from the city council, McNear & Company arranged for the City of Blue Island to borrow $96,500 by issuing a series of 97 funding bonds. The interest rate was 3.5 percent (considered to be exorbitant interest in 1937!) and the bonds were to be paid off incrementally and semi-annually. The first bond, due in 1942, would be in the amount of $500. Every other bond would be in the amount of $1,000. The last one would be paid off in 1957, unless the city was in a position to retire its indebtedness sooner. However, if the bond issue went the full 20 years, the city would pay $142,112.50 in principal and interest. This did not include the fees to McNear & Company, which were not detailed in the city council minutes. At that point, aldermen believed they had final numbers and they voted 12-2 to approve the bond issue in the specified amounts and interest rates.

In Blue Island, someone always is against everything, even when everything is good. In this case the opponents of the plan were the Fifth Ward aldermen, Harry Sutton and Otto A. Kasch, who used their votes as protests. Their goal was to delay the bond issue until they could stop the dumping of garbage at the Illinois Brick Company clayhole south of 123rd Street at California Avenue, which bordered their ward. Their plan worked, but only for a very brief time and with the help of their constituents. Residents attended the October 11 city council meeting—before final approval of the bonds—and voiced their complaints about the dump. Aldermen Sutton and Kacsch spoke out, as former did Fifth Ward alderman Stewart Sandberg, whose reputation they'd attempted to tarnish prior to the 1937 election. Mr. Sandberg let bygones be bygones and became their ally against the dump. The most vocal may have been Fifth Ward resident Oscar Klenk, the brother of the former mayor. According to the *Sun-Standard,* Klenk stated that the dump "was a problem for the whole city to solve."

Packing the little second-floor city council chambers and speaking out was effective. So was the submitting of petitions of protest, which indicates that someone involved had an attorney in the family. Professionally written and resembling resolutions like those passed by the city council, the petitions informed Blue Island officials that the bond issue could not be approved without a referendum. The last paragraph of each petition pointed out that the documents were signed by one percent of the voters in Blue Island (conflicting reports stated the number of signatures at either 197 or 161) and as such, by law, the transaction had to be put on hold until it could be submitted to voters by referendum.

Hart could have put an end to the political maneuvering by brokering a compromise, but he didn't. Thus the petitions put the kibosh on the bond issue until Illinois passed legislation enabling communities under 300,000 to approve bonds for purposes of eliminating debt. That reportedly came in mid-1938, at which time the hold up of the bond issue turned into a double whammy. Suddenly there were additional claims of indebtedness in the form of a lawsuit filed by the Standard Oil Company of Indiana for $3,182.53. Later, two lawsuits would be filed by Helen Boeber.

In the first *Helen Boeber v the City of Blue Island* lawsuit, the demand was for $54,249.33 for wage claims for virtually all city employees. The second *Boeber* lawsuit demanded $10,714.06 for material, merchandise, etc. furnished to the city by employees and businesses specified in the litigation. City Clerk Schwartz checked the claims and reported to the city council that they were accurate and should be paid. That was in addition to what the city council already agreed to pay.

Some prominent Blue Island names were listed in the *Boeber* filings. From the police department: George

J. Fiedler was due $985, Richard Sorgenfrei was owed a total of $1,470 and the controversial Arthur Fritz and Stewart Heim were due $1,470 and $1,680, respectively. John Link, at various times listed as fire chief, fire captain, and fire inspector, was due $1,520. Police captain and former acting chief William O. Hankey, the future father–in-law of prominent attorney, dealmaker, and judge Henry Gentile, was owed $1,320. Fireman and vehicle mechanic John Sauerbier was owed $1,575. Mrs. Boeber herself was owed only $290. According to the September tabulation, former mayor Fred Rice had $225 coming after all of the aggravation he had endured. For a reason not explained, he was not included in the 1938 settlement.

Then there were additional lawsuits, all of them legitimate. In the matter of *Wells Crockett v the City of Blue Island*, Crockett, the city commissioner of assessments and tax commissioner, claimed he was owed $4,061.63 for services performed in checking judgment records, searching titles, preparing publication of tax notices, obtaining tax deeds, and other unspecified services. There was a suit by local auditor Jonathan B. Cook for $1,204.47. (While the expression "cooked the books" did not originate in Blue Island, the city never had an unfavorable review during the many years Cook served as auditor.) There was litigation by Westinghouse Electric Supply Company ($794.08), Illinois Bell Telephone ($2,748.32), Sanitary District of Chicago ($7,240.50), and the Public Service Company of Northern Illinois, which is now ComEd ($15,739.87). To each suit, $19.20 was added for court costs.

There were the 45 businesses that did not sue individually. Eventually they became part of the *Boeber* lawsuit and their total of $10,714.06 due was included. Among the locals on it were the *Blue Island Sun-Standard Newspaper* ($2,171.36), Jebens Hardware ($377.85), E.B. Bronson and Company ($246.37 for auto repair work and parts), Fiedler Mohr Motor Sales ($282.11), Melvin Press ($277.55), various companies run by the entrepreneurial Pronger Brothers ($473.62), Habich Brothers Motor Services ($1,016.79), and George J. Roll & Sons ($170.12).

Because of the delay caused by the protest against the dump and by the lawsuits, the payouts were greater. The final cost of all judgments was $100,071.79 and the city was forced to pass an ordinance for a new series of bonds that allowed it to borrow more money at the higher interest rate of 3.75 percent. The transaction was consummated during the Monday, September 12, 1938 city council meeting. The makeup of the city council was the same, but Mayor Hart conned aldermen Sutton and Kasch into believing he would solve the garbage dumping problem. This time the vote was 14-0.

Who actually saved Blue Island? When it came to the greatest financial dilemma in the history of the city, most of the credit should be given to the taxpayers. While they were denied an opportunity to approve the bond issue via referendum, they did pay for it with their tax dollars. Over 18 years, the total bill for the borrowing was $157,960 and the taxpayers of Blue Island paid every penny.

In hindsight, paying off the debt was small and solvable. Larger and far more challenging problems pertained to controlling crime and convincing people that the fix worked for everyone. Those problems were solved, although some might say perfected, by a local hero. So perhaps the man who actually saved Blue Island was that guy.

"My Dad Was Making Moonshine in the Living Room"

Babe Tuffanelli, the man who may have done more than anyone else in history to "save" Blue Island, was so very adept at deception that few friends, acquaintances, and perhaps even the FBI knew his first name. Outside of family members, the few still around who remember him know his name.

Perhaps this was and still is the Blue Island response to the adage, "What's in a name?" No one cared about Babe's first name. All they cared about and continue to care about was that Babe maintained their way of life—the Blue Island way of life.

Babe Tuffanelli was born in Chicago and moved here with his parents and two older brothers not long after his birth, which reportedly was March 3, 1903. There is a ridiculous and completely false Internet story that says Babe and his brother stowed away on a ship from Italy to America, jumped ship just before the vessel docked at New York Harbor, and swam to shore so that they would not be arrested by immigration officials. This preposterous tale actually may be an offshoot of what happened to his father, Ferdinand Gaetano Tuffanelli, who was known in Blue Island as "Fred." A native of Ferrars, Italy, Mr. Tuffanelli was reportedly a seaman in his country's navy. According to family legend, Fred Tuffanelli, a headstrong young man, wanted shore leave so badly that after his request was denied he literally jumped ship off of the coast of Argentina and swam to shore. From Argentina, Fred eventually made his way to California and later to Chicago. No one is certain how he met his wife, Julia Gobet Tuffanelli, an Italian who reportedly was from Switzerland. They may have met in Chicago because the Gobet family relocated there too.

Fred Tuffanelli listed his occupation as "brewery agent" but there's a question as to whether this meant Mr. Tuffanelli sold product or manufactured it. The latter might begin to explain how Babe began to acquire his great skills as a bootlegger. Julia Tuffanelli was a housewife. After their three sons were born, the family moved to the East Side of Blue Island where the Italians lived in those days because they had to—first to a home on Division Street and later to 1832 York Street. The first listing for Fred Tuffanelli appeared in the "Blue Island Directory" in 1908.

Adolph, the oldest child, was born in Chicago in 1893. Another son, Ferdinand Jr, who was known as "Ferd," was born in 1898. Dolores and Helen were born in Blue Island in 1912 and 1914, respectively.

What was Babe Tuffanelli like growing up? Where did he go to school? Who were his friends? What was he involved in?

"My uncle used to tell us that when he was growing up, he and Babe Tuffanelli were in Boy Scouts together," recalled lifelong Blue Island resident Gary

Decker. Beyond that, little is known about Babe's boyhood. There are no school records that indicate he attended public schools, parochial schools, or any school at all; or whether he belonged to any organizations or ever got into trouble. It cannot be said that "Babe was no Boy Scout" because according to local lore, he may have been.

According to his daughter, Shirley, by the time Babe was eighteen, he had made the quantum leap to the working world, where of all things he started in law enforcement.

"He was the sheriff of Palos," laughed Shirley during a 2013 interview at the Palm Restaurant in Las Vegas, where the Babe Tuffanelli family moved during the 1960s. Asked how it came to pass that an untrained 18-year old was in charge of law enforcement for an entire community, even a rural one, she shrugged her shoulders and said, "He may have been the only one who wanted the job."

That part of Babe's legend certainly plays into another. According to Shirley and other family members, it was during his time as a law enforcement officer that Babe discovered and subsequently was discovered by Al Capone.

"I heard that Babe got in with the Outfit because Al Capone noticed his driving," said Babe's nephew, Charles Tuffanelli. "Babe was a police officer and something happened where Babe was chasing one of Capone's cars. Capone's driver couldn't lose him and Capone himself was so impressed by Babe's driving that he offered Babe a job. That was how he joined the Outfit."

Babe's granddaughter, Dawn Marie Tuffanelli, agrees. "That's exactly what happened," she said.

There are many gaps in Babe's biography and another one occurs here. At some point, Babe went from being on the right side of the law to the left. There is no doubt that he went to work for Al Capone in various capacities, most prominently as a bootlegger and that his career in law enforcement and as an Outfit member merged. Babe's older brother, Ferd, had pursued a similar path. According to the *Sun-Standard*, briefly during the 1920s, Babe was on the police force of the Township of Thornton. Ferd was an officer with the Cook County Highway Police. The Tuffanelli brothers were busted for bootlegging during the week of December 5, 1926.

According to the *Sun-Standard*, there was a raid at a farm at Crawford Road and Lincoln Highway in Chicago Heights. The Feds made the arrests when they discovered "a giant distilling apparatus in the process of [being] set up." The still belonged to Babe and Ferd. It is believed that the Tuffanelli brothers appeared in court, paid a fine, and continued bootlegging, although Ferd "was stripped of his star and credentials" and eventually was fired. He continued to serve as a deputy for some local law enforcement agencies before becoming a jack-of-all-trades. Later, among his employers were Majestic Cleaners of Blue Island, the Cook County Forest Preserve District, and Babe's juke box company, All-American Music.

By 1926, the Fred Tuffanelli family had spread throughout Blue Island. Fred Sr. and Julia lived at 625 York Street. Adolph resided at 242 Walnut Street, Ferd lived not far away at 283 Walnut, and Babe was at 352 Walnut, two blocks away. As for employment, there was no mention about whether or not Babe lost his job with Thornton Township, but either his arrest or a more lucrative business opportunity may have precipitated a temporary move to the West Coast. That was where he met a beautiful farm girl named Augustine Amore. Babe was making moonshine in Hollywood, California. The exact year is not known, but it was prior to 1930. Shirley Tuffanelli was not able to provide exact dates, but she does have other details as provided by her parents.

"My mother was raised on a farm in Bakersfield. She liked to sing and dance, but her father was very strict and didn't believe in those things. He didn't want her to leave the farm," explained Shirley. "Her brother had to sneak her out at night so that she could compete in dance contests."

Like Babe Tuffanelli, Augustine Amore was ambitious, adventurous, and creative. What she was *not* was long for farm life. Shirley explained, "My mother was talented. She wanted to find out if she could make it in Hollywood. She'd never waitressed in her life, but she moved to Hollywood and went to work as a waitress."

Can you guess the name of the talent scout who walked into the restaurant and discovered her?

"So my father comes in and my mom waits on him. He starts talking to her and she's not interested," said Shirley, who laughed as she told the story she'd heard from her mother. "When it comes time to pay the bill, he pays it and leaves her a five dollar tip. Big money in those days. My mother was offended and wouldn't take it. She threw the money back at him. My dad admired that, but he wasn't taking 'no' for an answer."

Babe liked the restaurant and he *loved* the waitress. The scene was repeated. It's what they do in Hollywood. The players do retakes until they get it perfect. Babe came in for coffee or to dine and to see Augustine. The former farm girl from Bakersfield didn't want anything to do with the smooth-talking big-tipping bootlegger from Blue Island. She continued to throw the five dollars back at him until finally Babe understood that Augustine could not be bought or impressed. Okay, she could not be bought, so according to Shirley, he tried a different tactic to impress her.

"Dad found out that mom had a roommate. He invited mom and her roommate to his home for Thanksgiving dinner. He told her, 'Everything on the up and up. No funny business, just dinner.'" That, of course, depended upon how you defined the term "on the up and up."

"Mom and the roommate get to the house for dinner and there's a still in the living room," laughed Shirley. "My dad was making moonshine in the living room."

Whether or not that turned out to be a dealmaker is not known. It certainly was not a deal breaker. Babe and Augustine began dating. Soon she agreed to his marriage proposal with a caveat: she had to meet his family back home. Cut. Print. Hollywood fadeout. Babe, Augustine, and her son Denny drove to Blue Island. It was the perfect ending to the story and the perfect beginning of their lives together. By the time they arrived, they already were a family.

"Mom had been married previously. I don't know much about it, but my understanding is that she only was married long enough for my brother to come along," said Shirley. "Anyway, they only made it as far as Las Vegas. That was where they stopped and got married."

The first listing for the new Mr. and Mrs. Tuffanelli at 2156 W. 121st Place was 1930. Babe listed his occupation as "tinsmith." The newlyweds also ventured back to Sheriff Babe's old jurisdiction, the Palos area. The business no longer was law enforcement, however. There was little money in it and Babe had a family to support. While a bit more risky, bootlegging was far more lucrative. The new Mrs. Tuffanelli had no issue with her husband's profession. According to Shirley, she was his partner.

"My mom, dad, and Denny would go out on deliveries together. The keg would be in the front seat with them. When the police stopped them, mom would hide the keg under her skirt to make it look like she was pregnant. It always worked. They never were arrested."

Those were the trademarks of Mr. and Mrs. Tuffanelli—Big Babe" and "Little Babe" as they would come to be known. They were crafty and they were entrepreneurial.

Thus Babe Tuffanelli became a full-time bootlegger, perhaps *the* bootlegger of the South Side, who was a master at the construction and operation of the apparatus known as the still. Not that there weren't occasional mishaps. In addition to the arrests at Chicago

Heights, there were other occasions when Babe's plans did not come to fruition.

There was what the *Sun-Standard* referred to as an "enormous brewery" that was discovered in a brick building on Broadway Avenue in Blue Island. Inside were five 500-gallon vats and six 100-gallon vats, "many containing beer." There also were four 400-gallon ice coolers. Two "employees" were apprehended, but they did not divulge the identity of the operator of the still, who the *Sun-Standard* said was reputed bomb thrower and bootlegger, Lorenzo Juliano. However, the operation was too large and sophisticated for Mr. Juliano, who reportedly did not have the means or the financial backing for such a set up. Because of his connection to Al Capone, Babe Tuffanelli did.

Then there was that mishap at the house two doors from Mr. and Mrs. Tuffanelli on 121st Place, empty of everything except a working still, which blew up in the wee hours one winter morning, scattering component parts and almost a next door neighbor. Okay, so even a master bootlegger, er...tinsmith, makes a mistake once in awhile. Despite these few setbacks, Babe was so good at his profession that he reportedly continued to make bootleg booze long after the end of Prohibition and operated stills in multiple locations. If you ever wondered whatever happened to the legendary machines no longer in operation...well, they didn't all go into museums.

"My grandfather had parts for over one hundred stills at the house on Bell," recalled his granddaughter, Dawn Marie Tuffanelli. That was in the place that Babe had built on a double lot at 11860 Bell during the 1950s.

It had garage space for the vehicles he loved: trademark Cadillacs and Offenhauers from his racing team. There reportedly was a tunnel which connected the Tuffanelli home to the home Babe had built next door on another double lot. In the basement of the Tuffanelli home, there was a family room with a bar and a bowling alley. Shirley had her parties there.

"We went to St. Benedict School together," recalled Gloria Rose, nee Rangel. "When Shirley had a sleepover or a birthday party, she would invite all of the girls over. Her mom would pick us up in the Cadillac and drive us there. They were the nicest people and what a house they had!"

So Blue Island was a good place to live and raise children. It also was a good place to make a very good living if you were a bootlegger...er, tinsmith. The fix always was in here. Eventually, Babe would control the fix in Blue Island so that he could practice his trades without fear of being arrested by local authorities.

By 1930, Al Capone had taken control of all of the bootlegging in Cook County. It is believed that Babe was Capone's representative in this endeavor in the South Suburbs. Babe had the bootlegging and another Blue Islander, James Hackett, had the gambling. They reportedly received permission from Al Capone himself to run those franchises. Babe and Hackett also had tacit understandings with the Blue Island mayors and the police chiefs. They could operate as long as they didn't let things get out of hand, which they never did. The problems came from those in Blue Island who did not have understandings: freelance criminals, pimps, and people on the lam.

From 1920 until mid-1937, Blue Island served as victim to all types of violent crime. Murder victims were dumped in the Cal Sag Channel. Armed robberies and truck-jackings were quite common. During September 1926, in response to what the *Sun-Standard* called "a rash of burglaries in the business district," Mayor Klenk gave Blue Island Police a "shoot-to-kill order." Because prostitution was not considered a serious issue for local authorities, most of the raids of local brothels were performed by outside law enforcement agencies. During one such visit to the Burr Oak Hotel, the Illinois Highway Police used tear gas. Patrons, prostitutes, and pimps fled. The joint was fumigated and reopened for business as usual.

It was no secret that Blue Island was a haven for criminals. Hoods came to Blue Island for recreation. On such visits, they held parties on commuter trains, commandeered street cars, fired their weapons in celebration, and in all things acted with impunity. There also were those who needed to keep a low profile. In search of these characters, Chicago Police and other agencies occasionally made surprise raids of Blue Island bars and pool rooms during which they frisked patrons and confiscated weapons. Then the Great Depression hit and things got worse.

In the minds of the local prim and proper, the damage to Blue Island's image eventually became worse than the crimes themselves. Something had to be done to save Blue Island.

If you believe in local legend, here's what some old timers say is what happened next. Two guys visited John M. Hart immediately after he was elected mayor and brokered a deal to control and clean up Blue Island. In all likelihood, no meeting that formal took place. No such ultimatum was given. Neither was necessary. John M. Hart was not a choirboy. He was a hedon. Based upon his proclivity for gambling, booze, and women, Mr. Hart probably was friends with some of the local unsavory types. He had to know the principals: Babe Tuffanelli, James Hackett, and perhaps even Mike "the Pike" Heitler. He needed money to pay for his expensive gambling habit. Operating a corner drug store during a time of economic turmoil may have paid the tabs, but it would not have provided the lifestyle to which John M. and Verna Hart aspired.

Suddenly things became even simpler and more profitable for two of the three business principles. During June of 1937, not quite two months after Mayor Hart took office, James Hackett died at a Chicago hospital after suffering a gall bladder attack. Mr. Hackett and his minority partner, professional bowling legend Jimmy Blouin, controlled all the slots and bookmaking and were able to operate their way. It was Mr. Hackett, however, who was the connection to the Outfit. According to family members, he made the original deal with Capone and the franchise did not pass to Blouin. Perhaps he did not have the Outfit connections or he had not earned Capone's trust. Or it may have been that someone else was a better businessman or had better connections. So the most accomplished bowler in Blue Island history was not allowed to control gambling in Blue Island. He was allowed to operate as a bookie.

Members of the Hackett family suspect that Mr. Blouin sold out Adeline Weiss Hackett, the widow of his partner.

"I don't know what happened with Jimmy Blouin after my grandfather died. He and my grandfather were friends and partners," said grandson and namesake James Hackett. "Somehow my grandmother got cut out of the gambling in Blue Island. It had something to do with Jimmy Blouin and my grandmother wasn't happy about it, but she didn't talk about it."

Actually, Jimmy Blouin didn't have any choice but to go along. The Outfit did not allow women any positions of authority. Mrs. Hackett was not the only one left out. The local bookies also were unhappy. Instead of the loose operation run by Mr. Hackett and Mr. Blouin, they either paid the Outfit to operate or they went out of business.

"In the old days every saloon also was a horse book. When the Mob took over, that changed," lamented Bob Withers. "The Mob took over the bookmaking and put little guys out of business."

For Babe Tuffanelli and Mayor Hart, the passing of James Hackett was fortuitous. Babe already owned the bootleg booze franchise. He provided gratuities to Mayor Hart so that he could operate it. Suddenly the local gambling franchise fell into his lap. The mayor already was getting a cut of the action from James Hackett. Instead of dealing with two different franchisees, now Mayor Hart was dealing with one.

Babe Tuffanelli and Mayor Hart made a deal that ended up lasting for as long as the latter was mayor. Babe could do whatever he wanted in Blue Island as long as there was no public violence or prostitution. In return, Mayor Hart and his police force looked the other way and received a cut of the action.

"The jar games could stay. The bookmaking could stay. The slots could stay," said Larry Price, who grew up in Blue Island and was a pharmacist who worked for and with John M. Hart at the drug store. "There couldn't be girls and there couldn't be violence. That was the deal between Hart and Babe."

It seemed to be a good deal for Blue Island. Over time, Mayor Hart and Babe became more than partners. They were friends who took trips together and whose families socialized.

"Mayor Hart and his wife came to our house for Christmas," said Dr. Denny Tuffanelli during a 2012 telephone call from his home in the San Francisco area. "That was before I went away to college. I don't know what happened after that."

It continued for years, according to Shirley Tuffanelli. "Mr. and Mrs. Hart came to our home for Christmas and on other occasions. He talked. She was quiet, very proper. She always wore a fur."

Shirley added, "My father and Mayor Hart were friends. They took trips together. Mayor Hart went up to my dad's cottage. My dad had a place near Rhinelander. He and the boys and Mayor Hart would go up there. They would go for weeks and fish and gamble. My father didn't gamble, but the others gambled."

Anyway, that's not how Blue Island was saved, but how it endured. The community was not rescued from financial ruin or other calamity; however, some might be of the opinion that the opposite occurred. The opposite is not what most people knew or even noticed, of course. What they knew and noticed was that murders and other violent crimes and prostitution disappeared. There were a few who understood reality. They knew that the reason was because those types of crimes no longer were permitted and that Mayor Hart profited from the deal that rid Blue Island of them. As for the more fun and profitable vices that Blue Island enjoyed for as long as anyone could remember that also were part of the deal...well, they flourished.

It was just the way things were done.

"Let's Go Find Earl!"

Teddy Aguilar and Zeke Benevides were angry and frustrated. It was the early 1960s just before Christmas. At that time, the two men were among the few Mexican-Americans ever employed by the City of Blue Island, but they weren't working, which meant they were not going to receive a paycheck. Mr. Aguilar and Mr. Benevides were members of the Public Works Department. Their boss, Earl Mager, told them to stay home so that Blue Island firefighters could pick up a few extra bucks before the holidays. In Blue Island of that era, it was just the way things were done. At least it was until Santa Claus showed up.

"We were mad about what happened and we were sitting at White Castle one morning complaining over coffee when Mayor Hart walked in. He asked us, 'Why aren't you two working?' I told him, 'Earl told us to stay home.'"

"He said, 'Oh, he did, did he?' We could tell when he heard that he didn't like it. He got mad. Mayor Hart thought for a second and then he said, 'Let's go find Earl!' So we went with him. When Mayor Hart found Earl, he chewed his ass out and told him to put us back to work," laughed Mr. Aguilar. "We went back to work right away."

For the record, that was not the only time John M. Hart played Santa Claus. Every year, he sponsored a

Christmas party for the children of the community. The event was held at either the Grand Theater or the Lyric Theater.

That was not the only time Aguilar was the beneficiary of a good deed by Mayor Hart. Not long afterward, Mr. Aguilar wanted to purchase a new car, but he was denied financing. "I must have looked depressed about it because not long afterward, when I ran into Mayor Hart, he asked, 'What's wrong?' I told him that I wanted to buy a new car, but couldn't get a loan.

"Mayor Hart told me, 'I'll loan you the money for the car and you can pay me back a little each payday. That's what we did until one day when I went to see him to make a payment and he told me, 'That's it. You don't owe me anymore.' I told him that I still owed him more money. He said he knew that, but he didn't want it. That was how I bought my first new car. It was thanks to Mayor Hart."

Few dispute that John M. Hart loved Blue Island and that he did some good things during the 28 years he was the city's chief executive. Mayor Hart's number one accomplishment, for which he does not get enough credit, if any, may be acquisition of the bridges that span the Cal Sag Channel at Western Avenue, at Division Street, and at Chatham Street. From the day in 1952 that the federal government announced the waterway would be widened, the U.S. Army Corps of Engineers was adamant the City of Blue Island would pay for the installation of new bridges. Mayor John M. Hart was more adamant that the City could not afford to pay for three bridges and would not.

And so it went into the early 1960s before the canal-widening project was completed. Not known for being reasonable or sympathetic, the Corps of Engineers continued to inform Blue Island that it would pay. Never known for parting with a buck if he did not have to, Mayor Hart insisted that poor Blue Island could not pay. The Mayor wrote letters and lobbied people in Washington. When the smoke cleared and the last rivet was secured, the Corps of Engineers proved no match for the stubborn mayor. The federal government installed three bridges at a minimum cost of $500,000 each, but no cost to Blue Island, with the caveat that after the bridges were opened, Blue Island owned them and was responsible for them. Forever. As Mayor Donald E. Peloquin learned during his last term in office, there would be no more free bridges. Nor would there be repair work on existing bridges.

Another Mayor Hart success story was modernization of the Public Works Department. According to the record and to some old-time Blue Islanders, DPW in Blue Island virtually was nonexistent. Hart grew the department's physical plant, its capabilities, and its services.

When John M. Hart was elected mayor, the city did not have a quality, secure public works facility. Trucks, machines, and tools were kept in a storage yard, were left on the street (in the case of heavy machinery and vehicles), or went home with employees. After April 20, 1937, there were more and better garbage trucks, dump trucks, and other equipment and responsibilities the city never had before. Thus there had to be a secure hub and in 1946, during Mayor Hart's third term, a new public works facility and firehouse were built adjacent to City Hall. Of course, the lion's share of the project was paid for "the Hart way"—with other people's money. Mayor Hart thought of local tax money as *his* money and to be used judiciously. Yet he thought nothing of putting the arm on local residents, businesses, and organizations to finance city projects. Hart paid for most of the new public works facility and fire station with donations. The remodeling of the city council chambers, another John M. Hart project, also was paid for by donations. Part of the latter project was a quid pro quo, according to Harry Robertson.

"The American Legion paid for some of the remodeling of the city council chambers," Robertson said during an October 2011 conversation, "but you have to understand that the Legion wanted to use it [an upstairs room at City Hall] for its meetings."

In those days on the second floor of City Hall were the city council chambers, the American Legion headquarters, and a gun range. The American Legion HQ and gun range were among the most popular local high society man caves of the era. These, as opposed to the working class man caves known as "saloons," which White males of any strata could enter. To frequent the Legion Hall or the gun range, you had to be a member or an invited guest. Invited guest Harry Robertson almost became the dearly departed one evening at the gun range because of an inadvertent one-gun salute.

"Some of the men were shooting at targets. I was sitting there watching near the spot where Frank Kasten Jr. was shooting. Kasten was a gun nut and on that occasion he was using a Spanish revolver," recalled

Robertson. "When he pulled the trigger, the gun exploded in his hand and the pieces went everywhere. One of them just missed hitting me. Fortunately, no one was injured, not even Kasten."

The American Legion missed the bull's-eye for a more costly, less hazardous reason when its members decided it was time for a new HQ. To understand the new order, it is helpful to understand the history of the old order. During July 1924, Mayor Klenk and the city council approved a sweetheart deal for American Legion Post 50 for a fifty-year lease of a large upstairs room in City Hall. According to the lease agreement, Post 50 paid $5,000 at the time the agreement was signed and $1,000 per year through 1929. For the next 45 years, Post 50 would pay the City only one dollar per year.

It was after "the Great War" when returning veterans were considered heroes. To give, lease, or dedicate property for a cause or group was popular. Memorial Park was created during this time to honor veterans. Local politicians believed it was the least they could do to repay Blue Island heroes by giving American Legion Post 50 a sweetheart deal for a lodge. After all, its members had defended America. Then after the war, the men returned, joined local service organizations, and played active rolls in the community.

No less important was for the community to have a man cave where members and guests could gather to drink, play poker and slots, and fire weapons. That the man cave was located at City Hall was convenient for John M. Hart and other elected officials. Gambling and drinking were among his favorite pastimes. Some say they were his *only* hobbies. So you can imagine how much he and members of his city council enjoyed being able to walk just a few steps from a city council meeting or his office to the poker table and the bar.

By the early 1960s, however, the executive board of Post 50 decided that it could do better. With the consent of the membership, it purchased land from the Mueller twins. Post 50 decided to construct a headquarters on the 12200 block of Western Avenue.

What did the American Legion have in mind? Its long-term plan must have been something great and profitable for it to opt out of its virtually no maintenance, no taxes, one-dollar-per-year lease. And speaking of poker, in deciding to build a new lodge, the executive committee of Post 50 determined that it held all the cards when it came to the lease agreement. The City needed Post 50 as a tenant far more than Post 50 needed the city. So the Post 50 executive board requested that the City of Blue Island pay their organization $5,000 to buy out the lease.

To further borrow from poker terminology, in this instance Post 50 overplayed its hand. Veterans were popular, but nowhere near as popular as during the 1920s, especially when it came to sweetheart lease deals. Even more important, Post 50 was negotiating with John M. Hart, who in Blue Island always held the best cards.

Yes, John M. Hart was a Navy veteran and was always partial to local veterans organizations such as the American Legion. He attended meetings, socialized at the Post 50 headquarters, drank, and gambled there. He did not like the organization enough to give it $5,000. So a terse statement came back that the City of

Blue Island would break the lease for $1,000. Post 50 negotiators must have believed they had Mayor Hart right where they wanted him because they rejected the city's offer and requested a meeting with him.

Did anyone ever have John M. Hart where they wanted him? Well, probably not until October 13, 1967. In the matter of the Immovable Force vs. the American Legion, a meeting was held, after which it was announced that Blue Island American Legion Post 50 gladly accepted the city's very generous offer of $1,000.

The American Legion was lucky to get anything. It was a rarity for the city to part with any money during the reign of King John I. The king was not disposed to pay out any of the city's money, *his money*, unless it was absolutely necessary. It should not have mattered that John M. Hart drank and played poker at the American Legion Hall, received a cut of the revenue from the slot machines, and got a kickback from the liquor license. He had the same deal at the Elks Club, the VFW, and everywhere in town where there was booze and slots. They needed him more than he needed them. Perhaps Mayor Hart was uncharacteristically generous to Post 50 because he won when he played poker there. Contrary to the autobiographical portion of his legend, John M. Hart may not have been quite as good a poker player as he claimed. He may not have needed to be a good poker player.

"The mayor used to play poker at the Elks Club and the American Legion. If you needed something in Blue Island, you played cards with Hart and let him win," Charlie Westcott said. Mr. Westcott is a long-time

American Legion member. His uncle, Ed Boyd, was Mayor Hart's last police chief.

The deal for property that eventually would become Hart Park could have come up during a poker game, a casual conversation, or anywhere. That acquisition of unknown origin was brought to the city council at the very end of the last city council meeting of 1943. On that Monday evening, December 27, Mayor John Hart informed everyone the city was acquiring recreation land at 123rd Street and Western Avenue. Here is the verbatim account from the city council minutes:

"Mayor Hart announced that the City of Blue Island will acquire title to a large tract of vacant land including the soft ball [sic] diamond at 123rd & Western which is owned by the Staffel family.

> *"The sum to be paid for this property is $4,750.00 plus a payment on unpaid taxes which may run $2,200.00 or may be settled for less.*
>
> *"This purchase is being made with the co-operation of the Blue Island Recreation Commission and will be operated as a recreation center by the Commission.*
>
> *"The Recreation Commission would probably [sic] as the Council to approve some Tax Anticipation Warrants in connection with this purchase."*

There was no public discussion. No one asked a question. After passing along that information, Mayor Hart wished the city council a happy new year and the meeting adjourned per a motion by Alderman Joseph Mausolf, a second by Alderman Louis W. Rauch, and a unanimous vote. That's how the city acquired the land that eventually was named for the man who brokered the deal. Over the years, it would serve as an athletic field (where sheep once grazed to cut the grass), the site of carnivals and circuses, and after John M. Hart was gone, a park named after the city's most famous mayor.

Mayor Hart also was instrumental in the creation of Blue Cap School. During the early 1960s, parents of children who had developmental disabilities formed an organization—"Citizens For the Mentally Retarded"—whose purpose was to ensure that handicapped individuals—especially children—received services. A difficulty was that CFMR wanted to build a school in Blue Island, the community where someone is against everything. Thus the new organization immediately encountered resistance. It wasn't that anyone was against services for the handicapped. Opponents did not want the handicapped and a facility that would serve them in their neighborhood. Chalk it up to human nature. The opposition was built on ignorance and fear of the unknown.

"The opponents were called NIMBs," recalled Ron Blouin, a lifelong Blue Island resident who served as executive director of Blue Cap. "It was an acronym for 'Not In My Backyard.' People weren't against a school being built. They just didn't want it near their homes."

One of the first Blue Island locations considered was the target area of "the Negro Invasion." The city owned a small parcel of land at 119th and Maple Avenue, and the members of the organization were interested in building a facility there. Mayor Hart reportedly was anxious to get rid of the land, which he determined to be virtually worthless. That was another characteristic of Mayor Hart. He seemed to think that undeveloped land had no value. When Mayor Hart tried to give the land to Citizens for the Mentally Retarded for its school, NIMBs from that area put the kibosh on the deal.

Romie Palmer, who would become city attorney under Richard W. Withers, was a founding member Citizens for the Mentally Retarded. His son Bruce was developmentally disabled. Mr. Palmer and the other members of CFMR refused to give up. Mr. Palmer and Mayor Hart were friends. They socialized together and played poker at the Elks Club, although not in the same game. During its heyday, the Elks Club was a social hub, according to Palmer.

"The big New Year's Eve party in those days was at the Elks Club, which was upstairs from Woolworth's. Everybody brought food and everybody got drunk. I remember that Norman Blatt, who was a big guy, threw Ferd Tuffanelli, who was a little guy, down the stairs. It wasn't a fight. Norman was just having fun and they were drunk. Well, when that happened everyone was alarmed because Ferd was Babe's brother. Ferd laughed it off, however, and there were no repercussions. After the party John made sure that everyone got home safely by providing rides in a police car.

"Thursday was poker night at the Elks Club. I played poker with the Watland brothers and with John," recalled Mr. Palmer. "John liked to play high stakes poker. The stakes did not matter to him. He just threw money into the pot."

Palmer believed his gruff friend, John M. Hart, really was a softy. Mr. Palmer's big gambling play pertained to the belief that Blue Cap School would become a reality.

"We wanted to develop a school in Blue Island. We didn't have property. I knew the city had property," said Mr. Palmer. "I took John to a school [for the developmentally disabled] in Chicago Heights. One of the kids there ran up and threw his arms around John's legs and hugged him. That picture always will be in my mind. When the kid hugged John, that was it.

The land at 119th and Maple was the first offer. After the NIMBs put the kibosh on it, Mayor Hart came up with another. It was the "town square" at Broadway and Chatham streets. Blue Island had acquired the land decades before after the town of Portland ceased to exist.

"John's word was magic. When he said something, it happened. John said to me, 'We have land at Broadway. I'll sign over the deed for it and I know a guy who has a construction company who will do it [build a facility] for cost.'"

Mr. Palmer also commented on Mayor Hart's frugality, the obsessiveness that went along with it, and he laughed about them.

"He inspected every [city] project personally. No one was paid until John inspected it. Other towns were having problems with money and projects. Not Blue Island. Not John," said Mr. Palmer, who implied that frugality and generosity can coexist."I heard that he even paid for kids' college tuitions out of his own pocket."

Blue Cap School officially opened in February 1966, ironically, after John M. Hart no longer was the mayor. Still, his efforts in the creation of Blue Cap School should not be forgotten. Nor should be forgotten his other less successful and not-so-generous endeavors, many of which are recounted in the following pages.

"If You're Ever Going to Do Anything, Make Sure There Are No Witnesses"

Unlike other Blue Islanders of the era, Pete Korbakes did not get his liquor license because he paid off John M. Hart or because he did the legendary mayor a favor. On the contrary, Pete Korbakes finally received his liquor license after what seemed to him like forever because the gruff Blue Island mayor felt remorse. For eight years, Pete was denied a liquor license because Mayor Hart did someone else a favor. That someone else was Pete's father, George Korbakes, who was a friend of Mayor Hart.

George Korbakes opened his fruit and vegetable market in 1915 at 12948 Western Avenue. He did not remain there very log, however. Ironically, in 1959 that store would become the home of another great Blue Island business, Iversen's Bakery. By 1920, Korbakes Fruits and Vegetables was at 12201 Western. George purchased a home with a garage there.

"His wife, Stella, wanted to kill my grandfather when he bought the house and garage there," said Jimmy Korbakes. "Then he trusted someone he thought was a friend and he ended up losing the place for back taxes."

In 1938, George Korbakes moved to 12734 Western, where Frank St. Aubin once had a tavern and where Elmer Witte Sr. would operate a Chevrolet dealership. Today the El Ranchito Grocery Store is there. By 1952, George had moved the store across the street and down the block to 12734 Western, near the building that was home of the Cavallini Ice Cream Company. In 1952, he moved to the current location, 12747 Western. At that time, he was across from the Stuebe's Grocery Store.

"It was a townhouse with units upstairs and down," said Jimmy Korbakes. "The family lived upstairs and he converted the downstairs into the store."

Starting in 1929, Bartle Flowers seemed to be following Pete around. Like George, Vera Bartle was peripatetic because she sought the perfect location.

"When my grandfather was at Prairie, Bartles opened there. When he moved down the block, they moved there. When he moved across Western to where we are now, they moved there. Everywhere my grandfather went, Bartles went, which was odd because they really didn't like each other" Jimmy explained.

From 1952 until 2009, when Bartle Flowers closed its doors after 80 years as one of Blue Island's great businesses, the two would be next door neighbors.

Through all of the moves, George Korbakes was a produce guy. On this, he never wavered. His son, Pete, however, was sure that selling alcohol was the way to go. Pete grew up in Blue Island, attended schools here, and knew the town as well as anyone. In those days, German Americans dominated Blue Island and were well-to-do and snobbish. Pete always got along even though the Korbakes Family had yet to make its mark or its fortune.

"The Germans dominated the city when I was growing up," said Pete during a conversation in early 2012. From his seat behind the counter at his liquor store, he pointed north on Western Avenue, and then south, and finally west down Oak Street toward Maple Avenue. "If you weren't German, you couldn't live there...or there...or there. I remember there was a guy who built a home down the street. He wasn't German, so they wouldn't let him live in it. That was just the way things were."

The guy may have been Salvatore DiNovo. During the early 1950s, Mr. DiNovo asked city officials if he could move one of his buildings—literally pick it up, transport it, and place it on another lot—from one location to another in town. His request was denied. In those days, sometimes you couldn't live there AND you couldn't move it. Everything was at the whim of the stubborn old Germans. Yet there are no hard feelings today. Sal's grandson, Joe DiNovo, and his family still live in the family home (not the same house) on Maple Avenue. His granddaughter, Betty Nagel, lives across the street. In the old days, if you were Italian, Greek, or Mexican, you had to dance to the tune played by the Germans. They ran the town. If you were African American, of course, you were not allowed close enough to so much as hear the tune. It was just the way things were done.

Pete told a story about the way things were for him during his years at Blue Island High School. "One day we were in the locker room during gym class and some of the guys—friends of mine said, 'Let's throw the Greek into the shower!' I said, 'No! No!' I didn't want to get all wet." Pete put up his fists like a boxer and remembered, "I started hitting them. The coach came along and took me to the principal."

Pete laughed a little as he finished the story about the well-dressed German kids and the one-outfit Greek kid from the produce market. "The principal asked me what happened. I told him, 'I wasn't going to let them throw me in the shower. Those guys have all kinds of clothes. These are the only school clothes I have. I don't want to walk around wet all day.' He understood, but he said, 'Well, I still have to suspend you.'"

Just as Pete stuck to his guns and would not allow himself to get soaked, he was just as adamant that selling alcohol was the way for the Korbakes family business to go. Even though his father disagreed, during 1946 Pete applied to the City of Blue Island for a liquor license. While applications always went to the city council license committee, that committee was a rubber stamp for Mayor Hart, who was the liquor commissioner. If Hart wanted you to have a license, you received a license. If not, you did not receive one. Hart made Pete Korbakes wait. Did Pete at first refuse to pay off before finally making a deal with Mayor Hart? He shook his head, but did not elaborate.

Asked how the Korbakes Family officially got its liquor license on April 12, 1954, one of Pete's four sons, Jimmy, picked up the story. "My grandfather was in the hospital. They thought he was going to die. My grandfather and Hart were good friends," said Jimmy, who crossed the index and middle fingers of his right hand to indicate how close Mayor Hart and George Korbakes were. "Before that, every time my dad would go to Hart and ask, 'When am I gonna get my liquor license?' Hart would open his desk drawer...[Here Jimmy Korbakes opened his own desk drawer to demonstrate], pretend that there was a list inside and say, "Oh, you're fifth on the list.'

"Finally, when he thought my grandfather was going to die, Hart told my dad, 'You know, I've kept you waiting a long time.' Pete said, 'Yeah, you've kept me waiting eight f------ years!'

Hart said, 'Do you know why?' My dad said, 'No.' Hart said, 'Because your father didn't want you to have one and he made me promise not to give it to you. Now I'm going to.'

"That's how my dad got the license and he didn't pay off Hart," Jimmy finished the story and he laughed. "Then my grandfather didn't die."

George Korbakes passed away during 1970. Thereafter, his only son, Pete, who died during 2012, and his wife Georgia ran the store. Two of their four sons, Jimmy and Steve, all but took over the major responsibilities during the last fifteen years. The Korbakes Family built and opened its new store at 12747 Western Avenue during November 2004. It is 14,000 square feet, which is ten times the size of the previous store, where the family lived upstairs until 2003. To accommodate its customers, during May 2004 the Korbakes Family purchased the southeast corner of Prairie Street for its parking lot. Over the years, the corner was the site of the legendary Pat's Tap, Weir's Tap, a laundromat, and finally a Brown's Chicken franchise. Pete was so right on the money that later the house to the east of the parking lot was purchased and demolished, and the parking lot was expanded further. Korbakes Liquors is so popular that it's the number two beer seller in the area.

The go-around that Pete Korbakes and Mayor Hart had over the business license wasn't their last either. Mayor Hart had one more surprise that raised Pete's blood pressure and cost him some money, although not as much as the eight-year wait.

"Our store was on one side of the alley and Bartles was on the other in the Masonic Temple building. Each of us owned their half of the alley. In front of the stores on Western Avenue, the sidewalk was broken and my dad was after the city to fix it," said Jimmy Korbakes.

"Finally, Mayor Hart himself came over. My dad was out there, the Bartles were out there, and the Masons, and Mayor Hart. So Mayor Hart looks at the sidewalk on both sides of the alley and he says, 'The city is going to pay for everything in this direction and Korbakes is going to pay for everything in that direction.'

"My dad got upset. He said, 'What! Why? That's city property! Why do I have to pay and they don't?'

"Mayor Hart just looked at him, pointed as he spoke, and announced again, 'The city is going to pay for the sidewalk in this direction and Korbakes is going to pay for everything in that direction.'

"When Hart made up his mind, that was it. My dad had to pay to have the sidewalk fixed," laughed Jimmy. "I don't know why he had to pay and the others didn't. It may have been Mayor Hart's connection with the

Masons. Hart didn't want the city to pay for anything if he could get away with it."

So the Korbakes Family reluctantly paid for a section of sidewalk. It did not pay off for a liquor license. Many others did willingly and for all manner of things during Mayor Hart's 28 years in office. Former Calumet Township committeeman and attorney Larry Petta, who knew Mr. Hart, offered an explanation via a story.

"Years ago, I owned property on the east side and needed a zoning variance because I didn't have enough parking for my building. I went to see Hart. I asked, 'What's it going to cost me?' Hart wanted to do business. He wanted to give me the variance. He told me, 'Let me have the price of a hat for me and my two aldermen.' It was ten or twenty dollars for each of them. Why? Because in those days, that was just the way things were done."

Mayor Hart received a percentage of the proceeds from Babe Tuffanelli's slot machines, which were prominent in bars and social clubs all over town. In return and to guarantee his cut, the mayor had to make sure that none of the joints got busted. With one exception, they didn't.

"One time the Sheriff's Department or another law enforcement agency came to town and raided joints with slot machines. Mayor Hart got real mad about that and raised hell with whoever it was," said the late Paul Talley, who was a longtime Blue Island resident and a friend and confidant of police officer, Harry Harczak. Between 1951 and 1965, Officer Harczak reportedly was one of the mayor's bagmen and drivers.

"Mayor Hart told them that they couldn't come into his town unless they notified him first. From that day on, Hart would get a call that there was going to be a raid. Then the calls would go out to everyone to hide their slot machines."

The hiding places varied depending on the type of establishment. Some proprietors had to be especially creative.

"Tom and Chuck Boza and I used to go into Bill Hughes' place when it was at 139th and Western and there were slot machines in there," said Andy Botte. "If we were in there when the call came in, Bill would have us wheel the slot machines into the restroom. Then we'd put a sign on the door that said, 'Out of Order.' When the Sheriff's Police or whoever came in, there were no slot machines."

Dick Reuss was a member of the Elks Club and he recalled what happened when the call came in from City Hall or the police station. "There was a fake wall and they'd push it in front of the slot machines. Then they would put couches in front of the wall to make it look good," said Reuss, who added, "There were slots at the VFW Hall too."

"I was a VFW member and there was a whole roomful of slot machines at the VFW Hall on Vermont Street," recalled Stig Nordstrom, who arrived in Blue Island in 1928 at the age of seven. Nordstrom has lived in Blue Island ever since and he knew Hart and the way things were done. "Mayor Hart must have been getting a cut. They couldn't have had slot machines there if he wasn't."

Former Blue Island police officer, James Base, didn't know about the slots or their hiding places until the old VFW Hall was being converted into the 9-1-1 Emergency Dispatch Center and City Council Chambers.

"At the end of my career, I was in charge of security when the VFW Hall was being rehabbed. Well, one day a bunch of old guys who were VFW members came in and asked if they could take a look around the place. I told them it was okay and showed them around. As we walked around, they told stories about the old days. One gentleman said, 'When the call came in that there was going to be a raid, we lowered the slot machines down a trap door.'"

"Hart got a cut of all the slot machines in town, plus some other things," said Harry Robertson. Those "other things" were women. There reportedly was a brothel in Robbins that was under Hart's protection. According to former city officials, the madam who operated the bordello had a book which listed all of her girls. Each girl in the book was color-coded based upon quality. As part of his gratuity, Mayor Hart was allowed to select whichever women he wanted.

"Hart liked women, but he was discreet," said Robertson. "I never witnessed anything, but Hart once told me, 'If you're ever going to do anything, make sure there are no witnesses.'"

As you have read, sometimes Mayor Hart did not take his own advice. Sometimes he was indiscreet about taking money and making deals, and sometimes there were witnesses when he did. Where and when did the payoffs start? Let's go back to the sale of alcohol. If you're looking for a specific date, it may be January 17, 1938—the night of a special city council meeting. During that meeting, an ordinance was created that called for the mayor to be appointed liquor commissioner and the number of taverns and package stores was increased to 50 and five, respectively. The new ordinance was "relating to the sale of alcoholic liquors" and was "to be construed to the end that the health, safety, and welfare of the people of this City [sic] shall be protected and temperance in the consumption of alcoholic liquors shall be fostered and promoted."

You could go back even further. The seed for that liquor ordinance may have been planted during April 1934. Looking for ways to regulate businesses and increase revenue, the city council debated creating license guidelines for regulating liquor and the sale of other items. Making the liquor license fee $400 was among the ideas discussed, but rejected. The debate found in city council minutes indicates that Alderman Rocco Guglielmucci may have been psychic. After aldermen were informed by City Attorney Roy Massena that state law provided the mayor be the local liquor control commissioner and have full power, Mr. Guglielmucci cautioned that "in the future there may be a time when a Mayor [sic] would take advantage of his power as sole authority on the granting of licenses, [sic] and felt there should be something specific in the ordinance providing that the application be referred to the License Committee. [sic]"

Attorney Massena assured the aldermen that he would incorporate Alderman Guglielmucci's request into the new ordinance. Rocco Guglielmucci also moved that there be no limit of licenses and his fellow Third Ward alderman, Charles Ulrich, seconded the motion. The vote was 10-2 against them, however. Aldermen Louis Rauch and Andrew Myers suggested a limit of 40 licenses. Alderman Gus Zavadil pointed out that there already were 48 licenses and that the number should be slightly higher. Joseph Lentz and George F. Fiedler recommended the license limit be 50. Alderman Stewart Sandberg inquired about the five applications on the waiting list. It was at that point that aldermen settled on the magic number, yet they did not pass the ordinance. Chalk it up to indecisiveness and a lack of leadership.

Under the strong leadership of Mayor Hart, who was supported by a local lobby group known as the Blue Island Tavern Owners Association, the city council revisited the ordinance that its predecessor never finalized. Yet there was no intent to abide strictly by the previous recommendations. The new discussion was for no increase in fees and all of the power to be with the mayor. Something else was amiss. The legislation did not have the usual rubber stamp. Aldermen George F. Fiedler and Henry Goesel were the sponsors. Kasch, Scanlan, Dewar, Gerdes, and Williams joined them by approving passage. Aldermen Rauch, Hayes, Guglielmucci, Leitzau, Ladwig, and Sutton opposed it because of the number of package stores. Alderman Joseph Lentz was absent. There is no indication how he would have voted, but had he dissented, passage would have failed. On the record, Mayor Hart remained mum, but only temporarily.

Enter the Blue Island Tavern Owners Association, the lobby group that advocated for the interests of local tavern owners and stores that made package sales. The BITOA announced its intentions in a letter (which looked suspiciously like a city council resolution) to Mayor Hart and the city council dated November 29, 1937. Tavern Owners officers were Henry Anderson, W. C. Hake, C. Wiessner, and Abe J. Chayken. Like any lobby group, BITOA wanted to make sure that regulation and enforcement favored its members and that competition was kept to a minimum. There were 50 taverns and four carry out stores at that time and the Tavern Owners wanted no increase in either.

To those ends, John M. Hart was their man. During his 28 years in office, the only legislation Mayor John M. Hart ever vetoed pertained to that liquor ordinance which benefitted the Blue Island Tavern Owners Association. Hart exercised his veto during the January 24, 1938 meeting when he announced in a letter to his aldermen that his opinion was that they had passed "special legislation" for the benefit of an applicant whose license was pending. Hart further stated that he completely agreed with all aspects of the revised ordinance and respectfully requested that they reconsider maintaining limits of 50 taverns and four package stores. Abe Chayken wasted no time in praising the mayor in a letter read into the minutes of the February 28 city council meeting. In a great understatement, but appropriate terms, Chayken said Hart's action "was in line with the draft by the Tavern Owners Association."

During the March 14 city council meeting, aldermen revised the legislation. The old fix was out and the new fix was in. The revised ordinance, #1441, was introduced by the chairman of the license committee, Alderman Fiedler, the same alderman who proposed the original license ordinance. Before the thirteen aldermen unanimously approved it (Alderman Lentz still was absent due to illness), they also voted unanimously to uphold Hart's veto. Yes, you read that correctly. Mayor Hart overruled the aldermen and they responded by rolling over.

Thereafter, Mayor Hart began to reap the rewards of his new legislation.

Harry Robertson became an usher at the Lyric Theater in 1935 when he was fifteen. He worked there until he was nineteen. The job enabled Harry two luxuries: he got to carry a flashlight ("I still carry a flashlight. I've found it useful my entire life.") and he got to see movies free. Young Harry also was able to see firsthand what went on behind the scenes at the Lyric and why the number 50 was important.

"Chief McEvoy was Hart's bag man. Hart reappointed him every year until he died. He was an Irishman with a huge nose and he was a real bullshitter," recalled Harry over lunch at Lumes Restaurant during 2010. "Every Friday night, he would come to the Lyric Theater, go into the office, and take off his coat. Underneath he wore a vest. Do you know how many taverns there were in Blue Island at that time? There were fifty. McEvoy's wife had sewn fifty pockets in his vest and each one was numbered for a tavern. McEvoy would go around each Friday night and collect ten dollars from each tavern. Then he would come to the Lyric office and count it. That's five hundred dollars a week. Big money in those days."

It was big money for 28 years. That $500 every week for 52 weeks came out to $26,000 per year. Over 28 years, (providing there was not an increase in fees) that was more than $700,000 from taverns alone. By 1949, that wasn't enough and during June the city council approved the line item by which the liquor commissioner was a paid position at $1,200 per year. Later, it was increased to $1,800. Mayor Hart received tens of thousands of dollars more for serving as liquor commissioner in addition to his kickbacks from the tavern owners.

Mayor Hart's cut from the slot machines installed in establishments along Western Avenue is not known because the tavern owners and Babe Tuffanelli received their cuts too. Hart also was rumored to receive a cut of fundraising, which, if he could not get a higher governing body to foot the bill, was his preferred method of paying for big ticket items such as municipal garages—as opposed to raising taxes or borrowing. While he didn't often use it for infrastructure (because he seemed not to understand the need for improved infrastructure) Hart used it to purchase city vehicles and to remodel the city council chambers.

Said Jack Sinese, who worked at the First National Bank from 1948 until 1980 and who knew Mayor Hart, "The city bought a new fire truck. It did this by taking up a collection. It was common knowledge that a portion of the donations went to the purchase of the fire truck and part of it went to Hart." Sinese laughed at the recollection. "Then to save money, Hart cut out the salesman who had done all the work with him. Hart told the manufacturer that the city would buy the truck only if it knocked off the commission. To sell the truck, that's what the company did."

Sure it was a lousy thing to do, but it appeared to save the city money, which is what Mayor Hart always touted. Pay in cash. Pay as you go. Purchase only if you can afford it. The reality was that Hart robbed Peter to pay Paul and then he undercut Paul. Peter and Paul took a real beating under Mayor Hart.

"If you wanted something done in your ward, you put something inside an envelope for the aldermen," added Sinese. "If you needed something bigger, you contributed something extra for the mayor. It was just the way things were done."

Mayor Hart may have pretended to keep his list of candidates of liquor licenses in his desk drawer. That drawer absolutely served another purpose according to Jack Heuser, who during Hart's last years in office owned the Blue Island Nursing Home.

"I needed some favorable legislation for my nursing home, so I went to see Mayor Hart and explained what I needed. I knew Mayor Hart and he and my father were friends," Mr. Heuser explained.

"Mayor Hart listened to me. When I finished, he leaned to his left and opened the top drawer of his desk, but he didn't say anything. I didn't say anything either, but he kept looking at that open desk drawer.

"Finally I asked, 'What's that?' Mayor Hart said, 'Put the money in the drawer.'

“I was surprised. I told him, ‘I don’t have any money.’ Mayor Hart closed the drawer and told me, ‘I don’t believe I’m going to be able to help you after all.’”

Mayor Hart took payoffs for years and no one seemed to care because they believed the mayor was entitled to it and because he saved Blue Island. Okay, they needed to get things done too. Hart was open about receiving gratuities and reportedly joked about it. His standard explanation about how he made his money, still repeated today as part of his legend was, “We made our money from iron and steel. My wife irons and I steal.” If anyone ever was offended by the half truth John M. Hart told on himself (Verna Hart did not iron to earn money), there is no record of it. Larry Petta believes John M. Hart took bribes but that he did not make his fortune under the table.

“All of the money he made wasn’t from graft. Hart invested wisely. He made money from the stock market,” said Mr. Petta. “In the sixties, after John [Rita] was elected alderman, we were at Mayor Hart’s home one day. Hart said, ‘I want to show you something.’ He went over to one of those big old radios or TVs that people used to have in their living rooms, picked up a check he had laying around, and brought it over to us. It was a dividend check from AT&T stock for $32,000. That would be what, $300,000 today?”

If Mr. Petta is being magnanimous, it is understandable. Graft is in the eyes of the beholder. An old-time politician himself, Larry Petta believed that payoffs were part of the system, a/k/a just the way things were done. Many Blue Islanders from Mayor Hart’s era conceded that the legendary mayor took money, but they professed not to care because he never took it from the city. Mayor Hart really loved Blue Island, they all said. Some still say it. They say he took money only from people in business and from people who needed favors.

They are wrong. The proof is on the record.

Mayor Hart had been raking in cash for over two decades when, in addition to his salary as mayor and stipend as liquor commissioner, his name began appearing in the city council minutes under "Accounts Payable." For reasons never explained, almost every pay period from June 8, 1953 until he left office during April 1965, John M. Hart received an extra $25 from the city of Blue Island. Also on the record, his city treasurer, Emil Blatt, a friend and vacation companion who for years operated a paint store in Blue Island ("Blatt the Paintman"), beat Hart to the punch when he began collecting his extra $37.50 on March 12, 1951. Police officer George Farning also received an extra $25 for awhile, as did all of Hart's police chiefs, including Edward W. Boyd, who was added to the accounts payable at $25 per pay period after he was appointed chief of police on September 10, 1956. Building Inspector William Gerdes must have been in very good standing with Mayor Hart because Mr. Gerdes received an extra $50. As usual, all of the expenditures were approved by aldermen without question.

That's an extra $7,700 for Mayor Hart, which doesn't seem like a lot to steal. There also was the $4,443 for Emil J. Blatt and the $5,700 for Chief Boyd, and there were the years of payouts to Mr. Gerdes and Officer Farning. All of the payments were extras. Would you conclude these men and others went above and beyond the call of duty for their mayor because they were paid above and beyond their salaries?

Some were not paid in cash, however. There were many who were paid in water. How many? The exact number is not known, but many friends of the mayor received free water during the 28 years John Hart was in office. According to reports from tradesmen of that era and from city officials who succeeded Mayor Hart, the numbers were substantial. Many meters reportedly had to be installed on homes and businesses after John M. Hart was out of office.

Okay, the water wasn't free. It was paid for by the same people who paid taxes and who donated money for big ticket items such as fire trucks and new public works garages. Hey, somebody had to pay and it wasn't going to be John M. Hart or his cronies.

These reports and others debunk the portion of the John M. Hart legend that he took money, but he never stole anything from the city. He did, and he did not mind sharing a portion of the money and water—taxpayer money and water covered by the taxpayers—with some of his most loyal followers and friends. The truth about John M. Hart was that he accumulated wealth and spent on himself and his friends, not on the community, as if there were no tomorrow. For Blue Island, unfortunately, there would not be.

"Like It Was the Little Hole at the End of a Funnel"

Annexation and the City of Tomorrow

In 1927, brothers George and Herman Wille bought dump trucks and began to haul stone for a living. The Wille Brothers hauled gravel that was used to make roads in Monee and out of the way places that dreamed of being Blue Island when Blue Island was a big deal. Because there was no road building during the winter, eventually the Wille brothers also began to haul coal.

In 1935, the supplier informed his customers that he would not sell stone to anyone who did not have his own facility. That was when George and Herman Wille decided to rent space at 2124 Vermont Street. There was a lumber yard in the back and they wanted the space in the front. The landlord was in the process of evicting the lumber yard. It was the Depression. As in the cases of many other businesses, the owner of the lumber yard could not pay his rent. The landlord informed George and Herman Wille that she would rent to them, but they would have to take the entire facility, back and front. It was all or nothing for the Wille Brothers.

George and Herman went for it all and Wille Brothers Building Materials and Lumber was created. They hired lumber yard employees and took over where the previous owner of the lumber yard left off with one exception—Wille Brothers became a very successful enterprise.

Initially, the Blue Island City Council did not want to grant a license to George and Herman Wille for their new building materials company. When they applied for their business license and explained to the city officials about the type of business they would operate, the news got out into the community. Thereafter, a few people complained because they did not want coal sold there. In Blue Island, someone always is against everything. It was just the way things were done. Eventually, the City Council came around and on July 29, 1935, Wille Brothers officially was licensed as a Blue Island business.

"After the first year, my father had a profit of exactly $1500," said Elaine Lentz, who is George Wille's daughter. "That wasn't much money considering he had a wife and four children to support, but he worked hard and he made it."

He not only made it. He became a hero to the community in general and the east side of Blue Island in particular. During the 1930s and 1940s when times were tough, Wille Brothers allowed residents to purchase building materials and coal on credit. The deal was simple. The purchaser shook hands with one of the Wille brothers and promised to pay what he could when he could until the debt was settled.

"My grandfather lived on the east side. Every once in awhile when I was at his home, he would hand me some money and say, 'Take this over to Mr. Wille,'" recalled Andy Botte. "I'll tell you, George Wille was a hero to people on the east side. He helped out a lot of people. He allowed them to purchase things on credit that they otherwise would not have been able to afford."

After World War II, George bought out Herman. Eventually Roy, Richard, and Harold joined the family business and the name Wille Brothers came to stand for George's sons. In his early days with the company, Roy Wille was a truck driver who delivered loads of building materials. He remembers delivering to the undeveloped areas west of Blue Island during the 1940s and 1950s.

"The area along 127th Street west of Kedzie past Pulaski was onion fields. That land was flat as a table and the soil was perfect for growing onions," said Roy Wille. "I don't think Palos Heights and Palos Park were even developed then. There certainly weren't any houses out that way before 1935."

The year is important because 1935 also was when another prominent Blue Island businessman, realtor Christian Krueger, sold property near 123rd Street and Harlem Avenue to Robert Bartlett, who was a realtor and developer. Bartlett reportedly built six homes on the land that year.

Bartlett's development, called Palos Heights, continued to grow. The death of another prominent Blue Islander contributed. After legendary Blue Island gambling boss James Hackett died in June of 1937, his family sold property he owned there to Bartlett. The July 7, 1937 *Sun-Standard* headlines said, "Hackett Eighty and Other Lands Sold To Bartlett" and "Palos Heights Development Nearly Double By Acquisition of New Tracts."

Here's what the story said.

"Eventually a population of 6,000 or more people who will look to Blue Island as their trade center can be expected at the Palos Heights community in the vicinity of 123rd and Harlem, which was enlarged by the acquisition of 320 acres this week by its developers, Robert Bartlett Realty company [sic].

"The new tracts purchased are adjacent to the 886 acres already owned in that vicinity. A deal was closed which gives the development the 80-acre tract at the northwest corner of Harlem and 127th formerly owned by the late James Hackett of Blue Island and the 80 acres adjoining to the west from Orland State Bank and 80 acres to the north from the Busch estate. West of the Busch property, 500 lots were acquired from the Continental Illinois Bank and Trust Company."

If the first paragraph of that *Sun-Standard* article didn't fully express the isolationist attitude of Blue Island then and for decades afterward, the following certainly made it clear:

"The trading influence of this population of 150 or so already living there is already felt in Blue Island, the natural trade territory for this region just four miles west. The territory is within Blue Island's Community high school district. Moreover, the development is a natural outlet for Blue Island's own crowded condition." Translation: your money is welcome here. So are you if you'd like to shop here, open a business, or move here, and by the way, it will help if you are German. No, thank you, we don't want your new community to be part of our established one.

Just prior to that *Sun-Standard* story, the Blue Island City Council added insult to insult when it refused the request of the Robert F. Bartlett Building Corporation for fire protection for its 60 new homes. Mayor Hart and the aldermen received a letter from Bartlett vice president W. F. Brown on May 3. The letter was well-written and flattering to Blue Island. In the second-to-last paragraph, Brown wrote, "We feel that we are justified in asking you to consider this matter because of the number of families now in the Community [sic] which is only in its infancy. Since Blue Island is a logical shopping center for the residents of Palos Heights, we understand that the businessmen of your city have already begun to benefit by the purchasing power of the new families."

The letter was read at the city council meeting seven days later and immediately was referred to the fire committee. The official reason for denial from that committee, issued June 28, 1937 reads as follows: "After careful consideration the Committee [sic] recommends no protection be given due to no available water at Palos Heights." The fire committee was Henry J. Goesel, William J. Gerdes, and Thomas Hayes. Mayor Hart called the shots, of course, even that early in his tenure. As one unit (one of Hart's favorite terms), the city council was in full agreement. Aldermen knew this because Mayor Hart told them that they were in agreement. Yes, members of the city council were aware that Palos Heights, new as it was, actually did have water. They also were aware that John M. Hart did not want his police or fire service to go beyond the city limits.

What the story did not point out, much bigger than merely providing services, was what Blue Islanders have talked about for years—that the City of Blue Island could have annexed much or all of the unincorporated land to the west along the 127th Street corridor and north and south of it for miles. Palos Heights, which did not incorporate until 1959 and was available for the taking, extends as far west as Southwest Highway.

"Blue Island could have had everything all the way past Harlem," Roy Wille said.

Most of the land west of Blue Island was zoned for farming. Rapidly after World War II, land owners began to request of Cook County that thousands of acres in those unincorporated areas be reclassified industrial and residential. Then Cook County notified Blue Island and other nearby municipalities that there would be a zoning hearing. Some of the hearings were held in Blue Island, like the November 1948 hearing for the 4.5 acres at Kedzie and Wireton Road. The owner wanted the land rezoned from F (farming) to I-1 (light industry). Blue Island was not interested and today that land remains unincorporated.

During the July 23, 1951 city council meeting, Blue Island was informed by Cook County that there had been a request to rezone 61.5 acres at 131st Street and Kedzie from farming to industrial and that a hearing would be held. City officials were not interested, but during that same meeting, at the urging of Alderman Charles Mosel, the city council voted unanimously to "dis-annex" land at 139th Street and Kedzie. Then during January 1958, the city council declined a request to annex 143rd Street to 144th Street between California and Kedzie, which was known as Sunset Manor. At the time this book is published [2014], it remains in unincorporated Cook County.

During September of that year, William C. Groebe, field secretary of the Ridge Council, sent a letter to Mayor Hart, cautioning him to keep an eye on the unincorporated land west of Blue Island and offering his assistance should he desire to annex it. The correspondence was read during a city council meeting. Neither Mayor Hart nor the city council ever reacted.

In those days, most land owners didn't care which community gobbled them up. Some were in the market to rezone, then build or sell. Often when they sold, they sold to industry. Yes, some land owners did formally notify Blue Island that they wanted to be annexed. There were reports that during the 1940s and 1950s, the Clark Oil Company wanted its property annexed by Blue Island. Mayor Hart and the powers that were wanted no part of an oil refinery in their town.

"At one point, Clark Oil was begging Blue Island to bring them in, but John didn't want to do it," recalled Romie Palmer. "Blue Island would have gone all the way to Cicero Avenue on both sides of 127th Street, which we should have done. There was a woman who had twelve acres that butted Cicero Avenue on the east side. She wanted to come in like crazy. I don't know what John had against wanting to annex land," Mr. Palmer concluded. "I think the door was closed by the time Dick got in."

The reference made by Romie Palmer was to Mayor Richard Withers. The door to annexing the refinery remained closed to Mayor Withers and every mayor who succeeded him. When Donald Peloquin was elected mayor in 1985, Blue Island was desperate for tax revenue. Mayor Peloquin did everything but wash the cars of the plant managers (another elected official did that) to get the owners of the oil refinery to sign annexation papers. Eventually it became a running joke. There would be an event at which Mayor Peloquin and refinery officials would be in attendance. The mayor would announce, "I have a copy of the annexation agreement in my pocket." Yet it was not a joke or a wise crack. The mayor really did carry the annexation agreement with him. Refinery officials were polite, but they wanted no part, or rather to be no part, of Blue Island. The tax situation and the economy were drastically different. It would have cost far more for the refinery to be in Blue Island than in unincorporated Cook County even if the city supplied emergency services. So the response, when there was one, always was a polite, "No, thank you, Mayor Peloquin."

No one got the refinery land, but Alsip gobbled up most of the rest of the area. The Termundes—first the father and later the son—were astute businessmen besides being mayors of Alsip. Mayor Hart was the biggest deal this side of Chicago until the mid-1950s, but he was not a good businessman and he lacked foresight. Mayor Hart could have had all of the land he wanted for Blue Island and he received warnings from others beside Mr. Groebe as to what might happen if he did not act aggressively.

Legendary Blue Island attorney Franklin Klein, in a May 23, 1953 letter, warned Mayor Hart not to allow Alsip to annex land at 127th Street and Central Park Avenue for the Martin Oil Refinery. Mr. Klein said that if Alsip controlled the land that it, not Blue Island would have some control over the refinery and benefit from its tax revenues. "Citizens of Blue Island ought to do all they can to prevent annexation of this territory for refining purposes," he cautioned.

Mayor Hart did not heed the warning letter, which already was too late. Mayor Raymond Termunde of Alsip was interested and his community had been annexing nearby land for years. Blue Island had sent Alsip a letter of protest as early as June 1952, but this may have been for show. The only way Blue Island could have stopped Alsip was to beat it to the punch and Mayor Hart was not inclined to do so. As for the city council, it seemed to be so unrealistically arrogant that it believed that Blue Island still was the biggest thing this side of Chicago and that it could bully other towns. Alderman Arthur Stuebe recommended that a warning be sent to Robbins and Alsip not to annex any property to be used for oil refineries. The "we-don't-want-it-but-you-can't-have-it" letter was sent after Blue Island "disannexed" land that would eventually become part of Robbins, putting more land out of its control.

Mayor Termunde also was interested in the 21.5 acres east of Crawford from 123rd Street to 127th Street. He was so interested that Alsip annexed it, but only after Blue Island received notice from Worth Township that there would be a zoning hearing November 12, 1954 because the owners of the property, classified for farming in unincorporated Cook County, requested that it be reclassified for heavy industry. The west side was rezoned during August 1956. Alsip eventually took that too. Blue Island officials displayed no interest.

Had there been anyone in Blue Island city government with a working antenna, they would have picked up the signal that farming was out and heavy industry was in. Post World War II homes, highways, and factories were constructed and big machines were needed to do the work. The owner of 23.5 farm acres at 127th Street and Central Park Avenue petitioned during May 1955 for a zoning change to heavy industry. Blue Island was not interested in annexing the land. Nor was it interested in the 46 acres on the west side of Homan Street at 123rd Street. Each was in unincorporated Cook County and each request was granted. Each now is part of Alsip.

Suggestions and warnings to annex had been issued long before that communiqué from Franklin Klein. They came before Mayor Hart. Alderman Joseph Lentz urged annexation of unspecified land during a May 1936 city council meeting. Frank Kasten suggested annexation as part of his successful 1929 mayoral campaign. In fact, Kasten suggested annexing property to the west of Blue Island several times, but the city council never pursued it. Jimmy Korbakes believes he knows why Joseph Lentz was ignored, why Mayor Kasten could not fulfill his campaign promise, and why Mayor Hart never appeared interested.

"The Seyfarths and the other people who controlled First National Bank did not want it," said Jimmy Korbakes, whose family has operated a business on Western Avenue since 1915. "They never wanted Blue Island to change."

The late George Simon, a lifelong Blue Island resident whose cousin, Francis A. "Skunk" Simon, was one of Mayor Hart's drivers when he was a member of the police force, said the same thing. "Electromotive wanted to build its plant in Blue Island. The company has a site picked out near the refinery. The Kruegers and the Kleins wanted Blue Island to be their town. They controlled it by controlling land," said Mr. Simon. They never wanted Blue Island to be any more than a farm town, their town, with a shopping district. Nothing ever was supposed to change. Can you imagine what Blue Island would have been like if it had the Electromotive Plant?"

George Simon's recollection appears to be correct. During the early 1930, a front page story in the *Sun-Standard* announced that Electromotive was considering Blue Island for its new plant. A follow up story stated that acquisition of land was near and a deal for the new plant was imminent. That was the last ever mention, however. Electromotive built its plant in LaGrange.

Fred Mansfield, who rose through the ranks at First National Bank from loan officer to chairman of the board of directors, does not believe Henry Seyfarth was against annexation, however. Mr. Seyfarth was chairman of the board prior to Fred Mansfield and he knew him well.

"I don't believe that about Henry. He was very progressive and he believed in growth," Mansfield explained. "He presided over the growth of a law firm and of the bank, from First National Bank to a network of banks. He was prominent in associations. Henry was a very sharp guy who would have wanted Blue Island to be bigger."

Wherever it came from, eventually it was only John M. Hart himself who perpetuated that philosophy. The mayor adhered to it for different reasons, some stated publicly and others privately. Whenever anyone suggested that Blue Island annex land to the west of the city, Hart told them that Blue Island could not afford to provide police and fire services and infrastructure. According to attorney and longtime Calumet Township official, Larry Petta, Henry Gentile received this stock response. Mr. Gentile reportedly made the biggest and last pitch to Mayor Hart during the late 1950s. Henry Gentile was Mayor Hart's police magistrate for most of the 1950s and into the early 1960s when he lost a re-election bid to upstart Earl Ebers Jr. His father-in-law, police Captain William Hankey, drove for Mayor Hart and reportedly served as one of his bagmen.

"Gentile went to Hart and told him, 'You know, everybody to the west [of Blue Island] wants you to annex them.' Hart responded, 'We can't afford the police and fire services.'"

Said Harry Robertson, "I was in the presence of John Hart when he said [about the land Alsip eventually annexed], 'We can't afford the police and fire services and we can't afford the infrastructure.'"

As an attorney, Henry Gentile was legendary as a dealmaker and as a shrewd businessman who reportedly made a fortune in real estate. Should there be any surprise that after he was appointed attorney for the Village of Alsip during 1961 that Alsip aggressively annexed thousands of acres that Blue Island could have had.

"I always heard that business leaders urged Hart to annex, Blue Island could have annexed that Alsip land and the land west. We could have had all of Crestwood," said Mr. Mansfield. "Can you imagine what Blue Island would be like if it had that airport land that became a shopping center? We would have been another Orland Park."

Prior to the 1965 mayoral election, a minor part of Richard Withers' campaign platform was annexation. Minor became major after Withers defeated Hart and became mayor because Alsip announced that it was annexing land along the Kedzie Avenue corridor between 127th and 119th Streets and parts west. Some of this was known as "the Mulder property." It was 200 acres just west of Blue Island on Kedzie between 127th Street and 123rd Street. Owner Herman Mulder entertained ideas of allowing some of the property to be used for an amusement park similar to Riverview and requested that Cook County rezone it for this purpose. While it was a vast improvement over what Mulder had there for years—a combination garbage dump and hog farm—his amusement park idea alarmed residents of Blue Island and Merrionette Park, who did not want the clientele an amusement park would attract. Merrionette Park held public meetings against an amusement park. Blue Island Park Board president James Anderson and others in Blue Island attempted to thwart the project by suggesting Blue Island annex the land and add it to the Park District. Hart sidestepped this suggestion by announcing that Mulder had not requested that his property be annexed.

Mr. Mulder never did get his amusement park and Blue Island did not get his land. Everything was settled shortly after the 1965 election.

"Hart and Termunde had a handshake agreement that no one would annex land that separated Blue Island and Alsip, and I intended to honor the agreement," Withers recalled. "When I heard Alsip was going to annex it, I called up Termunde and said, 'I thought we had a deal that no one would annex that land. Termunde told me, 'That deal was with Hart.'"

Mayor Termunde's response caused Mayor Withers to look to the west to annex. This caused Alsip village attorney Henry Gentile to publicly warn Blue Island not to attempt to annex land that Alsip already had designs on. "We will oppose any land grabs," Mr. Gentile said in a May 6, 1965 *Sun-Standard* story. "We believe in orderly annexation, parcel by parcel, and will oppose any mass expansion by Blue Island."

It was a needless threat. Raymond Termunde and Henry Gentile had waited for John M. Hart's time to expire while preparing Alsip to act when it did. Because of Mr. Gentile's foresight and Mayor Hart's lack of it, Alsip was so far ahead of Blue Island that there was virtually nothing left to annex. During Mayor Withers' twelve years in office, the city council was able to add only a few small tracts after Alsip grabbed thousands of acres. Years later, Richard W. Withers talked about John M. Hart's philosophy.

"Hart once told me that he did not see Blue Island growing out. He saw it growing upward," Withers explained. "Hart foresaw Blue Island as one day having skyscrapers like Chicago. It really was what he believed."

Instead of skyscrapers, Mayor Hart actually championed "widescrapers." During his last ten years in office, Hart perpetrated a boom in apartment building construction. The long row of apartments that runs along the east side of Vincennes Road from 123rd Street is one example. So are the apartments on Fairview Avenue between Birdsall and Cochrane streets. So are the apartment buildings built by the Mueller twins, Arnold and Archer, on Burr Oak Avenue between Elm Street and Highland Avenue. The list goes on. Apartments were built all over town during this time. Multi-unit buildings failed to make Blue Island bigger, only more cramped, and it precipitated a myriad of problems over the years. Blue Islanders of today believe that allowing so many apartments to be built was almost as monumental a mistake as failing to annex large tracts of free land available for the taking.

"John was a good businessman, but not annexing land to the west was a big mistake," said Fred Mansfield, who was an officer of First National Bank for forty years and knew John Hart as mayor and customer. "I'll never understand that. Blue Island really could have been a big city if it had done that."

Told that Henry Gentile urged Mayor Hart to annex the land and of Hart's response, Mr. Mansfield added, "You have to project how you are going to make money if you are going to spend money. I know John's philosophy was pay as you go, but that land would have more than paid for itself."

"Blue Island could have been as big as Oak Lawn," added Roy Wille. Frank Amato Sr. agrees. Amato has lived in Blue Island since 1956. His family owned and operated businesses in Blue Island for eight decades. Amato believes Hart's problem was "funnel vision."

"John's problem was that he saw Blue Island like it was the hole at the end of a funnel. John Hart did not see the big picture. Blue Island could have been as big as Oak Lawn, but John did not want that. He walked down Western Avenue and saw the business district and thought he was king. People who suggested annexation saw the big picture. John didn't see the big picture," explained Amato.

Mr. Petta defended Mayor Hart. "That was the way he thought and it worked for him. John Hart was very successful," he said.

During the reign of King John I, Blue Island saw itself as the center of the universe. It had the railroads. It had Western Avenue, Burr Oak, Vermont Street, and Broadway—all roads that lead to Blue Island. There were fewer other places to shop and no quick way to those that existed. The Dan Ryan Expressway, I-57, and I-294 were decades away. Blue Island had lumber yards and auto dealerships, St. Francis Hospital and churches, bars, and gambling. All provided reasons to visit even if some of them weren't the right reasons. Blue Island had Klein's Grain and Feed store. Farmers always would need grain and other farm supplies, wouldn't they? The Libby's plant at 137th and Western was going strong. Blue Islanders believed it never would close. As the letter from W.F. Brown stated, Blue Island had a shopping district. Kline's Department Store opened during 1927 and Montgomery Ward would open a store here during 1940. Sears Roebuck would follow. They would be here forever. Why would they leave? Business was good and it always would be good here.

Why should Blue Island change? Why should it expand? Blue Island would be the center of the universe forever. Mr. Mansfield added more counterpoints. Some were on the money. Others were, well, you be the judge.

"No one could have foreseen that retail was going to go from Mom and Pop stores to malls and the types of stores there are now," he said. "Look at banking. In those days, each bank was a separate corporation. No bank could own more than 49 percent of another and all it could do was banking business. Now there are big banks with multiple locations who sell insurance and other things."

Perhaps the thinking of Blue Island officials was reflected most accurately by another event. During the October 8, 1956 city council meeting, a correspondence was read. It was an invitation for the mayor and aldermen to attend the American Congress Municipal Convention in St. Louis during November. The theme was "The City of Tomorrow." According to the correspondence, the city council was informed that "Experts will include the surgeon general, the urban renewal commissioner, members of Congress, and other experts. A general session will be devoted to community improvements, residential development, planning for industrial development, and how to sell community improvement to the public."

Alderman Stuebe moved that the correspondence be placed on file and the other aldermen voted unanimously to approve his motion. That is what and where it is today—on file. No one ever gave a report to the city council on any aspect of "The City of Tomorrow" because no one from the city council attended the convention. Blue Island was not to be a city of tomorrow. It was sentenced to be a city of yesterday.

While it is not *The Land That Time Forgot*, Blue Island seems to be *The Land That Refused to Accept Change*. Whether or not the first families of Blue Island issued the mandate that locked Blue Island into its fate is not known for certain. Wherever it came from, John M. Hart and his city councils embraced the philosophy, put it into place, and kept it there.

"A Serious Matter That Money Cannot Fix"

See a Hole, Fill It Up. Part I

John M. Hart was a veteran of the U.S. Navy and a self-proclaimed patriot. During World War II, he organized scrap iron collections in Blue Island that benefitted the war efforts. In April, 1942, he announced a deal with the Works Products Administration to sell the rails of the defunct street car line so that the Department of Defense could use the scrap to make machine guns.

Before buses replaced them as a method of public transportation, street cars ran from Blue Island to Chicago and also points south. "You could ride the street car all the way to Riverview," recalled Charlie Westcott.

According to legend and at least one published report, gangsters also enjoyed riding the street cars in lawless Blue Island. Whenever they and their female companions came here for fun, they waylaid the conductor and commandeered the street cars. On those occasions, booze flowed and guns blazed.

In Blue Island, the street car rails dissected Blue Island streets from Vincennes to Burr Oak to Western and south. The rails and the stress of vehicular traffic caused the streets to become bumpy and difficult to repair. The Chicago Interurban Traction Company ceased operation in 1927. Not all of the rails imbedded in the streets of Blue Island were removed, however. Those on Western Avenue awaited their turn because during the Depression, the city could not afford to remove the iron railings or repair the streets. Looking to remedy the situation, the always-calculating Mayor Hart, then in his second term, came up with the idea that would allow Blue Island to do both.

The WPA could purchase the rails at the going rate, Hart told the agency, if it removed them, hauled them away, and repaired the streets with concrete, which streets were made of before WWII. The government agreed—with one exception: it would not use concrete. The substance was more expensive and difficult to come by during the war. The repair of the streets would be completed with the newer substance called "asphalt." Because Mayor Hart never was one to look a gift horse in the mouth, he took the deal, which aldermen unanimously approved during the July 13, 1942 city council meeting. Approximately 354 tons of steel went to the war effort. The materials were used to make .50 caliber machine guns. Apparently the mayor believed this was such a good idea that during the next city council meeting, he announced a scrap iron drive. Thereafter, Department of Public Works trucks drove around town and picked up the donations and deposited them in a storage yard at Gregory and New Streets. In the first two weeks of the drive, the city picked up 20,000 pounds of scrap.

There were two products of these initiatives. One was that Hart was introduced to George Krug Sr. The other was the mayor's introduction to asphalt. Each would help John M. Hart make lots of money.

George Krug Sr.'s Company, Krug Excavating, was hired to remove the street car railings and haul them away. Mayor Hart and Mr. Krug seemed to be perfect for each other. According to the reputations of each man, they would let practically nothing get in the way of their making a buck. Street car rails and waste hauling just happened to be two endeavors upon which they collaborated.

"I was a heavy machine operator for Krug and I was on the crew that removed the street car rails," said Blue Island resident, Bob Peterson, during a December 2010 interview. "We removed the rails on Western to 127th Street and then east on 127th. We dug them up with a backend loader, cut them up with a blow torch, and put them on trucks. I don't know what happened to them after that."

While that's an interesting anecdote about the transformation of one Blue Island era into another, what Peterson said next is more insightful.

"I worked for Krug Excavating for five years. George Krug was a conniver. You could not trust him," continued Peterson. "He told all of his dump truck drivers that every day when they returned to the yard they had to bring back a load of black dirt. It didn't matter where they got the dirt."

Mr. Peterson's recollection is supported by run-ins Krug had with James Amato, whose scavenger service did business throughout the area and had headquarters in Blue Island. Amato owned the northwest corner of 127th Street and Kedzie and adjoining acreage north and west. According to his descendants, Mr. Amato's company used the area as a dump site and storage for dirt and other commodities. During 1946, George Krug Jr.'s drivers carried out their boss's mandate when they trespassed on the Amato property and either dumped without permission or carried away dirt. James Amato found out about it and told George Krug to stop. Krug's trucks continued to sneak in, however. According to the *Sun-Standard*, in 1947, he filed a lawsuit against George Krug and his company to force compliance. The matter was settled out of court.

"You could not trust George Krug," Peterson concluded. "Eventually he went to prison for income tax evasion."

What John M. Hart and George Krug Sr. did regarding the removal of the street car rails was not historic. Nor was anything else they conspired to carry out of the city or the area. What they brought in, starting in 1943 when they teamed up to begin a garbage nightmare, forever stamped their imprints upon Blue Island.

Seeds of the con job were planted during the September 13, 1943 city council meeting when a letter from Hugo Filippi, vice president of the Illinois Brick Company, was read into the minutes. Mr. Filippi requested that the company be permitted to fill its 119th Street clayhole with materials from outside of Blue Island. Actually Illinois Brick Company had no intention of filling any of its clayhole with "materials." The clayhole would be filled with garbage and everyone knew this. There was big money to be made if you had a large hole in the ground and you found someone to pay to dump garbage into it.

For years, residents had complained about stench, rats, and wind-blown debris. Each was a byproduct of the garbage brought to Illinois Brick clayholes and other local dump sites. During the Depression and into the 1940s, Blue Islanders also complained about the hobos who set up shanties and lived near 119th and Vincennes, which was also near a rail yard.

"They would come to our back door," said Caryl Tietz, whose father, Bill Frey, was a Blue Island alderman and Calumet Township official. "Sometimes my mother gave them handouts, but my father didn't like it. He was concerned one of them might do something. He told my mother to keep the back door locked."

Anything brought into Blue Island from the outside—whether stowed away on a boxcar or hauled in on a dump truck—was not welcome. The letter from Hugo Filippi to Mayor Hart that was read into the minutes of the September 13 meeting stated that Illinois Brick wanted to help Blue Island by bringing something in. And why not? The company had a perfectly good hole in the ground that was going to waste. The correspondence, reprinted verbatim, follows:

> *"It would be extremely desirable, as a community improvement, to have the clayhole filled and with that object in mind, we have, for many years, permitted the city of Blue Island to dispose of the refuse on the premises. The progress of filling, has however,*

> *been very slow and it would appear desirable that the operation be speeded up in the future.*
>
> *"We have been approached by interested parties who are asking for the rights to fill the clayhole with refuse, but we hesitate to grant such right until your views and those of your Council are made known to us. We believe that filling the clayhole will improve the property and represent a definite civic benefit. We also believe that the proposed dumping operations can be carried on in an orderly and acceptable manner.*
>
> *"We are advised by the interested parties that the matter will be presented today, to your City Council, for its consideration and are hopeful that your decision will be favorable with respect to granting permission to carry on the proposed dumping operations. Please be good enough to advise us concerning any action that may be taken with respect to the foregoing matter so that we may be fully informed in the premises."*

Aldermen voted unanimously for the matter to be turned over to the health inspector, the city attorney, and to the committee on streets, bridges, and alleys for a recommendation to the full city council. Aldermen Joseph Mausolf and Frey also suggested that because the dump already was a problem, rat poison be purchased for use there. While there is no record of rat poison ever being purchased (Hart was too cheap even for basic items), during the September 27 city council meeting, it was requested that representatives from Illinois Brick and those wishing to dispose in the clayholes meet with the health committee, streets committee, City Attorney Paul Schreiber, and Aldermen Frey and Mausolf, whose Sixth Ward was closest to the clayhole. A meeting was quickly held. In addition to the aforementioned, also in attendance were Aldermen Rauch, Schaller, Fiedler, Britt, Williams, and some residents.

Everyone on the receiving end lived in Blue Island. When those Blue Islanders heard that Chicago garbage would be hauled in by a Chicago refuse company, they must have become steely-eyed. Their jaws must have jutted and their necks must have bulled. There was no way Chicago garbage was coming into Blue Island. Outside trash was viewed the same as outsiders. Neither was welcome in Blue Island. *Hrrrmph!*

The jaw-jutted-neck-bulled denial became official during the October 11 city council meeting. The committee made its recommendation to the full city council. The vote was unanimous. There would be no dumping of outside garbage. After almost two decades of complaining, Blue Islanders finally had someone on their side. It was the men they had elected to be on their side—aldermen of the Blue Island City Council. Finally, Blue Islanders would now begin to get relief from garbage dumping at the clayholes. Who is next? Bring on the hobos!

In Blue Island, there is only one thing stronger than disdain for outsiders. It is even stronger than rat poison and garbage stench. It is the fix. The reminder that it always was in came during a scripted performance at the November 22 city council meeting. As much landfill as George Krug's company did in all of his years in business, he never laid it on as thick as he did that night. He did not have to, of course, because the fix was in. Mayor Hart paved the way when he introduced Krug, Fillippi, and the president of Illinois Brick, John Goodridge.

Mr. Krug announced that the landfill (garbage) would be completely sealed with layers of dirt or slag using "the New York Method" which was approved by the Army and which had been used successfully at LaGuardia Field, at the New York World's Fair, and in San Francisco. He added that there would be no oxygen or water in the solidly packed mass and as a result there would be no decomposition or fire danger.

On the other hand, George Krug did not explain whose army, provide proof that the New York Method had been used successfully on any of the projects or how the landfill at Yard 17 would defy science and nature by not holding water, by being fireproof, and by not decomposing. Was magic garbage to go into Yard 17 and lie just below the surface of their community into perpetuity?

With Mayor Hart as their front man, Goodridge and Filippi did not have to say anything. Yet they did have speaking roles in the performance, probably because there was so much money at stake. The executives went on and on without telling the city council or the public anything. They assured everyone that the materials dumped into the clayhole would not contain "but a certain percentage of specified refuse on each load or loads." They said that no refuse would be blown beyond the limits of the clayhole. They promised that obnoxious [sic] odors would not emanate from the premises.

Goodridge and Filippi were not precise on the certain percentage or specific on the type of specified refuse. They did not explain how they would prevent materials and odors from riding the wind down the streets and into the neighborhoods. Had they been able to perform these possibilities, they would have made millions doing so, as opposed to making bricks, renting out large holes in the ground to people with garbage, and misleading the public. Instead they were pied pipers who would bring rats in, take money out, and disappear.

Even the *Sun-Standard* was in on the deception, although the newspaper must have done so unwittingly. The story about the agreement between Illinois Brick Company and the City of Blue Island was favorable, but at least it spilled the beans on how the deal came to fruition. It was the council and the mayor. Translation: fourteen aldermen who always had been adamantly opposed to anything from the outside suddenly realized that outside garbage wasn't so bad. It is quite possible they may have changed their minds because someone gave them the price of a hat. Specifics of the backroom deal were not made public, although the *Sun-Standard* did say, "The council and mayor feel that the property values will be greatly advanced [sic] in that area and that the city will have a new industrial site for future expansion as a result of the contract."

The deal which gave Illinois Brick Company and its subcontractors total freedom to dump whatever they wanted came despite decades of complaints. Those who lived closest to the dump always were the loudest and most frequent complainers and they included aldermen. Those aldermen often brought their complaints to the floor of the city council and the problem was not outside garbage, but garbage in general. Local businesses were taken to task as violators whether or not they actually were. Recently Libby's had been asked to stop dumping at the clayhole.

Not that dumping was limited only to the Illinois Brick clayholes. There were other dump sites in and around Blue Island that also were quite active. Operating a dumpsite or a scavenger service could be lucrative. At the very least, either would keep you busy. Frank Amato went to work for his grandfather's scavenger business during the 1950s. Here's what he had to say.

"There was the clayhole at 119th Street and there were clayholes on each side of 123rd Street. On the east side of Kedzie between 123rd and 127th was Mulder's dump. Across Kedzie there was a hog farm. My grandfather owned the land at 127th and Kedzie where O'Connor Chevrolet was and where the school is. People did a lot of things that they shouldn't have been doing in those days. We'd do our pickups in the morning and then come back and do a paper burn. We'd set fire to whatever we picked up. That was going on in the early 50s. After they built the homes across the street (at Homan Avenue), the people who lived there would call the cops and complain, so we had to stop.

"In those days, there was no EPA, so whatever people threw out, we picked up and dumped. We had no way of knowing what it was. My grandfather dumped at the clayholes. Later we dumped there. Go out to the Meadows Golf Course to the spots where no grass will grow. It's still bubbling up in some places too. Who knows what kind of toxic stuff was dumped there? Who knows how long it's been there? That means there's still gas underground."

The landfill project at Illinois Brick Yard 17, only part of which actually was in Blue Island, took approximately three years to complete. Garbage dumping was not limited to Yard 17. It was expanded on land west and south and there was also a burn pit there. The garbage dumping deal at Yard 17 and its surrounding area was so profitable that during the 1950s Illinois Brick Company officials decided to repeat the process at its 123rd Street clayholes. To that end, they subcontracted to a man who may have been more scrupulous than George Krug Sr., but who was absolutely relentless in the pursuit of his one goal. That man was John Sexton, whose mantra reportedly was, "See a hole. Fill it up."

Not long after he was elected in 1937, after receiving numerous complaints from residents and pleas to do something about garbage dumping at the clayholes, Mayor Hart acknowledged that the dump was "a serious matter" with the disclaimer "that money cannot fix." This did not prevent him from working quite well with both George Krug Sr. and John Sexton, which only goes to show that the viability of solutions can be a matter of the interpretation of one little word. In Blue Island, the word was "fix."

How Black, Inc. Nearly Led to Red Ink

From 1955 until the day John Hart left office in 1965, contractor Robert A. Black just happened to submit the low bid on almost every major paving job and a few small ones posted by the City of Blue Island.

What a coincidence, but what are the odds? Mr. Black's company, Robert A. Black, Inc., submitted a sealed bid that was lower than the bids submitted by other companies virtually every time. You would have to be a mathematician to calculate the odds and don't forget that was over a 10-year period and there were multiple bidders for each project. Do you think the odds would be a million to one? Would you have been able to get odds in Las Vegas or from legendary Blue Island bookie Jimmy Staes? With what would you compare this unusual string of events? There was no state lottery in those days, so you could not say that Robert A. Black would have had a better chance of winning the lottery.

Blue Islanders of that era who paid attention knew there was a local lottery. Unofficially, there was a City of Blue Island Paving Projects Lottery as administered by Mayor John M. Hart and his assistants, City Engineer Allen L. Fox, Fox's successor, A.C. Dunn, and approved by the city council. Mayor Hart personally created all of the paving projects. First Mr. Fox and later Mr. Dunn created the specifications, solicited sealed bids, and reviewed those bids. Finally, Robert A. Black won the lottery, which was paid out in the form of paving contracts. During the last ten of John M. Hart's 28 years as mayor of Blue Island, Robert A. Black, Inc. earned $1,549,803.96.

If there was one thing you could say about Mayor Hart, it was that everything his administration did was completely transparent: anyone paying attention knew that the deals were dirty and the fix was in.

Bill Klein is a lifelong Blue Islander and scion of one of the community's first families. To go along with his heritage, he is a student of Blue Island history. "Robert A. Black," he said without hesitation when asked if he recalled the name of the paving contractor that Mayor Hart favored. "The story I heard was he and Hart had a deal. If things were slow or he needed some work, all Black had to do was call Hart and his company could do a paving job in Blue Island.

"Keep in mind that for years Blue Island was the only south suburb that was in the black. Blue Island had the money and Hart had credibility," added Mr. Klein. "He could get away with a lot."

The observation about communities "in the black" is not completely accurate, but it is close. Alsip under the mayors Termunde, first the father and then the son, was solvent even during the Great Depression. One reason was because their philosophy was to accumulate money, not spend it. Another was because they had a plan to acquire land and develop it, not pave it.

Would the "a lot" Mayor Hart could get away with include bid rigging and accepting bribes from paving contractors? For the record, there is no hard evidence that bids were rigged or that any money changed hands between Robert A. Black, Allen L. Fox, A. C. Dunn, John M. Hart, or any of his aldermen. On the other hand, as Bill Klein and others have said, John M. Hart was king in Blue Island and he could do whatever he wanted.

Well known is that after World War II when the composition of streets changed from cement to asphalt, communities became cash cows for paving contractors and the elected officials who received gratuities from them. Whether a contractor such as R. A. Black approached John M. Hart or the mayor known for "pay as you go" put the word out that you could go far in Blue Island if you paid him, is not known. Either way, for a ten-year period Blue Island was a boom town for blacktop. Streets were repaved and parking lots were created whether the projects were necessary or not. Case in point: the city purchased the east side of Gregory Street between New and York Streets and created a parking lot. It was paved, striped, and wooden barriers and parking meters were installed at a cost of over $100,000. Robert A. Black received the paving contract.

"It was a good deal for St. Benedict because the people from the church and school used the parking lot," said Mr. Klein. "It didn't turn out to be a very good deal for the city. People did not want to park there and walk to Western Avenue to shop."

That's why just a few years after Mayor Hart and his city council created that parking lot the land was sold to First National Bank. So the city spent over

$100,000 on asphalt that was torn up and thrown away. Not to worry if you were a paving contractor, of course. For John M. Hart, parking lots were like buses—another always seemed to be coming along. The one that came along next was installed across from the public library. Black, Inc. just happened to be awarded that contract too.

Larry Price had the same quick recollection as Bill Klein when the subject of the parking lot across the street from the Blue Island Public Library was brought up. Ironically, he was standing outside of the library when he said with a smile and without prompting, "Robert A. Black. He used to come into the drug store and visit with Hart. They would go in the back room and make their deals. Once when I was there, an associate of Black's came into the drug store and handed Hart an envelope.

"I didn't know the man's name. I just knew that he worked for Robert Black because I had seen him around," Price continued. "The same night he came into the store, I happened to go to the city council meeting. I was a Cub Scout leader and I took the kids as part of their civic project. Well, Black's associate was there, probably to make sure his company got the bid they'd paid for. When he saw me, he got very nervous. I'd seen him give Hart the envelope and I think he was worried I was going to say something. After the meeting, he came up to me and asked why I was at the meeting. I told him about the Cub Scouts. He appeared relieved. All he said was, 'That's a fine thing you're doing.'"

There were many deals during the Black decade which began for Blue Island on March 14, 1955. Out of the blue, Black submitted a letter of interest to the city council. Aldermen already had approved the plan for the parking lot on Gregory between New and York Streets. Business was booming in Blue Island and the Chamber of Commerce and other local organizations strongly endorsed the idea of off-Western parking. Some local organizations contributed to the projects. Black sniffed out this one and it isn't difficult to determine how. Prior to the deadline for bids, Black's letter of interest was co-signed by city engineer A.C. Dunn. When the four bids for the project were opened during the May 9 city council meeting, Blacks submission of $73,238.40 was the lowest.

What a coincidence! Mr. Black submitted a letter of interest by the man who received and opened his sealed bid, A.C. Dunn.

There were other coincidences and they also illustrate just how much money poured into the city coffer via water bills. Hart recommended during the November 7 city council meeting that a $100,000 "excess" from the Water Fund be transferred. Aldermen approved the recommendation. Some of the "excess" money was put into the Corporate Fund and some was invested in government bonds. On December 12, the city council approved a $1,000 transfer from the Water Fund to the Police and Employees Benevolent Fund so that the traditional Christmas bonuses could be awarded.

Regarding those funds, under Mayor Hart, the City of Blue Island had a fund for everything and he used them like the operator of a shell game. Per the mayor's requests, money frequently was shifted from one fund to another. The transfers always were done with the full knowledge of Hart's alderman, City Treasurer Emil Blatt, and his city clerks—first Louis F. Schwartz, then John C. Joens, and finally William G. Schimmel. The accounting firm that audited the city knew, as did City Attorney Paul R. Schreiber. Why did none of them ever publicly question the transfers, which sometimes were illegal? Was it because the mayor was infallible? Or did they believe that the public, not them, was the victim? In these cons, the taxpayer was the main victim, of course. The money—from taxes, water bills, licenses, etc.—moved from one fund to the other so often that while John Q. Public provided for them, he could not keep track of them.

Complicit silence was golden for Mr. Black, who on June 9, 1958 almost tripled his previous contract when his low bid of $194,474.41 was accepted for the "resurfacing and improving various streets in the city and parking lots." On June 22, 1959, R.A. Black again struck pay dirt when his $241,271.93 just happened to be the lowest of four bids for the new parking lot across the street from the public library. The number landed on black again April 25, 1960 when the Black bid of $114,581.78 was the lowest of the four contractors who wanted to repave "various streets." His company was awarded another "various streets" contract March 13, 1961 when his $197,439.28 was the lowest of four bids. The appropriately-named Black, Inc. outbid four other pavers and was awarded a "various streets" contract during the January 22, 1962 meeting. The amount was $190,441.86.

During the same January meeting, City Clerk Joens informed aldermen that the Corporate Fund balance was $85,314.50. This was very low. If the city was to pay Black, Inc. and all of its other contractors—and there were many others, including a few who were awarded smaller paving contracts—then large sums of money would have to come from elsewhere. Where was elsewhere? Paving projects were supposed to be paid for with motor fuel tax revenue, but Blue Island received an average of only $9,000 per month in motor fuel tax funds. One year's MFT would pay only half of what the city owed Black for one job.

Mayor Hart literally went to the well. Again he "borrowed" from the Water Fund, which was blatantly illegal since he never paid it back. Money generated from water bills, etc. was to go for water projects. This was ironic since Hart refused to use water money for two projects Blue Islanders had requested for decades: an improvement to the local water system that would solve Blue Island's water pressure problems and a new storm sewer system.

On March 25, 1963, aldermen voted unanimously to award Black, Inc. another contract to pave "various streets." Of the four sealed bids, his $131,444 was the lowest. Then, during the May 27 city council meeting, Black's company defied greater-than-usual odds when it was the lowest of seven bidders competing for a contract to resurface portions of 123rd Street and Chatham Street. His bid was $77,041.80. Perhaps more significant and definitely a foreshadowing, Alderman Richard Withers, a rookie in just his second meeting, voted against the contract. The vote was 13-1. Withers and Sal Rende were the only aldermen ever to cast votes against a Black, Inc. award.

Robert A. Black continued to bid with impunity. He was even more spectacular January 27, 1964. During that meeting it was the lowest of nine bidders for each of three separate street projects. That's a total of 27 bids—nine for each—and Black, Inc. just happened to submit the lowest for each project: $52,461.30, $27,391.50, and $14,177.05.

It should be noted that the companies Mr. Black bid against were reputable pavers who had been in business for many years. Among them were Gallagher Asphalt, Ready Paving, Chicago Paving Company, Alpha Construction, and George Hayes. If any of those companies ever fired the accountants or engineers who prepared their failed bids or complained to Mayor Hart or the city council of the coincidences by which Robert Black beat them on almost every major contract, there is not a record of it.

One month later, Robert A. Black again steamrolled his competitors. He was the lowest of seven bidders at $252,179.41, which earned his company its biggest Blue Island payday for resurfacing "various streets."

There are records of the bids for paving contracts and there is no explanation on the record as to why Mayor Hart recommended during the April 13, 1964 city council meeting that $80,000 in cash be transferred from bonds and deposit accounts into the Corporate Fund. Nor is there any record of questions from the aldermen who unanimously approved the request. An inspection of the ledgers makes conclusion academic.

The city had huge paving bills on the horizon. Tax revenue and motor fuel tax money were nowhere near enough to feed the monster. Mayor Hart had refined pay-as-you-go to the extent that he paid out so much that Blue Island could go under.

City attorney Paul Schreiber should have informed Hart and the city council that what they were doing—paying paving contracts with money other than motor fuel tax funds, grants, or specific set asides—was illegal as well as fiscal suicide. He could have done this publicly, during a city council meeting, or privately and it would not have been out of character for Schreiber to do so since he reportedly was completely scrupulous. Yet Mr. Schreiber, who had an impeccable reputation, did not bring to an end the string of deals between Mayor Hart and Robert A. Black. Instead the city attorney became an enabler when he gave Hart and his city council legal remedy. Schreiber drafted a resolution by which the city could loan money to itself. Aldermen responded by unanimously approving that $55,372.71 be loaned from the General Corporate Fund to the Motor Fuel Tax Fund "without interest" and according to the agreement prepared by Schreiber, "to be repaid as soon as money therefrom is available." There is no record that the loan was ever repaid.

Attorney Schreiber and Mayor Hart almost shared a complete history. "Young Paul Schreiber" came in with Hart during 1937. He did not cross the finish line with the legendary mayor, however. This was by choice. During the September 14, 1964 city council meeting, Mr. Schreiber resigned after 27 years as city attorney. According to the letter read aloud by Mayor Hart, Paul

Schreiber wished to devote more time to his law practice and to traveling. It would be logical to wonder, of course, if Schreiber had had enough of Mayor Hart's manipulations of money and bestowing of favors. There were all of those asphalt contracts and recently Mayor Hart had rammed through "spot zoning"—blatantly illegal legislation that would allow the building of an apartment complex near Memorial Park. At the conclusion of his last city council meeting, City Attorney Schreiber was given a standing ovation. Mayor Hart appointed Earl Ebers Jr. to the post during the September 29, 1964 city council meeting.

Just as Blue Island was running out of money, John M. Hart and Robert A. Black were running out of time. Two contracts awarded to Black, Inc.—one for $176,944.57 and another for $18,333.45—were approved by Mayor Hart's city council on March 8, 1965. Mayor Withers' first city council, which convened two months later, was stuck paying it.

The change at City Hall and the draining of its coffers apparently worried Mr. Black. He sent a letter reminding the city of its obligation and requesting an installment payment plan. The letter from the paving contractor was endorsed by "our engineer, Andrew C. Dunn," the double-dipping engineer for the City of Blue Island. It was the same A. C. Dunn who, like his predecessor Allen L. Fox, always received the sealed bids, announced them after they officially were opened, and made recommendations to the city council. It was the same engineer who was paid seven percent of every engineering contract. Mr. Black's take over ten years was $1,549,803.96. That means the engineers' cut was

$108,486.28. That was only for Black, Inc. contracts. There were other paving contracts. There were engineering services that did not involve paving. The engineers received seven percent of all things engineering that involved the city.

That reportedly wasn't anywhere near what Mayor Hart received, according to Larry Price.

"One day at the drug store, Hart pulled a wad of bills from his pocket. A one hundred dollar bill was visible. 'That's a nice Kansas City roll you've got there,' I told him sarcastically. A Kansas City roll is when there's a big bill on the outside, but the bills on the inside are ones.

"Hart fanned the roll so that I could see," Price concluded. "They all were hundreds. He bragged, 'This is my cut from Robert A. Black.'"

Said Lou Lombardo Jr. "Ernie Barzycki told me this story. There had just been a big paving job on the west side of Blue Island. After that, Mayor Hart showed Ernie a lot of money, two or three hundred dollars in cash. Hart bragged to Ernie, 'This is my cut of the paving contracts.'"

After his letter of reminder to the city, Robert A. Black did receive payment for the two jobs. They were the last jobs he got from the City of Blue Island.

"Not long after I became mayor, Mr. Black asked to meet with me," recalled Richard W. Withers, who was the salesman for his brother's audio visual company when he became mayor. "I had a sales call at the Chicago Board of Education, so we met at a restaurant downtown. Mr. Black told me that he wanted to continue with the same deal he had with Hart. I informed him that he was welcome to bid on any city road project and that he would get the same consideration as any other contractor who did so. I think that was the last time I ever heard from Mr. Black."

That is how Robert A. Black's lucky streak of obtaining city paving contracts ended. There were thirteen contracts and no one ever asked hard questions or complained about them.

For decades, Blue Islanders had asked questions and complained about flooding. Every time there was a heavy rain, basements in homes and businesses flooded, causing damage, loss, and aggravation. Residents and business owners suggested that the storm sewer system be improved. The aldermen sometimes sympathized and agreed. Hart always resisted. With one exception, he did this in three ways. The mayor ordered the city engineer or another city official to do a study and report back—or the mayor ignored the complaints—or if he became exasperated, he launched into a long speech about endless red tape and insurmountable cost. The last was a reminder to aldermen not to agree with residents and business owners, and it always worked.

Let's take a look at what happened regarding storm sewers not long before all of those paving contracts were awarded.

During the October 25, 1954 city council meeting, a petition containing the signatures of 168 residents was presented. The Blue Island residents who signed the petition requested that the city engineer determine what needed to be done to alleviate flooding; however, this time the mayor did something out of character.

Mayor Hart commissioned an outside engineer, Edwin Hancock, to inspect the city's storm sewers and issue a report to the city council. This took another seventeen months, but the question of whether or not to install new storm sewers finally was answered during the February 27, 1956 city council meeting. Mr. Hancock told the city council that Blue Island did indeed need a larger storm sewer system. He explained that the current system was not adequate to handle all of the runoff, which caused water to back up into homes and store basements. According to Mr. Hancock, residential sewers were only 37 percent imperious while commercial sewers were 85 to 100 percent imperious. Engineer Hancock explained that the area in greatest need was north of Burr Oak Avenue. As part of the solution, he suggested that a larger main sewer line be installed along the Rock Island Railroad right-of-way on Vincennes Avenue.

Mr. Hancock was thorough, precise, and helpful. He told the city council that the cost of a new, larger storm sewer line would be exactly $908,944. He suggested that if the city could not pay up front for new storm sewers, a bond issue and a small tax increase would handle the cost. There were 5,000 water connections in Blue Island. A 30-year bond issue could be floated if each home and business with a connection would pay an additional $11.50 per year.

That was enough for Mayor Hart. He thanked engineer Hancock and announced the findings would be "referred to committee." Thereafter, Edwin Hancock disappeared from Blue Island. He did not work for the City of Blue Island ever again. To this day, there is not one additional mention of him or his data, which also vanished.

What Hancock's report failed to mention was that when it came to the decision about new storm sewers, the opinion of only one resident mattered and he lived at 2428 New Street, literally at the top of the hill. It's not known if John M. Hart's basement ever flooded, but it didn't matter. Nor was it that John M. Hart didn't want storm sewers. He simply would not spend one million dollars to install them no matter how necessary they were. Spending anywhere near that much on an underground public works project, on something that voters could not see, was not politically prudent to Mayor Hart. Showing them paved streets and parking lots and keeping them in a Depression-era mindset made much more sense. He believed they were what kept him in office.

Blue Island would get its new, larger storm sewers (at a cost ten times greater), but the project would not start for another 19 years under another mayor. Until then, under Mayor Hart, there were paving contracts and payoffs.

Part IV

The Man Who Tried to Save Blue Island

And Those Who Helped Him

Richard W. Withers

Born June 12, 1931
Elected April 1965
Mayor Number 11
Served Until May 1977
Number of Years in Office 12

Richard W. Withers did not want to run for mayor. When he did run, he was not supposed to win, but he won anyway, in part because of another candidate. Then he did not want to run for a second term. After his third term, when he appeared not to want to run again, he did anyway and lost, in part because of another candidate. In between, Withers, the eleventh mayor in Blue Island history, tried to save Blue Island by returning to the paths of prosperity and fiscal responsibility.

Unlike his predecessor, Richard Wayne Withers was born in Blue Island. The date was June 12, 1931. His father, Robert L. Withers Sr. was a milkman whose dedication to hard work and quality service led him to a series of executive positions by the time he retired. His mother, Leona, was a homemaker who over the years worked part time at Kline's Department Store and at Staes Produce. Leona was the daughter of Peter W. Heintz, who was a prominent insurance man and public official.

"My mother was the number two student of Blue Island High School Class of 1927. "The top student was Robert Field, who became a doctor," said Richard W.

Withers. “Mom didn’t go on to college because she and my dad fell in love and married right after high school.”

Robert “Bob” Withers Jr. Richard’s older brother, recalled that their Uncle Ed Kruse owned the Old Style Inn, which was next to the Long Bar and across from the Grand Theater on the 13100 block of Western Avenue.

“Uncle Ed was a tavern owner and a bookie in the days before the Mob took over all of the books in town. In the back room of the Old Style Inn there was a big board with all of the day’s horse races on it. When I was a kid, I would go there and put beer bottles into cases for Uncle Ed and he would pay me a quarter,” recalled Bob Withers. He added, “My wife and I were married on Derby Day in 1949. The ceremony was in the living room of my parents’ home because we didn’t have a lot of money. Uncle Ed came up to me after the ceremony and handed me an envelope with $100 inside. He said, ‘Bet it all on Ponder.’ He was joking. Ponder had won the Kentucky Derby that day and paid 13 to one.”

According to Bob Withers, Uncle Ed’s partner at the Old Style Inn was Dan Chamberlain, who had been an engineer on the Panama Canal. His daughter, Ruth Chamberlain Seyfarth, was born in Panama.

“Dad came to Blue Island when he was 13 or 14 and lived with his aunt and uncle, Mayme and Jimmy Blouin. In those days it seemed like everyone in Blue Island either was related or knew each other,” said Bob Withers.

By the time the Depression hit, Robert Withers Sr. was married and had a family. Thereafter, the Withers Family experienced the same types of hardships just about everyone did. There never was enough money. Often there was not enough food or supplies. So while Blue Islanders may have had it a bit better than people in other communities, times were tough here too. Though the Withers family was not wealthy, it was resourceful. The family's most prominent characteristics were closeness, hard work, and a determination to be successful.

"My father was not able to finish high school because he had to go to work," said Bob Withers. "Yet we always had a place to live and we always had food. My parents always provided for us."

Robert Withers Sr. became a milkman because of a bit of misfortune followed by a tip from his father-in-law, Peter Heintz.

"A milkman died and my grandfather was the insurance man," explained Bob Withers. "My grandfather told my father that the Blue Island Sanitary Dairy needed someone to fill the position, so my father got the job. My father believed in service and in taking care of his customers. He grew that milk route. It got so big that they had to divide it into three and hire two more milkmen."

By all accounts, Robert Withers Sr. was a very positive person. Bob Withers tells a story about how things were so tough during World War II that even a positive person could get down on himself, however. Yet the story had a happy ending thanks to a person some might call an unlikely hero—John M. Hart.

"I sometimes accompanied my father on his milk route. One of the deliveries was Hart's Drug Store. During 1943, things were really tough. The war was raging, and every-thing was rationed. Well, my father always whistled a happy tune on his milk route, but one day just before Christmas he didn't. We were at Hart's Drug Store. John Hart noticed and he asked, 'What's wrong?'

"My father told him, 'My wife wants to bake her Christmas cookies, but she can't because we can't get any sugar.' My father was very disappointed. Hart said, 'Maybe I can help,' but he didn't explain how. When we finished and went out to the truck, there was a 100 lb. bag of sugar in the back of the truck. John Hart did that."

That was the same John M. Hart who later would be opposed by Richard W. Withers. Or would it be that Richard W. Withers was opposed by John M. Hart? There will be more on that contest later and you can be the judge.

All three Withers children—Bob, Richard, and Susan—grew up to be very successful. Susan had a great job as manager of the TWA ticket agency at the Sheraton Hotel in Chicago. She is still in the travel business in Kansas. Robert and Richard eventually went into business together in Visualcraft, a company that supplied audio and visual products to schools. The company was created by Bob. It was first located in the basement of his home and he was the only employee. At the start, it succeeded because of Bob's energy and determination and thanks to some good advice from—who else?—his father.

"In 1953, my father was a vice president of the Young Films Division of McGraw-Hill. My dad asked me if I'd like to go into the business. He said, 'We need someone to sell to schools in this area,'" explained Bob Withers. "My father was 'Salesman of the Year' and his boss came in from New York to present him with the award. The boss told everyone at the presentation, 'Robert is the only one of my salesman who does not have a college degree.' Dad quipped, 'I don't even have a high school diploma.'

"Dad's boss offered me $52 a week to sell film strips to schools. I didn't know it then, but that was $52 against the commission," Bob Withers emphasized. "That is how Visualcraft was created. I was a distributor of McGraw-Hill School products.

"I remember sitting in my car with my dad in front of First Lutheran School. It was my first sales call and I was nervous. Before I went inside, my dad gave me some simple advice. He said, 'Give your customer service. That's all you've got.' I've never forgotten that.

"The first three years in business were tough. After that, things started to improve. When Dick returned from Korea, I asked him to join me, but he was still getting over the effects of the war. He was on the [front] line for thirteen months and wasn't the same person when he came back. Dick decided to use what he learned at the University of Illinois to get a job as an engineer at Argonne National Laboratory. So I grew the company and it became successful. It never had a year in which it didn't make money or increase sales. At one point, that little company supported 78 people."

Eventually, while he was still at Argonne, Richard Withers asked to become a partner. Bob agreed and Richard bought in. "The company wasn't ready to support two full-time employees, so I worked at Argonne during the day and during the evenings for Visualcraft," said Richard Withers, who also has great memories of growing up in a strong, close-knit community that included family, friends, competition, and work ethic.

"We lived upstairs from my grandparents on Union Street. That was across the street from the Boza Family. That's how I met Tom and Chuck Boza," recalled Withers. The Boza brothers and Richard Withers became lifelong friends. When Richard Withers was in high school, his father took a job out of town. Richard Withers often stayed with the Boza Family, whose home was across the street. Tom Boza eventually became an alderman in the Withers administration. Chuck served on the civil service commission.

"We were pretty close and spent a lot of time together," said Chuck Boza, who recalled how one of the gang would rally the troops for socializing. "One of us would stick his head out the window and shout across the street, 'Throw on some aftershave! We're going out!'"

When Richard Withers was a boy, he also accompanied his father on his milk route. That was how he came to know Blue Island, its homes and businesses—and John M. Hart.

"The Blue Island Sanitary Dairy was on Irving Street next to Patsy Ann Cookies, which was owned by Cookie Shay. When I was eight years old, I delivered milk with my dad. We delivered milk to Hart's Drug Store where they made those great milkshakes. So I knew John even then. Hart was friendly to me and everybody else.

"There's more. It goes back farther," Bob Withers added. "My grandfather, Peter Heintz, urged Hart to run for mayor and was instrumental in getting Hart elected. He also was Hart's police magistrate." Hart pointed out one of those facts to Bob Withers years later when his brother was a candidate for mayor. The story also illustrated just how competitive the Withers Brothers are.

"It was at the American Legion. Hart came up to me and said, 'Your grandfather got me elected. Now your brother is trying to get me out of office.' I told him, 'Let's hope he does.'"

"My grandfather was police magistrate under Hart for only one term because he wouldn't look the other way for Jim Hackett. There was some kind of legal matter or court case against Hackett's son or there was a problem related to his business," explained Richard Withers. "Hackett had a lot of power and he told my grandfather that if he didn't go along, he would not be police magistrate again. My grandfather refused and next election, Hart got himself another police magistrate."

What happened to their grandfather wasn't what motivated the Withers brothers to become involved in local politics. There were plenty of other incentives, however. For example, for as long as they could remember, Robert and Richard Withers knew what the community lacked. One of those deficits was water pressure, which sounds insignificant, especially seventy years later. Yet if you had to bathe or cook and the water only trickled from your tap as it often did in Blue Island during the Hart Administration, it was a very big deal. Neither of the Withers brothers ever forgot.

"During my growing up years, my family lived in the flat upstairs from my grandparents. If we wanted hot water upstairs, we had to bang on the pipes. You had to let the people downstairs know you needed water. If they were using water downstairs, you'd only get a trickle upstairs," recalled Withers. "It was like that all over town."

"It was a two-story flat. My grandparents lived downstairs and we lived upstairs. If we wanted steam [heat], we had to bang on the pipes to let them know," said Bob Withers.

For 28 years, Blue Island residents complained about water pressure to Hart and the city council. Some of the aldermen were sympathetic and proposed remedies. Mayor Hart always resisted. It was money-driven politics. John M. Hart hated spending the city's money, *his money*, on anything he thought frivolous or impractical, (i.e., projects that would not benefit him either financially or politically.)

"After I became mayor, before we approved the water tank project on the north side of town, I spoke to Hart," Richard Withers said. "He told me, 'Don't waste your time with anything underground. People won't notice it and it won't get you re-elected.'"

Mayor Richard W. Withers did proceed with the project and he considers the installation of the above-ground water tank at 121st Street and Highland Avenue to be one of his greatest accomplishments as mayor because it helped provide adequate water pressure to Blue Island residents, businesses, and for emergency response.

"There was a gauge at the fire station that measured the water pressure in Blue Island. If the needle on the gauge went below a certain point, the water in the community had to be shut off because if it wasn't, there wouldn't be enough water to fight fires," recalled Richard Withers. "I remember after I became mayor and before the water projects were completed when there were concerns about water pressure during hot weather. I was at the fire station watching that needle because I was the one who had to make the decision to shut off the water. Can you imagine the reaction in Blue Island if I had to shut off everyone's water? Fortunately, it never came to that."

That was a few years after Withers decided to enter local politics because of guess who? Yes, it was John M. Hart and there is a story behind it.

Richard Withers graduated from Community High School in 1949. He attended the University of Illinois at Champaign-Urbana until he was drafted into the army in January 1952. He served in Korea, was promoted to staff sergeant, and was discharged in October 1953. That may sound uneventful, but it wasn't.

"I was in school at the University of Illinois and it was suggested that I join ROTC. The recruiter told me, 'If you don't sign up, there's a good chance you'll be drafted.' Well, I didn't want to join ROTC. I could have avoided the draft if I signed up, but my friends Tom and Chuck Boza were in the service and I did not want to do that to avoid the draft. So I told the recruiter I'd take my chances. That was not long before Christmas," recalled Withers. "When I was at home during Christmas break, I received my induction notice. By January, I was in the service."

While in the army, Richard Withers and his unit experienced one of the scariest and most unusual events of the war.

"My unit was at the front line when Singman Rhee opened all of the prisons and set the inmates free. The inmates rejoined the population. They and the Korean and Chinese armies swarmed and surrounded us on three sides. Just like that, we went from being at the front line to being behind it. The only way out was over a mountain and across a river." Even while discussing serious subjects, Richard Withers enjoys a quip and does not mind taking a shot at himself. He added, "I was a pretty good swimmer growing up. Had the enemy attacked, I had a plan. I was going over that mountain, into the river, and I was going to swim that river to escape."

Serious again, Withers added, “It was a tense situation. We were trapped there for weeks and the only way the army could get supplies to us was to drop them in by air.”

The army eventually managed to rescue that entire unit from its precarious position. During his tour of duty, Richard Withers was promoted to staff sergeant. He completed his two-year hitch on October 16, 1953, returned home, and married his high school sweetheart, Shirley Faden, in 1954 at Grace Methodist Church. He also went to work at Argonne National Laboratory in Lemont, in the engineering division, where he wired consoles used to operate reactors and he took a few courses at the Chicago Art Institute. While life in prosperous post-war America might have been pretty good, Richard W. Withers, now an adult with a family and eyes wide open, did not like what he saw going on in Blue Island under Mayor Hart.

“I never had a personal beef with John Hart, but I didn’t think he should be mayor,” Richard Withers explained. “I came back from Korea, saw what was going on here, and said, ‘This is bullshit. Let’s see what we can do to get Blue Island straightened out.’ I tried to get some people interested in changing things, but I was unsuccessful. That was one reason I ran for alderman.”

The man who eventually got him on the path to helping get Blue Island straightened out was not the incumbent mayor. John M. Hart provided problems, not solutions. Robert Schrei, another local politician—a gregarious man with a big, bright smile and a soothing voice—was the impetus. Mr. Schrei was active in Calumet Township politics. He served for awhile as township committeeman and he wanted to be Blue Island mayor.

Blue Island history was shaped by a chance encounter at the Montgomery Ward's store here.

"It would have been early in 1961. I went into Ward's one day to buy some snow tires. The guy selling the tires said, 'What do you think about the election?' I asked, 'What election?' He said, 'For mayor. Hart's running.' I told him, 'I hope he loses. He's been in there too long.' The salesman said, 'Well, I'm running!' That salesman was Bob Schrei."

Robert Schrei convinced Richard Withers to help him with his campaign. At that time, however, there weren't enough Blue Islanders who felt like Richard Withers and Robert Withers, who also joined the Schrei campaign. Mayor Hart trounced Robert Schrei and the Withers brothers mistakenly believed they were through with politics.

"I said to my brother, Bob, 'That's it for me. No more politics,'" Richard Withers recalled with a chuckle. By that time, Visualcraft was out of Bob's basement and in an office on the 2700 block of Union Street. What Richard Withers did not foresee was that Mayor Hart would force him to reconsider.

"My brother and I campaigned for Bob Schrei. That was a no-no and it cooked my goose with Hart. One day Harry Harczak pulls up in the squad car. It wasn't Harry's idea. Harry was a gentleman and he seemed embarrassed about it. Hart sent him. We had some decorative rocks in front of our office. Harry told me that the rocks were against the law, which they were. We didn't know that, but no one brought it up until we opposed Hart.

"At that point, I started looking for someone to run for alderman. I must have talked to a dozen people, but no one wanted to run," Richard Withers explained. "So I told my wife, 'If I can't get anyone, I'll do it myself.' She said to me, 'You're nuts!'"

"After Hart sent Harry down to our building, Dick couldn't find anyone to help him. He tried Louie Lombardo, who was the alderman, but Louie wouldn't help," Bob Withers recalled. "We were in the supply room of our little office building on Union Street and Dick told me, 'I can't find anyone to run for alderman.' 'I'm going to run.' I said. 'Good! Let's get going!'

"One of the first things we did was talk with our cousin, Jimmy Withers, who was an alderman in Champaign," Bob continued. "Jimmy gave us some great advice. He said, 'One thing you must do is go out and meet every single voter.' That's what Dick did."

Richard W. Withers beat Louie Lombardo by 89 votes to become one of the Fourth Ward aldermen. That was the election of April 1963. Prior to that time, Richard W. Withers and John M. Hart had been passive, long distance opponents. Early within their first year together on the city council, they began to butt heads. This was because, as the rookie alderman quickly learned, the mayor's management style was to abruptly bring projects and purchases to the city council with little or no explanation, present them for approval, and bully any aldermen who opposed him. During the 26 years before Withers was elected, it was just the way things were done. Alderman Withers suggested a transparent process. During the June 10 city council meeting, he proposed that the city council pass legislation that all bids over $500 be held for 24 days for review and that bidders submit no-collusion affidavits. Mayor Hart's first reaction to the proposal was to bristle.

Then he grumbled. Finally the mayor decided his best response was to ignore the proposal. The suggestions by Alderman Withers were not approved.

Things became heated between the long-time mayor and the rookie alderman during the October 28 meeting. Mayor Hart informed aldermen that the city would purchase an Elgin "Street King" street sweeper at a cost of $13,450. There were to be no bids, just a vote to approve the mayor's request. Alderman Withers did not get on board, however. He drew Hart's ire when he questioned him on the purchase.

"We knew in advance the city needed to buy a new street sweeper. During that meeting we learned it was going to be done the John Hart way—without bids. Prior to that meeting, I asked, 'What about bids?' and Hart replied, 'We don't need to do that,' explained Withers. "Well, I happened to attend a convention after that and I brought a bid back to the next city council meeting, but Hart wouldn't acknowledge it.

"After Hart brought up the purchase of the street sweeper, I suggested that the purchase be put out for bid to get the best price. Hart waved me off. He said, 'We don't need to do that.' Then he tried to ignore me," Withers explained. "I'd read Roberts Rules of Order which said that anyone who wanted to be recognized during a meeting has to stand up. Well, Hart was ignoring me. So I stood up so that he couldn't ignore me."

"I was at that meeting," said Bob Withers. "Hart did not want bids, but Dick had gone out and gotten a bid. When Hart brought up the street sweeper, Dick stood up and said, 'I have a bid we should consider.' Hart told Dick,

'Sit down. We'll get this done on a roll call vote.' He ignored Dick. That was it."

Some people describe Richard W. Withers as stubborn, especially when he thinks he's right. Others explain it as competitiveness or even righteousness. Whatever Withers is, he's never been one to back down. When he continued to challenge Mayor Hart on the big ticket purchase, the mayor lashed back by verbally attacking Richard Withers and his family during the October 28 city council meeting.

"Hart got personal. He was a pretty rough guy, but I wasn't going to take that," Withers recalled. "I was still standing when I pointed my finger at him and said, 'If you ever attack me or my family again, you're going to think you grabbed a wildcat by the tail!'"

The *Sun-Standard* reported a much more civil version of the exchange in its October 31 edition. In the story, Richard Withers was referred to as "the dissident alderman." He told Mayor Hart, "Expenditures of that size should be by competitive bidding as a possible taxpayers' savings."

Mayor Hart responded that he "was not against competitive bidding, but in this instance the matter had been thoroughly investigated and he was sure the transaction was a good buy." Among John M. Hart's tactics were to embarrass and intimidate. He tried them on Alderman Withers when he added, "I've been elected seven times for saving the taxpayers' money and was saving it long before you ran for alderman."

Mayor Hart was a bully. He was very good at using confrontations and insults to make opponents back down. On that occasion, however, the mayor must have understood that he'd crossed the line. According to

Richard W. Withers, Mayor Hart never gave him trouble publicly after that. Privately, Mayor Hart must have fumed. Not only was an upstart alderman challenging him, after decades of the *Sun-Standard* covering for him, the newspaper had become a critic.

Nor was Richard Withers the only young lion with whom King John I had trouble. Third Ward alderman Sal Rende preceded Richard Withers on the city council. He and the mayor sometimes were enough at odds to the degree that they also exchanged barbs. When they did, the city council meetings were far from dull. The March 28, 1963 meeting had been one such event. During that meeting, Alderman Rende became one of the few aldermen ever to question a John M. Hart paving contract. Sal Rende wanted to know which streets would be paved according to the $130,000 contract awarded to Robert A. Black, Inc. Hart told Alderman Rende that he should have known the streets before the bids were let.

"If you had any brains, you'd have asked for the information at an earlier time," Mayor Hart acidly said to the alderman. "You're just asking questions to make a showing before some of your constituents. The east side must have been hard up for an alderman when they elected you."

"I'm going to continue to ask questions whenever I please, no matter what you say," Sal Rende shot back.

Because of the railway stations, parking has always been an issue in the Third Ward. During the July 8, 1963 meeting when Alderman Rende questioned cars parked on parkways in his ward, Mayor Hart ripped him without addressing him personally. According to the *Sun-Standard*, "Hart said that one alderman is not mentally, physically, or financially big enough to oppose him." The mayor concluded, "That question is a silly one. I'll give you an answer back in the same vein."

Theresa Rende, Sal Rende's widow, still lived on the east side in 2013. According to Mrs. Rende, Hart did not like to be questioned and he rejected every proposal that involved spending money on anything that didn't directly benefit Hart.

"My husband told Hart, 'We need to spend money to make improvements in the town.' Hart told him, 'We don't need to spend money. This is a retirement town.' My husband replied, 'It's going to be a dead town if you don't spend some money.'"

Mrs. Rende's assessment of Mayor Hart is not flattering.

"We got nothing down here in the Third Ward. It was like we didn't exist," said Mrs. Rende during a March 2012 telephone interview. "Hart thought he was king. He thought he owned the town."

At that time, Dale Elton was a member of the Calumet Township Democrats. Elton agrees. "I didn't live on the east side, but I remember what was going on. They couldn't even get a stop sign down there. To Hart, the only thing that existed was the business district."

Chris Disabato, who served as alderman, city treasurer, and mayor, agrees. "I confronted John Hart on the street one day. We couldn't get anything done on the south side or the east side. Mayor Hart was not interested. He spoke to me as if I didn't exist. I remember being so mad. That conversation was one of the things that got me interested in politics."

Theresa Rende believes part of the problem was a perceived class warfare: the People on Top of the Hill vs. the People Below the Hill.

"The people on the top of the hill resented Italians," said Mrs. Rende. "If you were Italian, they didn't want you to live up town. When my husband and I were looking for a new home in Blue Island, a guy who was a realtor here for 50 years told us, 'Why don't you buy on the east side with the other Italians?'"

Opponents of Mayor Hart and fans of good government and accurate reporting had allies in whoever wrote under the pen names Watchful Watson and Wiley Watson. "Watchful" may have been *Sun-Standard* editor Wes Volp. "Wiley" was Hank Savino.

Watchful Watson's column "While Wiley's Away" appeared in many editions for years, as did "The Town Crier" by Wiley Watson. In them, the Watsons wrote about any and all things timely, from local news to international events, although their submissions rarely appeared in the same edition, perhaps because they played off of each other. Often they used a few paragraphs to comment on what Hart was doing. The week after Alderman Withers suggested that the purchase of a street sweeper be put up for bid, Watchful Watson wrote:

> *The honorable mayor had me worried recently since everything seems to be going so smoothly at City Hall. It could not have been all moonlight and roses recently in Springfield since in his inimitable way he got back in stride with Alderman Withers over a new street sweeper.*
>
> *Such sensitivity!*

> *The man just asked if a better price couldn't have been obtained than the quoted $13,450. The best way to show it to be the 'good buy' that it was claimed to be was to have received bids in excess of $13,450, then everyone would have known it was a 'good buy.'*
>
> *What criteria they may have used I do not know. I am not certain, but so far as I can recall, the City could not have purchased more than a couple [sic] sweepers in the last six or seven years, if not longer. It certainly could not have been predicated on past experience.*
>
> *Evidently, Alderman Withers was not convinced or he certainly would not have raised the question.*

The Withers and the Watsons weren't the only dissenters. Since the late 1950s, there had been grumblings around town that Mayor Hart was out of touch, that he was too cheap, and that some of the things he did embarrassed the community. Watchful Watson voiced those concerns by chronicling the mayor's shortcomings. An issue Watson shined the spotlight on Mayor Hart was streetlights. To save money, the city turned off the lights on one side of Western Avenue between 119th Street and 139th Street. Members of the business community, among others, saw this as a detriment to business and a negative reflection on Blue Island. They complained to aldermen. One of the aldermen, Art Schaller, brought the subject up to the mayor during a December city council meeting. The alderman had the audacity to suggest that all of the lights be turned on. Mayor Hart attempted to bury the suggestion when he referred the matter to the electric and gas committee.

According to the *Sun-Standard*, during the February 10 city council meeting, Alderman Schaller again brought up the streetlights. He asked the mayor why the committee had not made a determination on his request. Hart was an atheist, both personally and politically. That is, he did not believe anything could be resurrected if it was not to his liking or benefit. This included requests by aldermen. In an effort to intimidate Mr. Schaller and create hostility between him and his fellow aldermen, Mayor Hart snapped, "I don't know. Why don't you ask them?"

This tactic was successful only in that it created chaos because, according to the *Sun-Standard*, "a heated discussion" followed between the mayor and aldermen. "Name-calling ensued." The mayor attempted to settle the matter by declaring Alderman Schaller out of order and threatening to have him removed from the meeting. The alderman stood his ground, however. He said that he was tired of disparaging remarks from businessmen and out-of-towners, the latter of which compared Blue Island to a hick town that can't afford lights. Alderman Schaller pointed out that it would cost the city only $95 more per month to have all of the lights on.

"In 1952, the city paid $148,883 for the lighting system on Western Avenue and it seems nonsensical to use only one-half the lights in order to save the city an additional $95 on its light bill," Mr. Schaller said.

If the matter was settled by the city council, there is no record of it. Eventually all of the lights were turned on. In a piece that appeared February 20, Watchful Watson took impractical and indecisive aldermen, but especially Mayor Hart to task.

> *Alderman Schaller makes a very good point when he states that if we are to burn only half of the Western Avenue lights, we should only have installed half the number of lights at half the cost. Unquestionably, this was not the engineering recommendation. Still, they do serve a useful purpose since we have poles to hang our Christmas ornaments on once a year.*
>
> *The most practical solution, which would require no electrical current at all, (happy day), involves but a little more concentration and effort on the part of those so economically-minded. They, like Joshua, could just command the sun to stand still.*

Watchful's harshest criticism of Mayor Hart came long before the 1965 mayoral election and it was precipitated by Hart's stinginess. The mayor decreed that his police and fire departments were not to respond to emergency calls from outside of Blue Island. Because of this order, on Sunday, September 1, 1963 a man died in a fire just seven blocks from the Blue Island firchouse. Firefighters from Blue Island, Alsip, and Dixmoor reportedly waited more than an hour before responding to the blaze at 3029 Vermont Street, which at that time was in unincorporated Cook County. According to the story written by Darlene Danaher that appeared in the September 5 issue of the *Sun-Standard*, "The charred body of Harry F. Davis, 48, was removed Monday morning. Burned beyond recognition, identification was made through a belt the victim was wearing at the time."

Mayor Hart defended his order and put a cost parameter on human life when he asked who would have paid in the event any of the fire department's $40,000 worth of equipment was damaged, if firefighters were injured, and the $500 he contended it cost for Blue Island emergency personnel to respond to an out-of-town call?

"Mayor Hart told us that the fire department was not to answer calls outside of Blue Island and that was it. We had no choice," said William "Sparky" Holdefer, a longtime Blue Island firefighter and deputy fire chief under Mayor Hart. "He didn't want to pay for the calls."

Watchful Watson usually covered a multitude of topics. His September 12 column was devoted entirely to the tragedy. In the column, he took King John I to the woodshed. The piece began:

> *THE HONORABLE Mayor's zeal for protecting thc public wealth verges on the ridiculous at times. It would be downright ludicrous if it weren't so tragic.*

In later paragraphs, it continued:

> *To me there is no question but that a fire department exists but for one purpose, to put out fires. The fire engines are purchased with that*

> *purpose in mind. They are not display pieces, and they are not toys.*
>
> *While it may be true that there was no legal duty to respond to the call, there certainly was an overwhelming moral obligation to do so. It is in keeping with our American tradition and heritage to help those in imminent peril.*
>
> *What would you think of a doctor who passed up an accident or disaster because there weren't any of his patients in the holocaust? What would you think of the seaman standing in his lifeboat with a life jacket and line in his hand but wouldn't throw it to his dying companion because he wasn't in his union; or of a mother watching a baby starve because it belonged to a different woman?*
>
> *It's that uncomplicated.*

Later in the column, Watchful refuted the mayor's contention that it came down to money when he wrote:

> *I might also add that $40,000 worth of equipment sent too late is worthless. We, the people, pay the firemen's salary. They get paid whether they are in the firehouse or at a fire. The cost of the volunteers wouldn't break the city. One more fire*

> *will not antiquate the fire engines. Fighting fires is a dangerous calling, and on occasion firemen do get hurt and/or killed. The firemen themselves know this, but in their dedication to their duty they fight the fires anyway. They wouldn't have it any other way!*
>
> *Equipment does get damaged from time to time. Again, the bill is paid by us, the people. So far as I know, there is no responsibility, obligation, or duty for any public official to cover these costs with his personal check.*

Mayor Hart defended himself by stating that no one in the area where the fire occurred ever requested fire protection services. Bessie Savich, who lived at 13119 Sheridan Road, refuted Hart's contention. A copy of her letter to Cook County Board president Seymour Simon appeared in the September 12 issue of the *Sun-Standard*:

> *"I hope you will read this letter and give it considerable thought. I am not writing just for myself, but for all the homeowners in the area between Sheridan and Sacramento St. This is in regards to the column that appeared in the SUN-STANDARD September 5, 1963 about a fire that destroyed a house and charred a body. In this column was printed that no one sought fire protection or even inquired about*

> *it. This is not true because my husband made two trips to the Fire Dept. and made three phone calls. He was told they were going to hold a meeting to take us into their fire call. Each time he called, he was told the meeting was postponed and so far as we know, no meeting took place. Two others at an earlier date had gone to see the Mayor and got no results. We did not seek fire protection before because we were under the impression we were protected by Blue Island Dept. We all thought that part of our tax money went for fire protection, as it is not used for any improvements in this town. But do not misunderstand me, we are all willing to pay for protection. All the people in this area asked me to write this letter stating we all want fire protection. We ask that Blue Island Dept. reconsider our problem and vote us in to their fire call as they are our closest neighbor. Seymour Simon, each and every one of us thanks you for your interest in our problem and for your interest to try to help us."*

In addition to Bessie Savich's signature, the letter also was signed by Mr. and Mrs. Lawrence Topolski, Mr. and Mrs. Stanley Baranowski, Mr. and Mrs. J. Cordero, Peter Topolski, Mr. and Mrs. Eli Jenin, Mr. and Mrs. Leo

Toploski, Mr. and Mrs. Alex Toploski, Mr. and Mrs. Michael Savich, Mr. and Mrs. Walter Fouts, and Charles Pyka.

"People just outside of Blue Island, near the oil refinery, for years had been asking for police and fire services. One of the drivers of a city garbage truck lived out there," recalled Sparky Holdefer. "Hart didn't like being told what to do. That may have been one of the reasons he wouldn't give in on the services."

Seymour Simon visited the scene of the fire the day after, but he took action before he received the letter from Bessie Savich. Mr. Simon ordered Cook County civil defense director Patrick M. O'Block to convene a meeting of area fire chiefs so that it could be determined which fire departments would respond to calls in specified unincorporated areas. In spite of Mayor Hart, residents who lived just outside of Blue Island city limits finally received fire protection, but it took a death for them to get it.

The mayor faced further opposition from his city council on December 9, 1963 when Blue Island was offered the opportunity to be the District Six headquarters of Cook County Court. The offer was made during a city council meeting by a Blue Island native, Judge Maurice J. Schultz, who was held in such high regard that the Illinois Supreme Court appointed him to the Cook County Judicial Organizing Committee. In that capacity, Judge Schultz assisted with the physical reorganization of the lower court by selecting locations. He explained to the city council that his selection of Blue Island was based in part on a desire to repay his home town because Blue Island had been so good to him. Judge Schultz added that he was not trying to sell the court to aldermen but was giving them the opportunity to decide.

The majority of the aldermen, including some in the mayor's pocket, enthusiastically endorsed Judge Schultz's offer. So did the Blue Island chapter of the American Bar Association, whose president, Leonard Carriere, presented to the city council a petition endorsing the proposal. Worth Township Justice of the Peace Romie Palmer also backed the endeavor. Yet Hart was against it. Whatever his real reasons, if there were any, the mayor mentioned only two.

Cost always was John M. Hart's primary concern—some said his only concern. "Who would pay for the necessary remodeling and related expenses," he asked? The mayor viewed the acceptance of Cook County District Six circuit court as a form of double jeopardy since his city court would be abolished because the larger court would force the local one out of its home. This would cost Blue Island thousands of dollars in revenue that city court generated in fines and fees. Unspoken, but understood was that the mayor, his police magistrate, and other city officials profited from the payoffs generated from city court. Hart did not want to relinquish control of a court that was a profit-making enterprise for himself and for those he allowed to supplement their incomes under the table.

Fortunately, those who favored accepting the proposal had Maurice J. Schultz on their side. Judge Schultz had been the first judge in the history of Blue Island city court. In addition to his affection for his home town, Judge Schultz also had an impeccable reputation as a great jurist and a man of reason.

"I remember Judge Schultz," said former Illinois Supreme Court justice and Cook County State's Attorney John Stamos during a 2011 telephone interview. "I tried cases before him. He was a terrific judge."

The majority of the aldermen supported the proposal made by Judge Schultz. Aldermen Withers, Rende, John Rita, Edgar Miller, and Joseph Mausolf told the mayor that for a modest expense, originally estimated at $10,000, Blue Island would more than earn the money back via court fees and revenue from parking and shopping. They pointed out that money spent by those who would have to come to court in Blue Island would be a boon to local businesses. They also mentioned the prestige that went with having a district court. Judge Schultz and the aldermen were so persuasive that the vote was 11-2 to accept the offer. In the process, the city council did something historic. Never in his 26 years had Mayor Hart been repudiated by his aldermen. Yet it was not a total victory for the opposition. The mayor's protests may have caused Judge Schultz to revise his offer because when he met with John M. Hart and a few aldermen the next day to discuss procedures when it was decided that Blue Island would have the District Six Court but not the records center.

During January of 1964, Mayor Hart and aldermen again sparred over the relocation. Aldermen Withers, Rende, and Mausolf wanted the mayor to appeal to Judge Schultz and reclaim the records center for Blue Island. For unspecified reasons—beyond that King John I did not like being told what to do, of course—the mayor was not interested.

Thanks primarily to Aldermen Rende and Withers and columnist Watson, the District Six record division eventually was relocated to Blue Island. Some of the aldermen were so happy about his victory that they showed up on moving day and helped Judge Schultz transport furniture and records. While Hart did not participate in physical labor, he did find $27,616.93 to spend on furniture and renovations for the courtroom. And, as was his habit, Mayor Hart approved the hiring of contractors and start of the remodeling without bringing any of the contracts or expenditures to the city council. Aldermen Rende and Withers criticized Hart for this and on December 23 some of the specifics were brought before the city council. Aldermen responded with unanimous approval, however, perhaps out of concern that construction delays would have forced the court to relocate somewhere other than Blue Island. As for Mayor Hart, he may have had an eye on the upcoming election when he made two grandstand plays. First, he threw a bone to Alderman Rende when he gave the alderman the no-bid contract to install the tile floors. He then announced during the February 24 city council meeting that he was "tired of the continued conversation that he hoarded money for the city." He said, "There is no other city in the area which has the record of being able to pay out in cash for such improvements."

Mayor Hart then went on vacation. Before he left, neither he nor his aldermen remembered to officially abolish city court. The court had been created by law and it had to be abolished by law, but it never was.

In Blue Island during the last term of John M. Hart, courts were not the only item in the news. Apartment building construction in Blue Island, Alsip, and Calumet Park also was a hot topic. Under the June 27, 1963 headline “More Apartment Buildings” the *Sun-Standard* gave details of new projects approved by Hart that eventually would be known as the dreaded “Vincennes apartments.” The Sheldon Heights Construction Company received the okay to build forty units between 121st and 122nd Streets for $70,000. R&B Construction got the green light to build 80 units at the corner of 122nd Street, reportedly for $80,000. During September 1963, Abbco Builders began an apartment complex at Chicago Avenue and 135th Street. It was thirty buildings with 180 units with parking for 250 cars. Watchful Watson linked Mayor Hart’s love of multi-unit housing, municipal parking lots, Alderman Schaller’s request for lighting, and aldermen fighting for District Six court in his January 2, 1964 column.

> *I would like to see a little common sense injected into the trend of apartment buildings as well as some reasonable, realistic regulations with respect to adequate parking facilities. City Hall can make a lot of friends along this line of endeavor. They [sic] may need them, too, in view of the political climate that prevails for the forthcoming municipal elections.*
>
> *The City Council made a good start in the right direction recently in its independent action on the new court. It is a hopeful sign. Another straw in the wind was Alderman Schaller’s desire for a brightly-lit Western Avenue, even if it jeopardized the old cliché*

> *'pay as you go.' It may no longer be sacrosanct. Besides, with it, where have we gone?*

Rookie alderman Withers and the legendary mayor continued to disagree on the construction of apartment buildings. During the spring of 1964, there was a proposed zoning change. The mayor wanted the city council to approve a variance so that an apartment complex could be built on the south side of Burr Oak Avenue between Highland Avenue and Elm Street. "The location was the old Lally property. Dr. Lally and his family actually had a home on it that was knocked down for the project," said Richard Withers.

The Mueller twins, Arnold and Archer, already acquired the property. They had a top flight architect, Robert Carlson, ready to design their apartment complex.

"We went to college with Carlson," said the surviving Mueller twin, Arnold, during a 2011 interview. "My brother and I drove to Thornton Community College for classes. Carlson was a student there too. We picked him up every morning. He was a friend and a classmate, and he rode with us to school."

More important than Carlson, the Muellers had "the dealmaker" on their side. Henry Gentile was their attorney and he hit the zoning board with everything, including (literally) the kitchen sink. During a zoning board hearing on June 14, Gentile brought in depositions he'd taken from the police chief, water superintendent, and street superintendent of Flossmoor, where a similar apartment complex had been built. All three had sworn under oath that the project had been a good one and that there were no problems with sewer, water, etc.

This was great theater, but Blue Islanders were not fooled. Okay, the ones who were not paid to be fooled weren't. John Hocheimer of 12719 Highland Avenue was one of the protagonists. He attended the hearing and countered Gentile's theatrics with information of his own. Actually, he stated what everyone already knew—that there were problems with low water pressure and drainage. Mr. Hocheimer pointed out that the problems might increase if the apartment complex was built.

Enter Zoning Board Chairman Joseph Brunswick, who played his part perfectly. A prominent attorney, Mr. Brunswick announced that the purpose of the hearing was to decide whether the requested zoning variance was in the best interest of the city. While Brunswick was convincing, he was incorrect. The purpose of the zoning board hearings was *to convince* people that the zoning board, the majority of the city council, and the mayor were looking out for their interests. They were not. The change Mayor Hart wanted was blatantly illegal and would drastically change the neighborhood for the worse. The trifling matters of legality and the effect on the neighborhood did not prevent the mayor's zoning board or his City Attorney, Earl Ebers Jr. from approving the change.

The rezoning of the Lally Property was against the wishes of the residents of the neighborhood, who were not fooled. Before the deciding vote by aldermen, exactly 52 of them joined Hocheimer and petitioned the city council to kill the zoning change. According to the petition presented to the city council, the residents believed that re-zoning the property from first residential to second residential "will not only break up the continuity of the neighborhood, but will also affect the value of our own personal property."

The deal wasn't done yet, perhaps because enough aldermen had not been paid. During the June 22 city council meeting, aldermen voted 12-1 to refer the matter back to the zoning board. This at least gave opponents more time to mount a defense and pray for a miracle. The project was in the Fourth Ward. Aldermen Withers and Merv Beattie were the aldermen. Mr. Beattie and his family lived less than a block from the site. Withers, Beattie, and Elmer Johnson proposed that any request for a zoning variance in their wards be made by them and based on a recommendation from the plats, public grounds, and buildings committee of the city council.

Just as he controlled the zoning board, Mayor Hart also had the plats, public grounds, and buildings committee in his pocket. The mayor and the three committee members teamed up to pull a fast one during the November 9 city council meeting. Led by a Hart crony, Alderman Niles Erfft, the committee announced that the recommendation of the zoning board be accepted.

At that point, another of those rare moments during the 28-year reign of Mayor Hart occurred. Thanks to Alderman Withers, a John M. Hart initiative was defeated. The vote was 8-6. Aldermen Jebsen, Collatz, Rende, Rita, Beattie, Withers, Johnson, and Schaller voted against the project. Erfft and the other two members of the committee, Edgar Miller and Sam Ruffalo, voted for it. So did Larry Witt, Joseph Mausolf, and Nick Splayt.

Richard W. Withers had been prepared to fight. He came to that November 9 meeting loaded for bear.

"You could not just rezone that parcel. The zoning had to tie into the surrounding properties and it didn't. What they wanted to do was spot zoning and that's illegal. To defeat the proposed zoning change, I brought in all kinds of charts and explained everything. I think that really confused John Rita because he voted against the zoning change Hart wanted and that upset Hart because John was supposed to vote with him. Hart got John outside after the meeting and chewed his ass out," explained Withers, who chuckled at the recollection.

Alderman Rita's vote would have given Hart a 7-7 tie, which the mayor could have broken with the deciding vote. Instead he had to wait one more meeting. The next time it was Mayor Hart who was prepared. He was so confident that he had City Attorney Ebers draft the ordinance, which he introduced for approval. That's what the price of a hat buys. It was so simple that even Alderman Rita got his signals straight. During that November 23 meeting, the vote was 10-4 to approve the project. Again, Aldermen Withers, Beattie, Rende, and Johnson voted against it. The four aldermen who changed their votes never explained why, but they did not have to because Withers and just about everyone else familiar with the zoning change believes there was a payoff involved. Arnold Mueller is adamant there was not.

"We never paid Hart anything," Mr. Mueller said during a 2011 interview. "We went to see Hart to ask for a zoning change. All he told us to do was build a good apartment complex. That was all he wanted. So we did."

The Mueller family came to America from Canada. The twins' grandfather was an hotelier. They and their father owned real estate in Blue Island. Eventually, Arnold and Archer went into cigarette vending where they made a fortune. The interview with Arnold Mueller also revealed why he and his brother decided to build apartments.

"We were making so much money so fast from our vending business that we had to do something with it," Arnold Mueller said.

The Mueller twins became Blue Island landlords at a perfect time politically and financially. Just one year later, they would not have received city council approval for their project. Also, during the era of prosperity, young white couples moved into apartments so that they could live in the community where they grew up, shop locally, and ride commuter trains to work. The revised American Dream that featured big houses in far away suburbs and open housing still was a decade away for Blue Island.

"Our apartments on Burr Oak were quality," said Arnold Mueller. "They were well-built and spacious—two and three bedrooms. Some of them had two bathrooms. We wanted something good for the tenants and the neighborhood and we had Carlson revise the plans over and over. The project took a long time because of all the changes. Every time my brother or I took a trip somewhere and we saw something, we brought the idea back and incorporated it."

While all of the apartments built in Blue Island didn't receive the detail the Mueller Brothers put into theirs, the construction was good and they were well-maintained at the start.

"When the Vincennes apartments were built, they were very nice. They were clean and well-kept, and there wasn't crime down there," said former city clerk Pam Frasor. "Young married couples lived there. Right after we were married, my husband John and I lived there."

According to Richard Withers, the Hart-endorsed apartment construction that overwhelmed Blue Island during the 1950s and early 1960s was part of Mayor Hart's unannounced vision.

"When he was mayor and I was an alderman, I asked John what happened to Blue Island. At one time, Blue Island was the biggest thing south of Chicago, but by then other communities were surpassing us because Blue Island stopped growing. I wanted to know why. So I asked Hart," said Withers. "Hart explained that his theory was Blue Island had to grow up not out. Hart told me that he envisioned Blue Island with skyscrapers, like Chicago.

"Hart believed that people would always want to live here and those who didn't would come from outside to shop here. He didn't notice that the lands he declined to annex now had homes and businesses on them or that communities that didn't exist when he became mayor existed. He did not understand that the new expressways built to bring people to Blue Island also would take them away," Mr. Withers explained.

Apartments were John M. Hart's alternative to annexing property in the vicinity of his town. Eventually, after many Blue Islanders decided their version of the American Dream existed well beyond the city limits and they refused to live in apartments here, Mayor Hart's "widescrapers" would house a transient clientele that brought a multitude of criminal, legal, and financial problems. For years after, Mayor Hart's apartment building boom would be a pox on Blue Island, just as multi-unit buildings were in other suburbs and in Chicago.

"Looking back at Hart's philosophy, I don't agree, but I understand," said Withers, who made annexation one of the planks of his campaign platform when he ran for mayor. "The mistake Hart made was not having another option to fall back on."

Mayor Hart wasn't the only local politician with whom Richard Withers had issues. Previously, Alderman Withers had an interesting encounter with Alderman John D. Rita. Like Richard Withers, John Rita was a rookie alderman in 1963. The two had run for aldermen together and won.

"John's brother Mike was a printer. Mike and my brother Bob went to high school together and were good friends. Mike did all the printing for our business," said Richard Withers. "In 1963, John made an offer to support me and in return, we all supported him. John and I had kind of a Tea Party movement going on back then. We had some good ideas that we campaigned on."

The Withers-Rita Tea Party movement did not last long.

"The day after the election, John came to my home to see me. He acted kind of funny and he told me, 'You know, we really can't do all of the things we promised to do.' The first thing I asked was, 'What do you mean?' Then I thought about it for a minute and said, 'Hey! You made a deal with Hart, didn't you?' John said, 'Yep.' Well, that was it for John and me," explained Withers.

Just as Alderman Withers broke from Alderman Rita, so were voters preparing to break from Mayor Hart. Wiley

Watson helped. His report of an inept police department and of a fire department that could not respond appeared in a "Town Crier" column that appeared September 24, 1964 after a fire at a trailer court. Weary of Mayor Hart and with the anniversary of the fatal fire of September 1, 1963 obviously in mind, Wiley Watson used the entire piece as an indictment of Mayor Hart and the first responders he had on a short leash. According to Watson, despite incidents that included loss of life, King John I continued to show a disregard for his subjects by refusing to bring about improvements in emergency services.

A wisecrack John M. Hart made may have been the impetus to that September 24 column. During the September 14 city council meeting, City Attorney Paul Schreiber resigned. This motivated Hart to quip, "It might be a good chance for Wiley Watson to be appointed to put into practice some of the things he writes in his column." Wiley Watson challenged Hart to make the appointment when he wrote:

> *We are this week making an exception by printing a letter which came to us unsigned. As you all know, this is contrary to policy, but being curious about the whole thing I made a few phone calls and found many confusing facts which I'm sure the public would be interested in hearing.*

The letter follows. The bullets were the newspaper's.

> *On the night of Saturday, September 5, 1964 the Blue Island Fire*

Dept. was called 3 times. It took 45 minutes to get to 139th and Harrison in B.I. The fire dept. was in doubt as to whether it was Blue Island or not. Now a 73-year old man had to find a place to live. Had they come on the first call, his trailer would still be standing and livable, but the firemen's axes were busy again—they ruined the trailer.

Thirty minutes later the B. I. police and Mayor Hart came down, looked around, and left the sick old man standing in the dark and cold—not asking if he had a place to stay that night or telling him why it took so long to get there.

The firemen were nice. They asked the man if he had a place to go.

* * *

Now the first item on the agenda was to call our Fire Dept. to find out if 139th and Harrison is within limits of our fire district. I was told by the man who answered that it was.

When I told him about the letter he stated that they answered the first call on the stated night of the fire. He said, though, that all fire calls came through the police dept. phone board and how many calls they received before one was relayed to the fire desk he did not know.

So then I called the Police Dept. and related the same message to the policeman that answered the phone. This man knew nothing and had no record of anything. This, of course, is nothing new for the department. They seem to have an aversion to keeping records of police calls because I've called on numerous occasions for information of various sorts and could never get any satisfaction.

I then called the Mayor's Office to verify the contents of the letter. The Mayor was out. I left a request for him to call this paper so that I might obtain some sort of enlightenment to this situation. No call was ever received.

So apparently things at the Police Dept. will continue on—in its merry confusing way. No one ever seems to care whether things run smoothly or not. Crime and thievery continue in our town—and who pays through the nose? We do, of course.

On one occasion a two-way motorcycle radio was pilfered from a police vehicle—shortly after two walkie-talkies disappeared from the police station, while a desk sergeant was on duty.

Yet neither item has been found and undoubtedly little has been done to make sure such thievery does not occur again.

We may be a rich town, paying-as-we-go, but I'm sure we can't afford too much of this nonsense.

* * *

I would very much like to accept Mr. Hart's idea that Wiley Watson "take over the city attorney's job so that he might put into practice his many ideas."But I'm afraid this does not fall in the attorney's realm of duties. Paul Schreiber has done a magnificent job for the city and it's in bad taste to unload his [Hart's] responsibilities on the city attorney.

I think it's high time our city council became interested in the goings on of our police department and determined why certain conditions are allowed in a department that is so vital to the welfare of our town.

* * *

And while the council is doing something about police reorganization, they can also consider a temporary lighting program at the foot of Vermont Street near the rail stations. With the cold and slippery weather and early darkness, this area has become a veritable haven for hoodlums to prey on unsuspecting women commuters. It might also prevent a broken leg on slippery pavement during bad weather.

We've needed this for a long time. It's been mentioned many times and like everything else, it never gets done. Surprise us, gentlemen, and give the poor commuters a treat. They deserve one.

Confusion still exists at every stoplight in town. Still no left turn signal. Still confused and angered motorists. Still lots of money in the bank.

And for a parting thought:

* * *

> *What's the big attraction for the police car that has been parked at a north side drive-in night after night, all summer long?*

Wiley Watson actually alluded to what some in the community had known for years. Mayor Hart's police chiefs were his bagmen and everyone else on the force was his henchman, chauffeur, or errand boy. Walter Wozniak learned about the mayor's private chauffeur service when, after joining the police force, he was assigned to switchboard duty. As he sometimes did on nights out when he either did not or was not in condition to drive his green Cadillac and needed a ride, the mayor called the police station and told the dispatcher where he was and to "Send a cab to pick me up." Everyone at BIPD knew that meant the mayor wanted a police officer to drive over in a squad car to transport him home or to wherever he was going. Everyone except dispatcher Wozniak knew. He called one of the local cab companies and had a taxi pick up Hart. Walter Wozniak took a lot of needling around the station after that.

As for the fire department, while the situation there was different, firefighters of every rank did what they were told. If they were told they were not to respond to a call outside of Blue Island, they did not respond. If they were called into Mayor Hart's office and told they were to complete a task or of an assignment of rank, they accepted it or else, according to Sparky Holdefer, who was a firefighter at that time.

"Hart had a group of unofficial advisors that met with him at his office. Niles Erfft was one of them," said Mr. Holdefer. "One day Hart calls me in and tells me, 'We want you to take such and such a position.' It was a promotion, but there was a problem. I wasn't in line for the promotion. There were others on the fire department that had seniority. That was what I told Hart and the others in his office. Well, you didn't do that. Hart told me, 'Either you take it or you're not the right man for the fire department.' I knew what that meant. If I did not do as I was told, I was out. So I had to take it."

All of that was done in private or after hours away from the public, in places where Mayor Hart did not care what Wiley Watson wrote because even if Wiley was right as rain, a mere columnist couldn't touch him. At election time, the mayor always tried to give the appearance of being responsive to the needs of the voters, however. Suddenly some of those suggestions weren't bad. After all, commuters were voters, weren't they? On October 8, the mayor announced new streetlights would be installed at Vermont and Irving near the railroad stations and that streets in the area would be patched. It was part of the John M. Hart's philosophy of getting re-elected: *Give the voters things that they could see.*

Richard Withers' brief time as an alderman, less than two years, only made him more determined to do something about what he saw as the decline of his community.

Chamber of Commerce Vice President Lloyd Holmlin declared his candidacy in a press release early in 1964. Michael Guglielmucci, an alderman from Hart's very first city council and since that time an elected official in Calumet Township, said via press release that he would run. The rambling announcement that appeared in the October 13, 1964 edition took shots at Hart.

> "I am a candidate for the office of Mayor of the City of the City of Blue Island," Guglielmucci wrote. "Many friends and well-wishers have urged me to run and many friends and acquaintances throughout the town have asked me so often about my candidacy that it is necessary at this time to make clear my intent. I shall run with a full slate of candidates for all major city offices and aldermanic posts. With me will be Norman Blatt as candidate for city clerk and Elmer Schwartz as candidate for treasurer. With them I pledge a forward-looking program of administration of the city to bring it up to date and give to it the services that a city of this size must have in the year 1965 and beyond."

Less than two weeks earlier, the well-respected Emil J. Blatt dealt Mayor Hart a setback when he announced he would not seek re-election to the city treasurer's post. Mr. Blatt was 76 years old and he had been treasurer since 1945. He also was a member of the high school board of education for fifteen years and he was a member of the Selective Service board during World War II.

"I feel that at my age, it is time for me to step down," the elder Blatt told the *Sun-Standard.* "I indeed am grateful for the confidence the public has shown in me for so many years."

"Blatt the Paintman" was a well-respected businessman and public official who could have generated enough support for the incumbent mayor to help him win an eighth term. Instead, he distanced himself from Mayor Hart and supported his son's ticket. Norman G. Blatt, who was the mayor's longtime city court clerk, took a less subtle shot after breaking ranks with Mayor Hart when he said, "I am proud to join Michael Guglielmucci as a candidate. I am well aware of the modernization necessary in the City administration."

The defections did not end there. Elmer Schwartz was the son of Louis Schwartz, another well-respected public official who for twenty years had served as Mayor Hart's city clerk. Louis Schwartz died in office, but he was far from forgotten in Blue Island.

"Louis Schwartz lived in the big house at the northeast corner of Greenwood Avenue and Union Street," recalled Harry Robertson. "He was a very well-liked and well-respected man."

Now the son would attempt to capitalize on the father's reputation. "My father devoted many years of service to the community as clerk of the city. As treasurer, I shall strive to be as worthy of the repeated votes of confidence that my father received as he was," said Elmer Schwartz.

Wiley Watson continued to stoke the fires of change when he wrote in the October 22 *Sun-Standard*, "We need more policemen, more firemen, a fire station on the isolated east side of Blue Island, a ban on railroads blocking traffic for extended periods of time, a study of out traffic in the uptown area to alleviate the mad confusion that exists and many other things too numerous to mention."

Richard Withers never made a public announcement. Nevertheless, by late October everyone in Blue Island knew he was a candidate for mayor. Wiley Watson stated in a column that there were four candidates for mayor and he mentioned each by name. Years later, Mr. Withers said he was not surprised that either Mr. Holmlin or Mr. Guglielmucci was on the ballot. He believes that John M. Hart put up each man to run for the purpose of stealing votes from the real opposition, who he perceived to be candidate Withers.

"Hart and Holmlin were friends. He really didn't have a chance at winning. I think Hart put him up to run so that people who didn't want to vote for Hart would have someone to vote for," Withers reasoned. "It was the same with Guglielmucci. Hart put him up to get the votes on the east side that he wasn't going to get. After Mike saw that he actually had a chance to win, he got serious."

Richard Withers was correct about Lloyd Holmlin, who was a longtime Hart supporter, a career bureaucrat, and businessman who never seriously sought public office. By all other accounts, Michael Guglielmucci's candidacy was a different story because he was a businessman (insurance and real estate) who always had been active in politics. Also, Michael Guglielmucci was a proud man with an ego. According to those who knew him, he would not have been a front for John Hart.

"I think he really wanted to be mayor," said Larry Petta, whose political career in Calumet Township was beginning at the same time Guglielmucci's was ending. "He thought he had a chance. So he ran."

"He would not have run unless he thought he could be mayor," said longtime east side resident Luigi LaRotunda, who knew Mr. Guglielmucci. "I don't think anyone put him up to run."

Mrs. Rende remembers Guglielmucci as a politician who knew how to milk the system as well as one whose ego would not allow him to be a front for Mayor Hart.

"Mike Guglielmucci was a big shot on the east side. He had a lot of votes and he wanted to be mayor," said Mrs. Rende. "He used to take the train downtown every morning to his political job, punch in, then get back on the train and come back home and take care of his own businesses."

Other trends support the opinions of Mr. Petta, Mr. Rotunda, and Mrs. Rende. Many members of the old guard broke with Mayor Hart either because they thought he could be beaten and they could assume power or because they believed it was time for a change. What other candidates—serious and otherwise—were doing did not matter to Alderman Withers. His initial strategy was to recruit a trustworthy mayoral candidate who could beat John M. Hart. He tried to recruit someone else to run for mayor so that he would not have to. Each person with whom he spoke rejected the overture, however. Alderman Withers finally decided to throw his own hat into the ring after a number of rejections and after a banker suggested he run for mayor.

"Sometime during early 1964, my brother and I wanted to borrow money to expand our business. I spoke to a banker in Harvey about getting a loan. He was familiar with Mayor Hart and knew that Blue Islanders were ready for a change. During our conversation he asked me what I thought was going to happen in the next Blue Island election. Well, I gave him my take, explained what I thought needed to happen, and told him that I'd asked 10 or 11 people to run for mayor, but they'd all turned me down

"He listened to me and then he asked, 'Why don't you run for mayor?' " Withers recalled. "That was the first time I thought seriously about it."

"About a year and a half after Dick became alderman, Dad and I and Dick sat down and talked about Dick running for mayor," Bob Withers said. "Mom did not want to be involved in the discussion because it worried her. Mom told Dick, 'I wish you wouldn't do this. I'm afraid for you because of Hart's connection to Tuffanelli.'"

Mrs. Withers was correct about the connection between John M. Hart and Babe Tuffanelli, the Outfit boss of Blue Island and the South Suburbs. What she didn't know was while the organized crime boss would not make threats or attempt any violence, Mr. Tuffanelli was concerned that Mayor Hart would not be re-elected. He wanted to protect his interests. To that end, he approached Larry Petta and John Rita.

Mr. Petta has told this story several times. The first was in the kitchen of Bob and Betty Harmeyer's home on Ann Street in Blue Island. Ironically, the home once belonged to legendary Blue Island mobster Lorenzo Juliano. During that 2011 conversation, Mr. Petta said, "Tuffanelli asked if John and I would help Hart. He set up a meeting with the four of us at his home on 119th Street. When John and I arrived, Babe took us downstairs to his basement. He had a beautiful basement with a full bar. Hart already was there sitting at the bar and we sat down with him. Babe didn't interfere. He went off to the side and let the three of us talk.

"I said to Hart, 'Babe asked us to meet with you. He thinks we can help you with the election.' Hart wasn't interested. He told us, 'I'm John Hart. Everybody knows me and my reputation for pay-as-you-go. I don't know what you could do for me.' John and I just looked at each other. That was it. What could we say? Hart wasn't worried and we couldn't make him take our help."

Mr. Petta told the same story during a 2013 conversation at his son's car wash in Blue Island. At the end of the story, he added, "When we walked out of Babe's house, after we were alone outside, I said to John, 'He's going to lose the election.'"

As John M. Hart admitted two and one-half years later in a deposition, he and Babe Tuffanelli were business partners. As such, they had a tacit understanding. Mayor Hart did not get in the way of Babe Tuffanelli's illegal businesses. When it came to politics no one, not even the powerful local Outfit boss, told Hart how to do things.

Mr. Petta summed things up during the conversation at the car wash.

"I understand why Hart didn't want our help. After years in office, you become complacent," he explained. "Hart had been mayor for 28 years. He thought everyone knew him and that he would get re-elected on his reputation. He didn't think he could lose."

Larry Petta's assessment may be right on the money. King John I seemed to believe he simply could throw his crown back into the ring and win re-election.

John M. Hart's re-election campaign unofficially kicked off November 19, 1964 when a half-page ad in the form of a letter urging him to run appeared in the *Sun-Standard.* It was paid for by The Blue Island Citizens Committee for Hart, whose chairman was E.J. Anhorn and whose office was 13017 Western. No one was fooled by the advertisement. Mr. Anhorn was Mayor Hart's longtime friend and barber, and the BICCFH "office" was Anhorn's barber shop where the King was coiffed and which provided him a throne outside of City Hall. For all anyone knew, Mayor Hart wrote the letter urging himself to run while having his shoes shined at Anhorn's.

"I can remember being in Anhorn's Barber Shop when Hart was there," said Bill Klein. "He'd sit there and have his shoes shined and talk about whatever was on his mind as though he knew it all. Hart was a very arrogant man."

The ad was transparent not only for its source. There also was a very unusual sentence—it could be interpreted as a scare tactic—in paragraph three of the letter to Mayor Hart. "In our opinion, there is no real need for change." With that statement, Mayor Hart attempted to plant the seed in the minds of those who feared new leadership would affect their way of life. Haven't your lives in Blue Island been good for the past 27 years? What will happen to Blue Island, TO YOU, if a new mayor is elected?

Richard Withers did not play on the fear factor, but he did not leave many other stones unturned. Unlike John Hart, Richard Withers was not above making promises and deals to help him in the election. Before he kicked off his campaign, he did something very unusual.

"The first person I spoke to after I decided to run was Mayor Hart. That was mid-1964. I informed him that I was running against him," Richard Withers said. "After that, the first person who I recruited to run with me was Earl Kough because he was so well respected."

It was Robert Withers Sr.—who else?—who urged his younger son to recruit Mr. Kough.

"It was Dad who suggested that Dick ask Earl Kough to run on the ticket. Dad and Mom and Earl and Mrs. Kough were good friends. Earl was a lifelong railroad man and a wonderful guy," Bob Withers said. "When Dick asked him, Earl said, "I've lived in Blue Island my whole life and I've never done anything for my town. I'll run."

Earl Kough, 66, was a World War I veteran. He was well-respected. By all accounts, he'd never let anyone down in his life. Then less than one month before the election, he almost did. On March 23, Earl Kough died of a heart attack.

"Dick was going to drop the whole thing, just drop out of the race," said Bob Withers. "Before he made the decision, he went to see Earl's widow. Dick told her that he was going to drop out. She said to him, 'No, you are not dropping out.' Mrs. Kough told Dick that he was running for mayor. That close to the election, you couldn't appoint a replacement, so Earl stayed on the ballot. It was a tribute to him when he was elected."

As it turned out, Withers' was able to recruit a formidable slate of good-looking, professional, thirty-somethings who challenged Mayor Hart and his stodgy group in the April, 1965 election. Their timing may have been perfect. Because Hart had grown complacent, he and the members of his slate did not campaign hard. This was a fatal mistake for Hart in particular. At age 72, he already was at the disadvantage of being perceived as too old and out of touch by many of his constituents. To them, "pay as you go" had gone from prudent point to passé. Mayor Hart had not spent enough taxpayer money on positive change. Blue Island voters were ripe for a change. And, as important as the issues and perceptions was the number of candidates. In 1965, there were more candidates on the ballot than at any time in the city's history.

After 130 years, there was also the acknowledgment that African Americans lived in Blue Island. African-American residents had been segregated across the Cal Sag Channel in the California Gardens section of the city on the far southwest side that bordered the African American community of Robbins. When Richard W. Withers campaigned for mayor, he did what no other candidate ever had done. He recognized them for what they were—residents and voters.

"During a meet-the-candidates event, Dick spoke to the people of California Gardens. He told them, 'You are part of Blue Island. If I am elected mayor, you will get nothing more than anyone else, but you will get nothing less,'" said Bob Withers. "The people of California Gardens asked Dick to come back again the following Sunday. As he drove in, there were 'Withers for Mayor' signs all along the road. The people of California Gardens helped Dick get elected."

Richard Withers also made two very shrewd moves that generated him votes east of Western Avenue, which is in Calumet Township. That is Petta, Rita, and Guglielmucci territory. Candidate Withers made a deal with Calumet Township committeeman Earl Kistner to become city clerk in the event Earl Kough won the election. Earl Kistner and his Home Rule Party Slate were running for re-election. Bill Frey, another popular local politician was on the slate and Mr. Kistner and Mr. Frey controlled many Blue Island votes. Richard Withers also garnered the support of John Carriere, the father of attorney Leonard Carriere and an Italian-American who was very popular on the east side of Blue Island where there was a heavy Italian-American population. Richard Withers needed Carriere, Kistner, and Frey to help him offset the votes the popular Michael Guglielmucci would get from the heavily Italian American population in the Second Ward and the Third Ward.

"Grandfather wasn't involved in politics," said John Carriere, "but he did get involved for Withers and he went against a big shot [Guglielmucci] on the east side."

"My grandfather helped Dick Withers get elected. He got him a lot of votes on the east side," said Ed Wencloff. "I remember hearing that in return, Dick promised to name the new firehouse down there after my grandfather, but that never happened.

"Afterward, Dick Withers was man enough to explain to the family that he could not do it," added Wencloff. "I respect him for that. Dick Withers was a straight shooter."

Bob Withers agrees with Carriere's grandsons and then some. "John Carriere was 'The Godfather' on the east side and he supported Dick," he said.

Richard Withers acknowledges the help he received from John Carriere. "The votes he got me on the east side offset the votes there for Guglielmucci and Hart," he said. Richard Withers insisted that he did not make any deals with Carriere or Kistner. He did explain, however, why he selected Mr. Kistner as the replacement for Mr. Kough. "I didn't know Earl Kistner, but he came very highly recommended by Larry Hupe Sr. That's why I selected him."

Candidate Withers also made one good proposal and one promise he could not keep during a meet-the-candidates event just before the election. The proposal was that an incinerator be built in Blue Island by a private company. Had the city council approved this initiative in any era, it might have been very beneficial to Blue Island. As for the promise, Richard Withers said if elected he would resign from Visualcraft and be a full-time mayor. This he could not do. The total compensation package for the chief executive was $6,800, which was not enough to support a wife and a three-year old son. He already had the perfect job for a suburban mayor: he was a salesman who worked out of the community where he lived. Sure he traveled, but often times the travel was local and he sometimes could make his own hours.

Fortunately, no one took Withers' promise any more seriously than they took Mayor Hart's, which was to lower property taxes and double the sales tax. He could not do the former and to perpetrate the latter on the business community would have been disastrous. Mayor Hart's promise was a sign that he was not paying attention to what was happening in nearby communities where homes and stores were being built. Just down the road, the Dixie Square Mall was under construction on the site of the old Dixie-Hi Golf Course. Dixie Square and Evergreen Plaza were the first shopping centers to siphon customers from Blue Island. One would disappear and the drawing power of the other would wane, but many others would take their places more effectively.

On the eve of the election, Emil J. Blatt took out a quarter-page ad endorsing Guglielmucci and the Blue Island Independent Party. Ultimately, it was the ideas and energy of the VIP Party that ruled the day.

"Bob Withers lived in my neighborhood. So I saw firsthand what was going on. The Withers brothers were very organized, they had energy, and they got out and campaigned hard. They had people out early in the morning putting door hangers on door knobs—things like that," said Arnold Mueller. "Before the election, my brother and I tried to talk John Hart into campaigning harder. We offered him help and advice. He wasn't interested."

Promises, ideas, and deals aside, Richard W. Withers had the best of all worlds. He had the youth vote generated by the vitality of his own youth, the loyalty and sympathy votes for the popular and well-respected Earl Kough, and the machine votes from Kistner and his organization. Also, Withers wisely didn't risk upsetting anyone by announcing in advance that the Calumet Township boss would be the replacement. Why take the chance of losing the Kough supporters? As for the Calumet Township Republicans who lived in Blue Island, Kistner and Frey could tell them who to vote for. After the election, Calumet Township and Worth Township Republicans not previously united, remained cozy for awhile. There are stories and photos of the elected officials together in various editions of the *Sun-Standard.*

As for John Carriere enabling candidate Withers to secure the east side vote, there is no doubt Mr. Carriere helped despite his not being a politician. And it was no small task. He was a mechanic for the Rock Island

Railroad, not the career politician and local businessman as was Michael Guglielmucci. In his roles as township supervisor, insurance man, and restaurant owner, Mr. Guglielmucci had been doing business in Blue Island for decades, primarily on the east side. Michael Guglielmucci knew almost everyone there. He had done business with many of them and he had done favors for many more.

The system went something like this: Guglielmucci advised immigrants about how to obtain citizenship, registered them as voters, and helped them get jobs and places to live. After he'd provide so much help, who else were they going to vote for? It had to be Michael Guglielmucci because once he did you a favor, you owed him a favor for life.

Unlike other Blue Island elections, the election of 1965 did not come down to one ward. It was all about the prevailing mood in the community. Did enough Blue Islanders want change?

The response was an overwhelming yes: 2,695 wanted it so badly that in the race for clerk, they voted for the late Earl Kough and entrusted whoever they elected mayor to appoint a replacement. Mr. Kough received 169 more votes than Peoples Economy Party candidate Norman G. Blatt. Incumbent city clerk William G. Schimmel had 2,416 votes.

It was the same result for a different reason in the five-man contest for city treasurer in which popular Edison P. Heintz, a Withers cousin, defeated three strong candidates. World War II flying ace Heintz received 2,921 votes. William J. Shipman had 1,812 and Elmer H. Schwartz received 1,714. Popular longtime Fifth Ward

Alderman Elmer Johnson, who ran as an independent, had 1,063 and 294 votes were cast for Guy W. Egbert.

VIP candidates dominated the aldermanic races too. Lawrence H. Witt Sr. edged William J. Gaertner and two other candidates in the First Ward. The very popular Ray Rauch overwhelmed incumbent Arthur G. Collatz and two others in the Second Ward. Vernon Umgelder made the difference in the Third Ward. Umgelder did not win, but the 45 votes he received helped Angelo Esposito squeak out a victory over incumbent Sal Rende. Mr. Esposito, the only Better Blue Island Party winner, defeated VIP incumbent Rende by 44 votes. The total was 565-521.

In the Fourth Ward, independent candidate Louis D. Lombardo made a comeback and edged VIP candidate and future city clerk George E. Heitman. Mr. Lombardo received 407 votes to 371 for Mr. Heitman, 172 for incumbent Merv Beattie, 115 for Winfield Nash, and 19 for Frank F. Bilotti.

The Fifth Ward was the most interesting because at that time it had had the greatest number of registered voters in Blue Island. The 1,065 votes cast for Howard E. Heckler were the second-most for an aldermanic candidate in Blue Island history. Robert Charlesworth Jr. would have won any other aldermanic race with his 710 and the well-respected Joe Johnson would have won contests in three other wards with 397 votes. Frederick G. Abrahms Jr. received 77 votes. There 2,249 votes cast in the Fifth Ward are believed to be the most in an aldermanic contest in city history.

In the Sixth Ward, John Clapek received 332 votes. He narrowly defeated longtime alderman Joseph Mausolf, who was on the city council since a special election held in

1939, and newcomer Ronald E. "Gene" Harmeyer. The 61 votes cast for Thomas M. McQuaid could have put either incumbent Mausolf (320) or challenger Harmeyer (310) in the alderman's seat instead of Mr. Clapek.

There was a similar story in the Seventh Ward where only 22 votes separated winner Clarence Wick (200) of the VIP Party, incumbent Niles Erfft (193), and William J. Gerdes (178). The difference-maker was Raymond J. Sossong, who was the fourth man in the race. The 62 votes he received were insignificant for him, but they would have been significant for the other candidates.

As you might expect, Mr. and Mrs. Withers played a role through Election Day.

"Mom told Dick, 'I'm going to bake klotchkis for every one of your events until you get to City Hall,'" said Bob Withers. "Dad campaigned. He was outside of the polling place at Memorial Park greeting voters on Election Day. People came up to him, shook his hand, and said, 'There's my old milkman!'"

Richard W. Withers was elected mayor with 3,297 votes. That was 40.5 percent of the total votes cast. John M. Hart was second with 2,615. Michael Guglielmucci received 2,045 votes, and Lloyd Holmlin had 176. There were 8,133 votes cast in what may have been the most contested, most exciting and second-most important election in the history of the community. The most important election? Well, John M. Hart was elected in 1937 and it took almost three decades for Blue Islanders to oust him.

Hindsight is supposed to be no worse than 20-20. If so, it could be speculated as to what would have happened had Mayor Hart not been so arrogant as to refuse the help of up-and-comers Larry Petta and John Rita, who could have gotten him more of the east side vote. Or had the mayor not been repudiated by the sons of the old guard, Norman J. Blatt and Elmer H. Schwartz. Or had he made a deal with Michael Guglielmucci to keep the first alderman he'd taken to the woodshed out of the race for mayor.

"Guglielmucci being on the ballot hurt Hart on the east side," said Danny Savino, who campaigned for Withers. "If both of those old timers hadn't run, one or the other could have been mayor."

Was John M. Hart too stubborn or arrogant to make that deal? Or was it that he did not know how to make one? The longtime mayor may have been the only politician in Cook County who did not seem to know how to make political deals. He did not appear to understand the concept of trading jobs or favors for votes. He understood money and he was used to getting his way. Whether it was the guy who needed a zoning variance or his dealings with Babe Tuffanelli, almost everything John M. Hart did was for the purpose of enriching John M. Hart or because John M. Hart wanted it.

Politicians made deals. Kings issued decrees. Former kings had no power. This may have been why when the election was all over, Richard Withers did not incur the wrath of Mayor Hart's business partner, Mr. Tuffanelli. It was just the opposite, as you will read in Volume Two of this history. Bob Withers, on the other hand, was on the receiving end of a threat, though he did not learn of it until after the election.

"Chris Krueger and I were friends. He and I and our wives played bridge together. After the election, Chris told me that a Blue Island police officer, Yale Green, threatened me," explained Bob Withers. "Chris said, 'You know, Yale Green told me he was going to beat the hell out of you.' I asked, 'Why didn't you tell me?' But it didn't bother me. I'd served in the Marines. I wasn't really worried about Yale Green and nothing ever became of it."

Richard W. Withers, not Bob Withers, would have problems with members of the police department, but the problems would not be physical and they would come much later. In April of 1965, Mayor Withers had other issues. He had been catapulted to the leadership of a kingdom that for decades had been allowed to grow or prosper and where people had no say in government. Would he be able to turn the kingdom into a functional democracy? Would he be able to convince people who never participated in government or experienced positive change that each could be good?

INDEX

A

B

C

D

E

F

G

H

I

J

K

L

M

N

O

P

Q

R

S

T

U

V

W

X

Y

Z

ABOUT THE AUTHOR

Joseph Thomas Gatrell was born and raised in Blue Island, Illinois. Like everyone else who grew up here, he heard the legends and rumors about politicians and dirty politics, local cops, gambling, men whose names you had to whisper if you even said them aloud, and the fix. Years into adulthood, when he published *The Blue Island Sun Newspaper*, he heard those and some new ones. By July 2010, he had heard enough. Mr. Gatrell began doing research and interviews with those who had information about the way things were done in Blue Island.

Just The Way Things Were Done is volume one of a political history of Blue Island. It tells the story of how the community went from Paul T. Klenk, a visionary who began to modernize Blue Island during the Roaring 20s, to John M. Hart, a corrupt and ultra-conservative mayor, who brought change to a grinding halt. Mayor Hart willed that the city never would change and the force of that will was so great that it seems to have become a curse. In many ways, Blue Island never has changed physically or philosophically.

"I had to find out what happened and why," said Mr. Gatrell, "and I did. When I did, I was very surprised, sometimes pleasantly, but too often I was disappointed. The result is a political history book for those who want to know the story of the real Blue Island. Anyone who prefers the fairy tale version...well, this book is not for them."

Joseph Thomas Gatrell still lives in Blue Island in a somewhat historic brick bungalow on a usually quiet street. He is referred to as a "retired teacher and marathoner," but he says this is inaccurate. "I'm not retired from anything and no one ever will retire me." He adds that Blue Island is a great place to live, work, write, and be virtually anonymous. "Decades ago mobsters and crooked politicians lived here and operated with impunity because the fix was in. They could live here today for a different reason. Blue Island is a quiet, peaceful little town that no one seems to be paying attention to. That's probably one more reason it never has changed."

Mr. Gatrell published the novel COUNTERPUNCH in 2012. It is available from Amazon and Barnes & Noble. Contact Joseph Thomas Gatrell via joegatrell@att.net.

CPSIA information can be obtained at www.ICGtesting.com
Printed in the USA
LVOW06s1031261014

410554LV00002B/616/P

9 781495 223198